CRAFTING TEXTILES IN THE DIGITAL AGE

BLOOMSBURY VISUAL ARTS
Bloomsbury Publishing Plc
50 Bedford Square, London, WC1B 3DP, UK
1385 Broadway, New York, NY 10018, USA

BLOOMSBURY, BLOOMSBURY VISUAL ARTS and the Diana
logo are trademarks of Bloomsbury Publishing Plc

First published in Great Britain by Bloomsbury Academic 2016
This edition published by Bloomsbury Visual Arts 2020
Reprinted 2020

Copyright © Nithikul Nimkulrat, Faith Kane, and Kerry Walkton, 2016

Nithikul Nimkulrat, Faith Kane, and Kerry Walkton have asserted their right under the Copyright,
Designs and Patents Act, 1988, to be identified as Authors of this work.

Cover design: Evelin Kasikov

All rights reserved. No part of this publication may be reproduced or
transmitted in any form or by any means, electronic or mechanical,
including photocopying, recording, or any information storage or
retrieval system, without prior permission in writing from the publishers.

Bloomsbury Publishing Plc does not have any control over, or responsibility for,
any third-party websites referred to or in this book. All internet addresses given
in this book were correct at the time of going to press. The author and publisher
regret any inconvenience caused if addresses have changed or sites have
ceased to exist, but can accept no responsibility for any such changes.

A catalogue record for this book is available from the British Library.

Library of Congress Cataloging-in-Publication Data
Names: Nimkulrat, Nithikul, 1974- editor.
Title: Crafting textiles in the digital age / edited by Nithikul Nimkulrat,
Faith Kane and Kerry Walton.
Description: New York: Bloomsbury Academic, 2016.
Identifiers: LCCN 2016003647 | ISBN 9781472529060 (paperback) | ISBN
9781472532046 (hardback)
Subjects: LCSH: Textile design—Data processing. | Textile
design—Technological innovations. | Handicraft—Philosophy. | BISAC:
DESIGN / Textile & Costume. | DESIGN / Fashion.
Classification: LCC TS1475 .C73 2016 | DDC 677/.022—dc23 LC record available at
http://lccn.loc.gov/2016003647

ISBN: HB: 978-1-4725-3204-6
PB: 978-1-3501-8560-9
ePDF: 978-1-4742-8622-0
eBook: 978-1-4742-8620-6

Typeset by Fakenham Prepress Solution, Fakenham, Norfolk NR21 8NN
Printed and bound in Great Britain

To find out more about our authors and books visit
www.bloomsbury.com and sign up for our newsletters.

CONTENTS

List of Illustrations vii

Contributors xiii

Foreword xix
J. R. Campbell

1 Introduction 1
Faith Kane, Nithikul Nimkulrat, and Kerry Walton

PART ONE DIGITAL TECHNOLOGIES INFORMING CRAFT 15

2 Crafting Textiles in the Digital Age: Printed Textiles 17
Cathy Treadaway

3 Digital Embroidery Practice 35
Tina Downes, Tessa Acti, and Donna Rumble-Smith

4 Textile Illusions—Patterns of Light and the Woven White Screen 47
Anne Louise Bang, Helle Trolle, and Anne Mette Larsen

5 The Intelligence of the Hand 61
Monika Auch

PART TWO CRAFT INTERVENTION IN DIGITAL PROCESS 75

6 The Digital Print Room—A Bespoke Approach to Print Technology 77

Helen Ryall and Penny Macbeth

7 Maintaining the Human Touch—Exploring "Crafted Control" within an Advanced Textile Production Interface 91

Martin Woolley and Robert Huddleston

8 *Garment ID*: Textile Patterning Techniques for Hybrid Functional Clothing 103

Kerri Akiwowo

9 Processes within Digitally Printed Textile Design 121

Susan Carden

PART THREE CRAFT THINKING IN A DIGITAL AGE 137

10 Hand Knitting in a Digital Era 139

Josephine Steed

11 Hidden Values and Human Inconsistencies in Hand Stitching Processes 153

Emma Shercliff

12 Perspectives on Making and Viewing: Generating Meaning through Textiles 171

Sonja Andrew

13 *Closely Held Secrets*: Embodied Knowledge in Digitally Crafted Textiles 189

Katherine Townsend

Index 207

LIST OF ILLUSTRATIONS

Plates

Plate 1. Printed motifs exhibiting the pixelated quality of early CAD, Cathy Treadaway, 1987.

Plate 2. Digital inkjet print on silk crepe de chine, Debra Bernath and Cathy Treadaway, 2004.

Plate 3. Integrating draped pattern cutting with embroidery design, Yuri Nakamatsu, 2011.

Plate 4. "Harlequin Cloven Red," Danica Maier, 2010.

Plate 5. Detail of the TWEEN screen by "Textile Illusions." The digital patterns of light appear to have a physical surface texture when they are projected onto a woven screen consisting of matt and shiny areas. The effect can be so intense that it appears as if the projected patterns are integrated as luminous threads in the woven screen.

Plate 6. The white-on-white TWEEN screen consists of four woven lengths in a double-layered complex structure of matt and shiny areas. An animation showing various transformations of the two basic block patterns is continuously projected on the screen.

Plate 7. An Installation at the Museum Vrolik for Anatomy and Embryology in Amsterdam in 2011. It shows a 3D woven object of the embryologic series together with a fetus in the museum's collection.

Plate 8. Stitched brain. The needlework of printmaker Jo Ganter from Glasgow, reflecting her very subtle graphic work.

Plate 9. Stitched brain. The interpretation of a brain by a Dutch high school student during a workshop.

Plate 10. Inkjet printed silk chiffon, generated using lace resist effects, Helen Ryall, 2009.

Plate 11. Silk habotai and chiffon (reactive dyes), Helen Ryall, 2010.

Plate 12. Screen printed knit patterns onto neoprene using discharge print paste, 2008.

Plate 13. Laser etched Polartec® fleece fabrics: fragmented digital patterns, 2008.

Plate 14. Digitally printed and hand-crafted silk sample, randomly textured textile with cooling properties, 2010.

Plate 15. Digitally printed silk chiffon, silk with discrete cool areas, 2011.

Plate 16. "Anchor and Crown" tea cozy, Andrea Williamson, 2011.

Plate 17. Crocheted model of a geometric manifold, Daina Taimina, 2004.

Plate 18. Samples from the third workshop held at the Arts University Bournemouth with a small group of textiles students, all able stitchers. Samples on the left are the originals and samples on the right are the reproductions.

Plate 19. Digital trials of image, texture, and color overlays for the second triptych.

Plate 20. *Closely Held Secrets* exhibition catalog, designed by Geoff Diego Litherland et al., 2010.

Plate 21. "Hold Your Beliefs Lightly," Grayson Perry, 2010.

Plate 22. "All the Stars," Geoff Diego Litherland, 2010.

Plate 23. "Invaders," comprised of multiple layers of embroidered threads to suggest different colored pixels, Geoff Diego Litherland, 2010.

Figures

Figure 2.1. Visual characteristics of printed textile process. Top left: engraved roller printing. Top right: silkscreen printing. Bottom left: block printing. Bottom right: digital inkjet printing. 19

Figure 2.2. Left: designing on an Apple IIe microcomputer, 1983. Right: CAD design, 1983. 22

Figure 2.3. CAD-generated printed design with hand-rendered watercolor and gold pigment, designed for Precision Studios, 1984. 23

Figure 2.4. CAD repeating pattern designed on the Pluto Designer system, Cathy Treadaway, 1987. 24

Figure 2.5. "Cape Cornwall," digitally printed starch with pigment and metallic foil embellishment, Cathy Treadaway, 2009. 25

LIST OF ILLUSTRATIONS

Figure 2.6. Digital code: "Evolving Lace," Gail Kenning, 2010. 27

Figure 2.7. Left: Z Corp 3D printer. Right: haptic tool. 27

Figure 2.8. "Thunderstorm" dress, Amy Winters for Rainbow Winters, 2012. 29

Figure 3.1. "Closely Held Secret," "Extreme Scale Stitches," Tessa Acti, 2010. 38

Figure 3.2. "Signatures Exchanged for Passwords," Donna Rumble-Smith, 2009. 39

Figure 3.3. 3D digital embroidery structures, Luisa Gil, 2011. 41

Figure 4.1. Weaving on the TC-1. 49

Figure 4.2. The outdoor piece in the TWEEN exhibition at the Design Museum Denmark is simply a pattern animation projected on a raw wall in the museum yard. In the animation two block patterns are transformed from one to the other and back again in a fast continuous loop of yellow light. 54

Figure 4.3. Each of the four pieces of the TWEEN screen built on a still image from a morph animation between two block patterns. The four still images represent the continuum between the two original patterns and are used as the "block pattern" for the woven TWEEN screen. 55

Figure 4.4. Detail of the TWEEN screen. During the exhibition at the Design Museum Denmark, an animation composed of a rich variety of colors with many subtle nuances was projected on the screen. Two basic block patterns served as inspiration for the pattern sequences. 56

Figure 5.1. A collage of rendered MRI-scan imagery of the author's brain and a drawing by her daughter Nora at the age of five. 61

Figure 5.2. Engraving on paper by Henricus Wilhelmus Couwenberg, 1830–45, shows postures and gestures of the thumb and other fingers. Dimensions: 150 × 108 mm. 63

Figure 5.3. Morphology studies, three objects from the "Ludens" series, 2011. Left: "Incompleta." Middle: "Spina Aperta." Right: "Spina Occlusive." Materials: plastic yarn, surgical drains, horsehair, paper yarn, and heat-reactive yarn. Dimensions: approximately 13 × 5 cm each. 67

Figure 5.4. The author is wired up while knitting at the Netherlands Institute for Neuroscience for EEG registrations, mapping dexterity through scientific data. 69

Figure 5.5. Two objects of the morphology series, "Neurotubes." Dimensions: approximately 20 × 25 × 10 cm each. Materials: fishing line, horse hair, and heat-reactive yarn. Technique: 3D weaving on a computerized loom. 71

Figure 6.1. Inkjet printing in action, demonstrating a lace fabric acting as a resist. 82

Figure 6.2. Lace resist print, silk habotai, Helen Ryall, 2009. 82

Figure 6.3. Inkjet printed silk habotai, generated using pleating resist effects, Helen Ryall, 2009. 84

Figure 6.4. Silk habotai and chiffon (reactive dyes), Helen Ryall, 2010. 85

Figure 7.1. Hand/material proximity and "crafted control." 94

Figure 7.2. The position of craft/manufacturer at Schlaepfer. 97

Figure 7.3. Improvised and predetermined treatments. 101

Figure 8.1. Design practice. 108

Figure 8.2. Iconic Capsule Wardrobe, 2008. 108

Figure 8.3. Puff print onto reclaimed knitted fabric, 2008. 113

Figure 8.4. Dye sublimation printed pre-colored Polartec® fleece fabric with photo-generated knitted pattern, 2008. 115

Figure 8.5. Dye sublimation printed neoprene: photo-generated knitted patterns, 2008. 116

Figure 8.6. Laser-etched neoprene: vector "knit" design, 2008. 117

Figure 9.1. Hand-crafted silk sample, tied and saturated with water prior to applying the alginate solution, 2010. 125

Figure 9.2. Digitally printed constructed silk sample, masked and coated with the alginate solution, 2010. 126

Figure 9.3. Testing temperatures of silk samples in laboratory, using thermocouples, 2010. 127

Figure 9.4. Coated silk samples and cooling process being explored in the sketchbook, 2011. 130

Figure 10.1. "Hamefarers' Kist," Hazel White, 2009. 142

Figure 10.2. "Knitted Homes of Crime," Freddie Robins, 2002. 143

Figure 11.1. Samples from the first workshop, held at the Royal College of Art, made by participants with varied skill levels. Left: skilled in the basics, having to pay attention to the placement of the needle. Right: moderately skilled, having to pay attention not to pull the tension of the thread taut. 157

Figure 11.2. With bowed head and work held close to the torso, the body manipulates itself to facilitate the close attention and focused concentration required for hand stitching. 158

Figure 11.3. The participant initially ranked the sample on the left, executed by me prior to the workshop, as the least aesthetically pleasing. After executing the task herself, shown in the sample on the right, she then ranked it the most aesthetically pleasing. 160

Figure 11.4. "Blending In": subtly intervening on a found fabric by neatly outlining and filling in the gingham checks. 162

Figure 11.5. "Hating Flowers": stitching a strongly personal mark onto a found fabric. 164

Figure 12.1. Early sketchbook page, wood stain and heat transfer experiment. 174

Figure 12.2. The first panel of the first triptych with a visual syntagm created to communicate the family as singled out for their pacifist beliefs. 178

Figure 12.3. Additions to the digitally printed textile surface via heat transfer, bonded frayed fabrics, stitch, screen printing, and flocking. 181

Figure 12.4. The second textile triptych panels in situ at the Bankfield Museum and Art Gallery, West Yorkshire. 182

Figure 13.1. Left: an interpretation of "Yew Tree Avenue–Children's Nightgarden" as an embroidered artwork, Simon Beck Mather, 2010. Right: section of embroidered appliqué based on the series of wave drawings and paper cuts, Charlotte Hodes, 2010. 194

Figure 13.2. Views of the installation, "What a Load of Shit" by Craig Fisher, 2010, Bonington Gallery, Nottingham Trent University. 195

Figure 13.3. "Harlequin Slit," Danica Maier, 2010. 196

Figure 13.4. Left: Tessa Acti working on Danica Maier's "Harlequin Slit." Right: detail from one of Maier's panels, illustrating how the artist accentuated the negative space of the background silk by applying smooth and raised stitch effects. 197

Figure 13.5. Left: "girl with fish" from "They Are Taking It to the People," showing satin-style stitches superimposed over digitally printed imagery, Stella Whalley, 2010. Right: "Part of Evidence of 20,000 Saints" and detail of motif based on oil smear, Derek Sprawson, 2010. 199

Figure 13.6. Left: "Lace Flow 1–3" by Katherine Townsend in *Closely Held Secrets* exhibition, Bonington Gallery. Top right: horseshoe collar motif on digitally printed silk surface. Bottom right: detail of a lace-inspired motif showing the use of short and elongated stitches within the same design. 201

Table

Table 8.1. Experimental Parameters and Methods. 111

CONTRIBUTORS

Tessa Acti After completing an MA in Textile Design and Innovation in 2010, Tessa Acti has developed her own highly innovative digital practice. In 2010 Acti worked collaboratively with visual artists as an embroidery technician to translate a series of original artworks into digital stitch for the *Closely Held Secrets* exhibition. She was employed for three years as a research assistant in Nottingham Trent University's advanced textiles research group investigating embroidered electronic antennae. She is currently working as a manager in an artist's studio, overseeing the day-to-day running of a busy arts practice. She has coordinated the publishing of a book and a vinyl record, and has jointly curated two international exhibitions.

Dr Kerri Akiwowo is a textile practitioner-researcher and lecturer in Textiles at Loughborough University. Her interests focus on new processes and materials, existing and emerging digital technologies, smart fabrics, performance sportswear and technical textiles, experimental approaches in printed textiles, patterning and surface design. Areas of investigation include digital laser-dye coloration and patterning approaches for PET textiles, and thermochromic and liquid crystal temperature-sensitive screen printing technologies for sports apparel. Kerri has disseminated her research and practice internationally via conferences, symposia, journal papers, and exhibitions. She has formerly held technical and academic roles including: research associate at the Textile Futures Research Centre, University of the Arts London; dye technician at Central Saint Martins College of Art and Design; and senior lecturer in Printed Textile Design at De Montfort University.

Dr Sonja Andrew is a senior lecturer in Textiles in the School of Materials at the University of Manchester. Crossing the disciplines of design, semiotics, and narratology, her research focuses on textile semantics and multimodal communication through cloth. Her work particularly examines the textile artifact as a signifying object and investigates the influence of image, medium, and site on audiences' perceptions of textiles. Sonja's commissioned work includes textile installations for UK clients such as the Diocese of Wells and Royal Bristol Children's Hospital. She exhibits internationally, with work most recently selected for the International Textile Art Kunststichting Perspektief (Belgium 2015), the "Craft and Conflict" and "Narrative Remains" exhibitions (UK 2014), the Scythia 9th and 10th International Textile Biennials (Ukraine 2012 and 2014), and the Kaunas International Textile Biennial (Lithuania 2011). In 2014 her practice-based research was selected for an Arts and Humanities Research Council Image Gallery Award.

Monika Auch lives and works in Amsterdam where she received her education in medicine and art. While practicing as a medical doctor she obtained a degree in textile design and printmaking in 2000. Her medical background is reflected in her detailed work, which is often suggestive of the growth patterns found through the lens of a microscope. The clash of digital and tactile methods in Auch's work heightens the material impact of the viewing experience, a combination of traditional, time-consuming methods and contemporary, instantaneous technology. Her hybrid background informs her practice-based research on hand–brain creativity, resulting in visual work, international projects, and publications. Auch received several grants and is an editor of *kM*, a Dutch magazine that publishes about artists' materials and techniques. She contributes to the exchange between art and science as an appointed member of several juries and boards.

Dr Anne Louise Bang, Helle Trolle, and Anne Mette Larsen all with a background in weaving and textile design—have been working together as—"Textile Illusions" since 2003. From the very beginning a declared goal has been to challenge "old-school" weaving and show the potential of the traditional craft in contemporary textile art and design. Textile Illusions works in a field combining animated patterns of light with the woven white screen. Over the years the group has exhibited in major Danish exhibitions for contemporary art (e.g. Charlottenborg Spring Exhibition) and in galleries and museums in Denmark and abroad. The website www.tekstile-illusioner.dk has an English entrance which contains information about various projects. Helle and Anne Mette also produce and exhibit their own work. Helle and Anne Louise both teach weaving at Kolding School of Design, and Anne Louise works as a researcher in design.

J. R. Campbell is professor and director of the Fashion School at Kent State University. Campbell has been researching, designing, and creating artwork with digital textile technology for nearly twenty years. His work pushes the limits of imaging technologies as they relate to clothing, our environment, and the human form. Campbell's art/design work has been shown in over seventy national or international exhibitions, receiving twenty awards, including the International Artist of the Year Award for the South Korean Fashion & Culture Association in 2010. Campbell has consulted for a number of academic institutions as they have integrated the technology into their teaching/research labs, and has published on subjects of design issues, controlling color, and integrating the technology into the design process for textiles and apparel. Campbell launched his TechStyleLAB concept in the Fashion School at Kent State University in 2009. The TSLAB functions as a research, teaching, and commercial environment to investigate the broadest range of digital textile and fashion design technologies and their implications for new business development and sustainable practices.

Dr Susan Carden is a practicing designer and associate lecturer at Northumbria University. Her practice explores the relationship that is forged when craft, hand making, and advanced technology are brought together through studio inquiry. She uses her practice to build theories through craft and design research, and to generate new multidisciplinary investigations. Her monograph *Digital Textile Printing: Art, Design, Culture* is also published by Bloomsbury as part of the series *Textiles That Changed the World*.

Tina Downes is the course leader for BA (Hons) Textile Design at Nottingham Trent University with responsibilities for postgraduate and research supervision. Her research interests lie in the field of smart materials and advanced textiles, specifically the aesthetic integration of new technologies and material interfaces within a cross-disciplinary design context. She has specialist knowledge of digital embroidery and works collaboratively to stimulate innovation, combining materials and processes in new ways or unexpected contexts to create fabrics with a considered aesthetic and added functionality. Examples of her practice-based research have been exhibited in Europe and published internationally. As a design educator with over twenty years' experience, she is concerned with theories of social learning and the enhancement to creative practice that occurs when differences in design thinking and experience meet in collaborative scenarios.

Robert Huddleston is interim Associate Dean of Student Learning Experience and Academic Quality, Faculty of Arts, Design and Media, Birmingham City University. With an MA in Fine Art from the Royal College of Art, his university teaching has encompassed visual studies, graphic arts, and textile design. Robert has designed for textile producers such as Ratti Spa., Como, Italy, and through his interest in the relationship of drawing and printmaking to new technologies, he contributed with the designer and maker Cheryl Welsh to a research and development project at the Swiss textile company Jakob Schlaepfer.

Dr Faith Kane currently leads the Textile Design Research Group (TDRG) at the School of the Arts, Loughborough University. Faith's research interests include: sustainable materials, process and design approaches for textiles with a current focus on laser processing; textile thinking; the role of drawing in textile design; and interdisciplinary research in textiles. Recent projects include "Textile Thinking for Sustainable Materials" and LEBIOTEX – Laser Enhanced Biotechnology for Textile Design. Her work has been published in several peer-reviewed journals and books and her design work has been exhibited internationally, including at the Museum of Textile History in Boras, Sweden; Izmir State Art and Sculpture Museum, Turkey; the Design and Architecture Gallery in Tallinn, Estonia; and the Centre for Contemporary Art and the Natural World, Exeter, UK. Faith is also an editor of the *Journal of Textile Design Research and Practice* (Taylor & Francis 2013), which provides a unique platform for publishing practice-led research in textiles.

Penny Macbeth is head of the Department of Art and Associate Dean for Student Experience at Manchester School of Art, Manchester Metropolitan University; she is also a writer and a practicing artist. Macbeth was a member of the supervisory team for Dr Helen Ryall's PhD, contributing her experience of hand-crafted textiles. Her current research focuses on the practitioner's engagement with cloth and specifically cloth as a catalyst for change, hope, and activism. She co-convened the international conference,

Outside: Activating Cloth to Enhance the Way We Live at the University of Huddersfield (2012), leading to a co-edited book of the same name published by Cambridge Scholars (2014).

Dr Nithikul Nimkulrat intertwines research with textile practice, focusing on experiential knowledge in craft processes in the context of design research. Her PhD research completed in 2009 at Aalto University in Finland examines the expressivity of textile material that is beyond visible, touchable qualities. Nithikul has worked at Aalto University (2004–10) and Loughborough University (2011–13), and is currently professor and head of department of Textile Design at the Estonian Academy of Arts (2013–present). She is an elected council member of the Design Research Society (DRS) and the convener of DRS Special Interest Group on Experiential Knowledge (EKSIG). Nithikul has published her research in peer-reviewed publications and exhibited her textiles internationally. She is co-editor of *Journal of Research Practice*'s special issue "Experiential Knowledge, Expertise, and Connoisseurship" (2015) and *Studies in Material Thinking*'s special volume "Experience·Materiality·Articulation" (2016).

Donna Rumble-Smith Since completing an MA in Textile Design and Innovation in 2009, Donna Rumble-Smith has developed a conceptual, textile art-based practice from a background in embroidered textiles. Her starting point is handwritten letters, poems, and reflective stories. Often the concept dictates the materials and techniques she uses and the outcome. Donna exhibits her work nationally, runs textile workshops, and is a sessional lecturer at Nottingham Trent University.

Dr Helen Ryall is a senior lecturer at the University of Huddersfield, with a background in textile print design and technical expertise in textile CAD and digital print technology. Helen joined the university in 2001 and has helped to lead the specialist textile CAD area for the university. She completed her PhD entitled "An Exploration of Digital Technology Over a Number of Manipulated Textile Surfaces" in September 2010. Her research explores the potential that digital technologies offer for the craftsperson and the future designer, encouraging the use of the technologies as a creative design tool, and as an integral part of the design process.

Dr Emma Shercliff is a textile maker, writer, researcher, and educator. Having previously worked in Paris as a textile designer in trend forecasting, she is currently senior lecturer in Textiles at the Arts University Bournemouth, specializing in stitched textiles. She completed her PhD "Articulating Stitch: Skilful Hand-stitching as Personal, Social and Cultural Experience" in 2014 at the Royal College of Art, London. Her research explores textile making in social and educational contexts, considers the differences between implicit and explicit forms of knowledge, and the meanings of hand making within post-industrial digital cultures. She continues to make large-scale textile pieces, video, drawings, and writings; her works have been published and exhibited in France and the UK, but also exist in homes, community centers, and other people's memories.

Josephine Steed is course director for BA (Hons) Fashion & Textile Design at Gray's School of Art, Robert Gordon University. She studied Constructed Textiles, specializing in Fashion Knitwear at the University of Middlesex and also has an MSc in Textile Technology from Huddersfield University. She has a broad range of experience of knitted textiles from designer/maker practice to textile design for mass-manufacture and has produced knitwear collections for a number of international clients. Her research focuses on the pervasive nature of textiles as a key component of contemporary material culture. One of her main interests is exploring the role and relevance of traditional hand skills in contemporary textiles and the value and status of craft process. She is the author of a number of research publications on the future of textile crafts, textiles, and industry and has a long-standing interest in the development of smart textiles through interdisciplinary collaboration across design, social sciences, and engineering.

Dr Katherine Townsend was awarded her PhD in 2004 for "Transforming Shape," a practice-led research project into the impact of CAD/CAM and inkjet printing technology on the integration of surface print and garment shape. The investigation was informed by her tacit knowledge as a designer/maker, running two independent fashion labels. Since achieving her first degree in Printed Textiles, Katherine has also worked as a lecturer, culminating in her current role as course leader for MA Fashion, Knitwear & Textile Design at Nottingham Trent University. She was appointed as a reader in Fashion and Textile Crafts in 2014, where she leads the Digital Craft and Embodied Knowledge research group in the School of Art and Design. Her ongoing research is focused on the synthesis of traditional hand and digital crafting approaches to create sustainable fashion and textiles. She is co-editor of the *Craft Research Journal* (Intellect 2010) and has published and exhibited her work internationally.

Dr Cathy Treadaway is professor of Creative Practice at Cardiff School of Art and Design, Cardiff Metropolitan University. She was one of the founder members of CARIAD (Centre for Applied Research in Inclusive Arts and Design), is a fellow of the Royal Society of Arts, fellow of the Higher Education Academy, and visiting scholar at the University of Technology Sydney. Cathy graduated in textiles and fashion design, has an MA in ceramics and PhD in digital technologies. She began her design career working for London-based design consultants Indesign and later Queensberry Hunt. She ran a design consultancy based in Wales for seventeen years, selling designs to industry around the world. She returned to academia in 2003 as a research assistant at Cardiff School of Art and Design and in 2006 successfully completed her PhD, which was an investigation into digital technologies and their influence on creative practice.

Kerry Walton is a lecturer at Loughborough University and the programme director for Textiles: Innovation & Design. Trained as a weaver, Kerry is principally interested in textile design, construction, and associated processes. Current research is based around the exploration of relationships between drawing and textiles, both within her own practice and in the context of a contemporary textiles education. As a member of the Drawing Research Group at Loughborough she has been involved in a number of drawing-related activities: exhibiting work and speaking at conferences in the United States and in the UK. Further practice-led research has developed in a number of directions, with a particular interest in non-traditional approaches, using heat and laser applications. In collaboration with the Textiles Research Group she was involved with developing the *Lasers and Creativity* symposium held at Loughborough in November 2009, and the *Textiles Research in Process* symposium, 2011.

Dr Martin Woolley is Associate Dean of Research, School of Art and Design, Coventry University. With a background in three-dimensional and industrial design, his research interests have broadened to encompass technology transfer, new product development, the crafts, environmental sustainability, and user-centered design. He has supervised and examined numerous research degrees, been active on several research bodies, and is a fellow of the Royal Society of Arts. Over the last two decades he has combined funded research with the challenge of directing research within several top universities. He has also undertaken advisory work for worldwide academic institutions. Martin is a fellow of the Design Research Society, has chaired two national subject associations, and in 1977 was one of the first people in the UK to undertake a PhD in Industrial Design. He has served on the RAE panel twice, and was a member of the AHRC Research Panel.

FOREWORD

As an artist, designer, and researcher who tries to champion the integration of emerging technologies into textile and clothing design practices, I find that I am still in a dissonant state of mind about how to navigate a definition of "craft." In *Thinking Through Craft*, Glenn Adamson poses that "skill is the most complete embodiment of craft as an active, relational concept rather than a fixed category" and suggests that craft might be most effectively conceived as a process.[1] At my core, I believe the concept of craft represents a particular way of knowing and working that can be formalized and is distinct but interrelated with design and art. As such, *Crafting Textiles in the Digital Age* functions as an insightful selection of case studies from accomplished makers and researchers in textiles. The collection of chapters leads to a strong emergent understanding of digital, craft, and textile intersections, starting from "digital technologies informing craft" through "craft interventions in digital process" and finally with "craft thinking in a digital age."

In 2007 I wrote a paper for the *New Craft/Future Voices* conference hosted by the University of Dundee, Scotland. The paper, titled "Digital Craft Aesthetic: Craft-Minded Application of Electronic Tools," attempted to introduce principles or considerations to evaluate, as part of an emerging coalescence of what I called the "digital craft aesthetic." In it, I noted that early use of digital design tools in textile design and craft practice initially fell into two fairly well-defined approaches: first, the use of digital tools to intentionally show a digital effect; and second, the use of digital tools to mimic a traditional effect or technique, thus attempting to "hide" the use of the technology. By 2007, approaches that explored more deeply the advantages and the unique aspects of digital tools were already being demonstrated to develop entirely new artifacts and products.

In his book *The Nature of Design* (1964), David Pye wrote: "The aura of a crafted product is a unique accumulation of responses to a material and is derived from the hands-on workmanship of risk involved in human manufacture."[2] This idea of the "workmanship of risk" is still incredibly relevant in how it addresses both the purposes and ways of knowing through craft. What has changed is the concept of what is a "material." In this way of thinking, all technological innovations addressed through craft practice have the iterative role of presenting new ways of making while also leading to the knowledge required to advance the technology. The imperative is not simply based in a desire to experiment with the new, but growing from the recognition that digital tools provide enhanced means to communicate craft goals. The desire to connect and communicate, to use crafted objects and ideas to enhance our sensory experiences of the world, is directly parallel to the role of developing technology. Ultimately, as humans develop and interact with new technologies, what we are doing is attempting to make better connections: connections to each other, connections to our abilities, perhaps even connections to the divine.[3] In viewing or experiencing crafted expressions, we are inherently drawn to thinking about their connections to the body and to how we navigate our existence.

The assumption that ever-advancing technology replaces craft can be challenged.[4] As artists/craftspeople, we can choose to be intentional about the use of digital technologies as we seek to convey their properties, failings, and beauty, or we can simply use the technologies as tools to convey our already existing needs (expressions) in more effective ways.[5] In either circumstance, the technology becomes part of the perception. Hybrid approaches to the integration of materials, technologies, and processes now dominate research and the development of products that once were more clearly held in the craft traditions. In order to enhance the interactivity, awareness, and responsiveness of textiles and garments, designers/craftspeople are employing technologies from information technology and medical sensing, nanotechnology, and electromechanical engineering.[6] Insights from these areas lead to new forms of craft practice.

In his article on the impact of information technology on design, Kalay makes the following assertion: "[R]ather than how can the new tools *assist* designers, one should ask how do the affordances they provide *change* the practice of design itself?"[7] The traits and potentials of the technology should lead us to question how "communication via digital files and video screens fundamentally changes the culture of the practice" and how "knowledge, once invested only in the designer but now ingrained in the tools, even in the products themselves, affect the practice of design."[8]

Is there a digital craft aesthetic? Rivka Oxman asks this question directly of design practice in "Theory and Design in the First Digital Age" from the journal of *Design Studies*.[9] One of these central questions relates to whether, in fact, digital design is a unique phenomenon, "a new form of design," rather than merely a conventional design accomplished with new media. If this radical assumption is valid, then a comprehensive theoretical formulation of digital design might also contribute to new interpretations of certain root concepts of our extant design theories.

One of the routes to elicit ways of knowing through digital craft is to define the characteristics and unique properties that are emerging in new forms of craft practice. The following are brief descriptions of the principles I introduced in the *New Craft/Future Voices* paper:

Ability to alter dimensional rules/expectations: When working with digital tools, craftspeople have the ability to conceptually modify their work in such ways that the resulting work is inside out, upside down, or potentially defying the normal laws of physics.

Ability to alter the natural material's normal working properties: In addition to intentionally modifying or manipulating dimensional experiences of a craft expression, craftspeople can also use digital design and production tools to alter a material's normal working properties.

Ability to enhance interactivity/communication: By merging digital tools with traditional materials, intentions to use the crafted product to enhance interactivity and/or communication are possible.

Abstraction: Abstraction is particularly relevant to the creative process in digital craft, as it helps to simplify the degrees of complexity in working with elements of digital tools.

Allowing imperfections (flaws) to be used to express the presence of technology: "Flaws" are in some respects a paradox when discussed with the application of digital tools. In many senses, digital technology allows for a degree of precision that can potentially eliminate flaws in a designed or crafted product. If, in using a digital tool, the craftsperson wishes to incorporate flaws, there can be difficulty in creating these to seem convincing.[10] Indeed the insertion of flaws can be intentional, not in a replicatory way, but as an aesthetic in its own right.[11]

Control over destruction or disintegration: Digital works can be designed to self-destruct or disintegrate over time. This is an option which has some aesthetic potential that may be considered at some point in the creative process.

Degree of individual control: To expand on the concept of control over destruction, it is important to note the more holistic degree of individual control over the entire development process. What has become characteristic of complex and integrated design systems is the degree of individual control provided the designer/craftsperson in digital processes. This has led to an increased importance of user interface design, and the need to encompass the realm of interface design in the effective creation of digital craft expressions.[12]

Loss/error: In working with digital tools, the concept of "loss" and "error" are greatly modified. With the exception of a computer "crash" in which an entire set of working files is lost prior to saving, objects or processes created in a digital environment are rarely lost. Errors can often be quickly and easily reverted with the "undo" capacity built into most software environments. This has two obvious impacts: (1) it might produce a tendency to create too many iterations of an idea; or (2) it could impact the creative ability to respond to errors in the work that could spawn completely new directions in the work.

Representing fractal, algebraic, and/or data-driven visualizations: The creative potential to express complex algebraic, algorithmic, or fractal structures visually in crafted products was mostly unattainable prior to the use of digital design tools. The massive processing power that the designer/craftsperson has access to currently allows for incredible calculations to create visual representations of mathematical concepts.

Sensory attachment/detachment: An aspect of working with digital tools that must be addressed and understood is that of the hand-tactile experience of creating. Though research into haptics and the activity of designing hardware and software systems is allowing for improved sensory coordination and experience, it is important to realize that the actions used to create digitally crafted expressions do not always need to mimic traditional actions, but could involve entirely new techniques and experiences.

Time: As designers/craftspeople become more experienced with technology, their degree of mental immersion into digital crafting environments becomes more fluid in a way that is similar to a master-craftsperson's knowledge of their own hand tools. Time-based experiences can potentially be incorporated into digitally created work in ways that transcend analogue media.

Viscosity: Related to time, error, and loss, Green and Blackwell define viscosity as "*resistance to change*, the cost of making small changes."[13] They describe two different types: (1) repetition viscosity, in which "a single goal-related operation on the information structure (one change 'in the head') requires an undue number of individual actions"; and (2) knock-on viscosity, in which "one change 'in the head' entails further actions to restore consistency."[14]

Visibility and juxtaposability: The ability to witness multiple views of a crafted object during the creative process is greatly enhanced through the application of digital tools.

Variations on these elements and principles are found in each of the chapters in this book. Through the insights presented by this fantastic array of authors, a clearer definition of *what craft is now* becomes evident. By exploring the variety of approaches, technologies, and perspectives presented, the reader can build a solid understanding of the emerging realities for crafting textiles in the digital age.

J. R. Campbell

Notes

1   Glenn Adamson, *Thinking Through Craft* (Oxford: Berg, 2007), 4.
2   David Pye, *The Nature of Design* (London: Studio Vista, 1964), 60.
3   J. R. Campbell, "Digital Perceptions: Visually Expressing the Potentials of Digital Textile Technology and Simultaneously Making its Perception Disappear," in *Digital Perceptions* [catalog and DVD] (Glasgow: Collins Gallery, 2006), 4–5.
4   Cathy Treadaway, "Digital Imagination: The Impact of Digital Imaging on Printed Textiles," *Textile: The Journal of Cloth and Culture* 2 (3) (2004): 256–73.
5   Campbell, "Digital Perceptions," 4–5.
6   Anne Farren and Andrew Hutchison, "Digital Clothes: Active, Dynamic and Virtual Textiles and Garments," *Textile: The Journal of Cloth and Culture* 2 (3) (2004): 290–307.
7   Yehuda E. Kalay, "The Impact of Information Technology on Design Methods, Products and Practices," *Design Studies* 27 (3) (2006): 378.
8   Ibid.
9   Rivka Oxman, "Theory and Design in the First Digital Age," *Design Studies* 27 (3) (2006): 229–65.
10 Jane Harris, "'Crafting' Computer Graphics—A Convergence of Traditional and 'New' Media," *Textile: The Journal of Cloth and Culture* 3 (1) (2005): 20–35.

11 Harris, "'Crafting' Computer Graphics," 20–35.
12 Oxman, "Theory and Design in the First Digital Age," 229–65.
13 Thomas Green and Alan Blackwell, "Cognitive Dimensions of Information Artefacts: A Tutorial," October 1998, 24. Available online: http://www.cl.cam.ac.uk/~afb21/CognitiveDimensions/CDtutorial.pdf [accessed July 20, 2015].
14 Andy Dearden, "Designing as a Conversation with Digital Materials," *Design Studies* 27 (3) (2006): 402.

Bibliography

Adamson, Glenn, *Thinking Through Craft* (Oxford: Berg Publishers, 2007).
Campbell, J. R. "Digital Perceptions: Visually Expressing the Potentials of Digital Textile Technology and Simultaneously Making its Perception Disappear," in *Digital Perceptions* [catalog and DVD] (Glasgow: Collins Gallery, 2006), 4–5.
Dearden, Andy, "Designing as a Conversation with Digital Materials," *Design Studies* 27 (3) (2006): 399–421.
Farren, Anne, and Andrew Hutchison, "Digital Clothes: Active, Dynamic and Virtual Textiles and Garments," *Textile: The Journal of Cloth and Culture* 2 (3) (2004): 290–307.
Green, Thomas, and Alan Blackwell, "Cognitive Dimensions of Information Artefacts: A Tutorial," October 1998, 24. Available from http://www.cl.cam.ac.uk/~afb21/CognitiveDimensions/CDtutorial.pdf [accessed July 20, 2015].
Harris, Jane, "'Crafting' Computer Graphics—A Convergence of Traditional and 'New' Media," *Textile: The Journal of Cloth and Culture* 3 (1) (2005): 20–35.
Kalay, Yehuda E., "The Impact of Information Technology on Design Methods, Products and Practices," *Design Studies* 27 (3) (2006): 357–80.
Oxman, Rivka, "Theory and Design in the First Digital Age," *Design Studies* 27 (3) (2006): 229–65.
Pye, David, *The Nature of Design* (London: Studio Vista, 1964).
Treadaway, Cathy, "Digital Imagination: The Impact of Digital Imaging on Printed Textiles," *Textile: The Journal of Cloth and Culture* 2 (3) (2004): 256–73.

1
INTRODUCTION

Faith Kane, Nithikul Nimkulrat, and Kerry Walton

Textile designers and makers have traditionally operated in a complex environment where craft and technology, structure, process, and materials interact, interrelate, and interchange on many levels. In an era of digital technology, many textile designers and makers find themselves at an interesting juncture. Knowledge and experience of traditional craft processes have, within the current generation, been supplemented by opportunities offered by digital technologies, presenting them with a rich variety of options for consideration. Highly specialized craft and design practitioners may now elect to make use of digital processes in their work, but often choose not to abandon craft skills fundamental to their practice, aiming to balance the complex connection between craft and digital processes. Craft still provides the foundation for thinking within the design and production of textiles, and as such may offer some clues in the transition to creative and thoughtful use of current and future digital technologies. Considering craft, as Glenn Adamson suggests, "in a simple but open-ended manner as the application of skill and materials-based knowledge to relatively small-scale production"[1] enables us to draw connections with digital processes and to understand the implications of this approach across various forms of cultural production[2] relating to textiles. Within the framework of current challenges pertaining to sustainability, globalization, social concerns, and economic constraints, it is important to interrogate and question how the integration of both established and emerging digital technologies in textile practices might contribute in a positive manner. It is also essential to address ideas around how textile designers and makers utilize and advance craft knowledge in the creation of their work, given the scope and potential of rapidly expanding and increasingly prevalent digital technologies.

Making the digital tangible relies upon a connection with the material world.[3] The emergent integration of digital technologies within the creative field of textiles requires contemporary textile designers and makers to adopt new visual and material languages in order to communicate something of relevance.[4] Current digital textile technologies including digital embroidery, digital printing, jacquard weaving, laser processing, and rapid prototyping have provided new opportunities for designers while enhancing the manufacture of textiles. For example, the advance of digital jacquard handlooms TC-1 and TC-2, cleverly integrating computer functionality into an essentially traditional hand-operated machine, has enabled textile designers to gain access to digital weaving. These handlooms facilitate more sophisticated and complex results outside of the manufacturing context and at an affordable cost. The digital thread controller permits warp ends to be lifted independently from each other, allowing the weaver to more freely create patterns with large or no repeat and to sample jacquard woven textiles more easily than on an industrial jacquard loom.[5]

As creative tools, however, these technologies may limit, restrict, or exclude a degree of creative spontaneity and intuition in terms of materials and production due to the "distance" that technology creates between the maker and the designed artifact. By adopting a digital tool as a mediator between the material artifact in progress and the designer's hand, the design process can become easier and faster but may lack character or the unique touch of the designer. It could arguably lead to a more superficial approach to the origination of the designs and artifacts, inhibiting conceptual content and promoting mechanical and uniform characteristics. Irregularity and subtle variety may then be less evident in the final textile outcomes if the digital tool dominates and controls the process of designing. Therefore, it would appear that it is crucial for textile designers to consider adjusting an approach, which might be described as "designing through making" and a "designerly way of knowing,"[6] to accommodate and handle technology with caution, so that their individual creativity can be maintained in the process and evident in the product.

In contrast, characteristics and irregularities arising from human inconsistency within traditionally produced artifacts have the potential to be understood and promoted as positive qualities, by embedding a degree of uniqueness into the textiles. Serendipity—the "happy accident"—is well known as a contributing factor where innovation comes about through hands-on experimentation, and is often at the root of new thinking and approaches. If craft is understood as "a way of thinking through practices of all kinds"[7] and as "a dynamic process of learning and understanding through material experience,"[8] handling digital tools in a textile design process can be considered craft, and learning through experience. The designer not only designs through making but also learns how making is a way of thinking innovatively through the practice of textile design with digital tools, the result of which is an unexpected outcome. The unexpected can contribute a visual and conceptual depth that is exciting and potentially unique.

Within this context a craft approach to textiles has acquired a new value and respect in recent years: bespoke and handmade products that acknowledge their craft origins have become increasingly sought after. It is the consideration of this broader context where textile practitioners are working from diverse perspectives, often rooted in traditional approaches to making and embellishing textiles—printing, knitting, weaving, and embroidery—that provides new insight into the current position regarding the integration of digital techniques.

Aim and approach of this book

The essays collected in this volume reflect on what might be considered a transitional phase in textile practice, predominantly from the viewpoint of aesthetic opportunity given by digital technologies. While this is the focus, it is acknowledged that this transitional phase not only involves aesthetics but also economic, social, and environmental implications for the way in which textile designing and making is practiced. In particular the impact of the digital movement more broadly on the communication and accessibility of textile knowledge, for example the rise of open-source design and the contribution of communities of practice often facilitated by social media, is seen as an important consideration in understanding the future direction of textiles.

The collation of the essays was first conceived as a result of the Textile Research in Practice (TRIP) symposium held at Loughborough University in November 2011. The symposium brought together textile designers, makers, and researchers from across the globe, not only from the UK but also from other European countries and the USA, to consider the value of traditional textile processes within the context of evolving digitization. The chapters are the result of ideas emerging through the symposium, and their content represents reflections on various forms of production in textiles.

The book is structured into three parts: (1) *Digital Technologies Informing Craft*, (2) *Craft Intervention in Digital Process*, and (3) *Craft Thinking in a Digital Age.* Each part consists of four chapters that present leading-edge research and practice relating to the value of craft in textile design processes and production. At a time of increasing digitization and the proliferation of digital textile technologies, many of the chapters evidence and describe the latest implementation of digital technologies within creative contexts. These are presented alongside reflective and theoretical accounts of practice which provide insight into collaborative and hybrid working methods and diverse creative approaches.

Part One: Digital Technologies Informing Craft

Part One considers the transference and integration of textile knowledge within digital design and production. It asserts the need for prior knowledge of textile materials and processes to develop an intimate understanding of the potential of digital textile technologies within different creative contexts. In Cathy Treadaway's chapter, "Crafted Textiles in the Digital Age: Printed Textiles," developments in digital print technology are traced from their early availability to textile designers in the 1970s to the present, in terms of software, process, and design practice. Her discussion provides several important insights gained from a long association with printed textile design practice, and specifically digital printing. What is of particular significance in Treadaway's contribution is her identification of the potential of digital technologies to inform and even direct the creative process. Highlighting the creative practices of Casey Reas, Ben Fry, Hilary Carlisle, and

Gail Kenning, Treadaway explores the notion that approaching digital printing via the designers' engagement with software development, programming, and the language of computer code provides a greater sense of intimacy with the digital as a medium.

The materiality of textiles requires, however, more than a visual and computational understanding of digital working to achieve crafted objects. As in emerging architectural practices that involve algorithmic methodologies, close connections between computational design and the materialization processes are needed.[9] This interplay between computation and materials, as Treadaway concludes, provides a future site for interdisciplinary innovation within digital printing. This section begins to touch upon the notion of active materials,[10] emerging in Part Two, that form a rich dynamic with digital processes and a further dimension to the creative and functional potential of textiles that can themselves become programmable. This presents the opportunity for smart and responsive textile design propositions.

Moving away from digital printing, "Digital Embroidery Practice" by Tina Downes, Donna Rumble Smith, and Tessa Acti provides in-depth case studies of creative practice to explore the acquisition and application of tacit knowledge within digital embroidery. As discussed in relation to digital printing and laser processing, central to their study is a probing of the pivotal relationship between human engagement, machines, tools, and materials. In turn, they interrogate the role that prior knowledge of the machine and the materials in question plays in the realization of creative design outcomes. In particular they consider how this impacts upon the potential for spontaneity within digital embroidery.

The creative privilege and opportunity created by the spontaneity resulting from the intimate relationship between the maker and the material, discussed by Downes, Rumble Smith, and Acti, is an important facet of the current discourse around the value of craft. Significant to this chapter is the exploration of the disruption to this spontaneity caused by the digital. This relates to the immediate physical distance created between the hand and the tool/machine, but, from an industrial perspective, further disruption is created by global systems of design and manufacture. Often, as the chapter highlights, the design and manufacturing processes are completely divorced from each other, leaving no space for material knowledge to inform design. The authors conclude that although knowledge of digitization is necessary for the fabrication of digital embroidery, direction of the interface is more successful from a creative perspective when the designer has prior knowledge of textile materials and stitching. This, they discuss, is not to deny the creative opportunities of the digitization process.

"Textile Illusions—Patterns of Light and the Woven White Screen" by Anne Louise Bang, Helle Trolle, and Anne Mette Larsen explores the creative opportunities offered by digital animation processes. The TWEEN project discussed in this chapter uses this digital space as a visual and conceptual source of inspiration. It provides an example of a digital approach leading and informing the design process in woven textiles. Further, it prompts us to consider the range of opportunities for crossover between disciplines and forms of output using common or familiar digital language—in this case, that between textiles and animation. Due to the historic symbiosis between weaving and computing, it is not surprising that textiles, and in particular jacquard weaving, provide a space where digital and material languages meet: pixel and interweaving joining seamlessly to create—as the chapter title indicates—visual and textural illusions. Several prominent digital practitioners such as Jane Harris[11] and Hussein Chalayan[12] have found that the intersection between textiles and animation provides much scope for creativity and innovation both within and beyond the screen.

Monika Auch expands on the discussion around weaving and the knowledge generated by its practice in her chapter "The Intelligence of the Hand." Auch's background in medicine naturally prompts an examination of the connection between anatomy and digital weaving in terms of both process and outcome. The chapter reveals an approach to practice which aims to uncover the creative process by exploring the connection between hand and brain using scientific methodologies. The practice discussed highlights and pinpoints the disruptive moments in making and the moments of creativity. What is significant here is the ongoing exploration of the impact that digital crafting might have on this hypothesis and approach. Auch's work demonstrates the connections between the inherent principles of textile construction and biological structures, built upon shared mathematical principles, the foundations of which are widely recognized. Intuitive exploration in this area, as Auch's chapter evidences, can lead to the abstract materialization of biology. Scientists, in particular mathematicians, have utilized textile making to materialize or visualize their scientific concepts. Referring to a knitted hyperbole, Kerstin Kraft suggests that our understanding of such scientific and mathematical principles might be assisted by such physical manifestations.[13] Evidence of how a mathematical concept is visualized through textile making is further provided in Part Three, in Josephine Steed's chapter entitled "Hand Knitting in a Digital Era," which discusses the mathematician Daina Taimina's crocheted hyperbolic curve.[14]

Part Two: Craft Intervention in Digital Process

Part Two considers hand-based crafted approaches to digital outputs: the intersection between material and process, digital-crafting, digital aesthetics, and invention at the newly defined perimeters of hybrid activity. "The Digital Print Room" by Helen Ryall and Penny Macbeth provides a personal account of applying the principles of "designing through making" to digital printing. It describes the realization of highly "crafted" digitally printed textiles using physical resists, such as barrier methods, restraints, and manipulations. The chapter provides a useful point of departure to reflect upon the textile practitioner's physical relationship with digital textile technologies in terms of both designing and making. In particular it explores our interaction with what we might consider "digital tools" within the context of creative production—an important theme throughout this volume. When considering designing through making, tools, which are often perceived as an extension of the hand,[15] are instrumental in the conceptualization, development, and realization of textile design. As such, the association between tools and hands suggests a creative dynamic. A tool, as one element of a toolkit, suggests Malcolm McCullough, directs your attention and enables "specialization" in terms of creative output.[16] McCullough observes that tools and toolkits benefit from the context of a studio,[17] supporting and giving place to a particular practice. Ryall and Macbeth's metaphorical understanding of the "digital print room," referring to traditional textile design and making practices, helps us to integrate digital technologies into our traditional vernacular of studio and workshop practices. As stated in the chapter, "the computer and printer became the palette, paintbrush, and dye vessel, while the print medium became the canvas on which the creativity could begin."[18]

The perception of the computer as a creative tool (computer-aided design: CAD) in all fields of design has been widely argued.[19] Exploring the notion of digitally driven "output devices" and processes (computer-aided manufacture: CAM), which give materiality to digital design, being an equally important creative tool is where Ryall and Macbeth's chapter provides an important contribution. In the practice described, the digital printer moves beyond being a mechanized device or "machine," perceived as being controlled but not directed by the maker. It moves towards being a creative tool which, when used as part of a broader understanding of textile media and where the maker maintains a physical presence/influence in the making process, can result in highly crafted outcomes that retain an aesthetic association with a creative individual. The performance of the printer and the quality of the outputs realized rely upon the prior knowledge and expertise of the maker.

The relationship between tools, machines, full automation, and maker within the context of digital design and production, in particular the use of laser processing for decorative effect in textiles, is considered further in Martin Woolley and Robert Huddleston's chapter "Maintaining the Human Touch—Exploring 'Crafted Control' within an Advanced Textile Production Interface." Central to Woolley and Huddleston's discussion is the position of the medium or material within this association. By modeling the impact of digitization and automation upon this dynamic, and identifying the gap or separation between the maker and the medium created by digitization, they arrive at a position which suggests the notion of "active materials" as a way of maintaining the interplay between perception, skill, knowledge, and creativity required in realization of "smart" textiles. Embedding crafted control capabilities into production technologies can result in a flexible means of adding value through unique design processes and outcomes. Their discussion of "active materials" draws further on McCullough's idea that within the use of digital process it becomes difficult to define where the tool ends and the medium begins,[20] identifying a production space in which materials find a new level of responsiveness, contrasting the "traditional one-way encounter between tool and material/surface."[21] The maker mediates this responsive encounter and the use of technology to enable creative manipulation of both the medium and the machine, compelling a deep understanding of materials.

As Woolley and Huddleston allude, this often leads to a requirement for interdisciplinary working where various bodies of scientific and technical knowledge can be drawn upon to enable creative manipulation of technology. Encompassing aspects of art, design, and engineering, textile design and production forms a natural site for interdisciplinarity. The unique and multifaceted way of working possessed by textile practitioners enables them to navigate and often lead creative collaborations utilizing new technologies, as evidenced in this case study on Jakob Schlaepfer. Here we see that the space between design, science, and engineering, mediated by a craft approach, becomes a rich site for creativity. The bringing together of scientific and poetic approaches that is often second nature to textile practitioners can, as Rachel Philpott suggests, "illuminate different perspectives, allowing for investigation of the metaphysical, the emotional and the imaginative alongside the technical."[22]

Moving from material to object, Kerri Akiwowo considers the possibilities presented by the use of digital technologies to manipulate the identities of iconic everyday garments in her "Garment ID" project. Akiwowo describes that central to the transformation of the garments in the project was the appropriation of traditional hand-knitted structures, again considered iconic, via digital processing. The notion of the iconic used here, "symbolic or representative of a particular period of time, event, uniform, fashion trend, generic term, textile development or process,"[23] leads us to consider the influence that digitization has on our reading and understanding of textiles and the impact of this on their cultural functions. These ideas are further developed in Part Three of this volume.

Although the meaning of textiles, and indeed the products they are part of, can be attributed neither to inherent qualities nor external projection,[24] it is possible to derive from the "digital look"—or the "look of code," as Braddock Clarke and Harris put it[25]—an association with technology, be it actual or conceptual. When this is "crafted," the relationship between process and product is perhaps more accessible or transparent, creating the potential to restore the connection between making and using.[26] This connection enables end users to form an association with the values, skill, and creativity of the maker. It is interesting to note that Akiwowo chose to appropriate the familiar hand-crafted aesthetic of a knitted garment in applying digital techniques. This in some way maintains an association with the values and qualities of traditional textile crafts, supplanting or supplementing the aesthetics of code often associated with digital technologies, and indicating the potential cultural value of a craft approach to the digital.

Finally, Susan Carden's chapter, "Processes within Digitally Printed Textile Design," provides an example of craft sensibilities creating an environment for invention. Carden's project supports established theory that craft practice, and more specifically hands-on interaction with materials and processes, facilitates tacit knowledge leading to new insights about a given field of inquiry. Her discussion draws us back to the dynamic between maker, medium, and digital processes, machines, and tools, but from an alternative perspective. It provides an example of a different and perhaps unexpected outcome that can be considered as cross-disciplinary invention. Carden's discovery of new technical capability within her medium and her reflection upon that discovery suggests that a craft approach to digital technologies supports intuitive practice that operates creative and aesthetic knowing, leading to technical or scientific insight and ultimately innovation.

Part Three: Craft Thinking in a Digital Age

Part Three explores the status quo and hierarchies of quality, knowledge, experience, and communication within the context of textiles. Josephine Steed discusses a deeper and more nuanced understanding of "Hand Knitting in a Digital Era" and the value of the embodied knowledge gained by its practice. Her articulation of hand knitting as complex, multilayered, and "living" helps us to consider this knowledge against emergent digital landscapes from personal, social, cultural, and technical perspectives. She suggests that we go beyond our basic identification of knitting as a transformation of linear thread to interwoven construct, towards a fuller comprehension of the haptic, temporal, and cultural indices that inform hand knitting. There are echoes here of Tim Ingold's imperative, when discussing the phenomenon of lines, to not only focus on "the lines themselves and the hands that produced them" but also to consider "the relation between lines and the surfaces on which they are drawn."[27] In doing this we are encouraged to see the broader personal, social, cultural, and technical "connections" and interconnections—a notion highlighted within the foreword[28]—that are inherent within the practice of knitting, and that are further facilitated by digital technology which enables communication, storage, and translation of craft practice. This is similarly significant in the practice and research of makers such as Angharad Thomas, who focuses her work around knitting gloves.[29]

This notion of connection is explored further in Emma Shercliff's chapter, "Hidden Values and Human Inconsistencies in Hand Stitching Processes." Shercliff explores the revived interest in and acknowledged value of hand stitching within the context of a screen-based culture of making. She focuses on the physical connection between humans and material facilitated through making by hand. Although her discussion is posed in opposition to technology, it leads us to consider at a deeper level the connections formed through digital crafting. What inner biological, psychological, and emotional responses are activated? How does digital crafting impact our interconnectedness with material, natural, virtual, and human dimensions? Employing Shercliff's reference to Ellen Dissanayake, what might digital "making-special" entail?[30]

Linking to the connections that are shaped by digital crafting, Sonja Andrew leads us to consider those made through our interpretations of digitally crafted artifacts. In "Perspectives on Making and Viewing: Generating Meaning through Textiles," Andrew explores viewers' responses to emotive printed textile artworks. Informed by personal narrative, traditions of making, and cultural identity, the visual language analyzed is the result of a hybrid approach to digital and traditional textile processes. Using semiotic theory, Andrew's study indicates that the tactile and textural qualities of textile materials provide a unique semiotic vocabulary, which adds a further dimension to the meaning constructed by the maker and that interpreted by the viewer of digital works. This further emphasizes the potential of hybrid approaches, which embrace both the digital and the material, to extend the communicative possibilities of textiles in both physical and virtual spheres.

Finally, Katherine Townsend's chapter "Closely Held Secrets: Embodied Knowledge in Digitally Crafted Textiles" extends our consideration of ideas around communication, meaning, and interpretation within digital making, but this time within the context of digital fabrication. In particular the chapter prompts us to interrogate the connection between the maker and the technician and, more specifically, how this relationship impacts upon the expressive potential of digital embroidery as a creative medium within a visual arts context. The significance of the process of "translation" within such creative partnerships is highlighted and, in particular, the unique dynamic of these relationships. Townsend identifies distinctive differences in outcomes defined by either precise or exploratory translations of non-digital gestures, marks, surface quality, and so on. This revelation of the often "hidden dialogue between the originator of an idea and the agent of interpretation" highlights the importance of embodied knowledge of digital processes in the creative use of technology.[31] It also draws our attention to the new collaborative and interdisciplinary spaces that open up at the intersection of digital and material craft.

Conclusion

Textile designers and makers today work in an interesting period of transition; the majority of contemporary practitioners have had a traditional training, rooted in one or other of the craft specialist practices: knitting, weaving, hand printing, and embroidery. They may have extensive craft skills and knowledge supported by education and years of expertise, but are increasingly dealing with the integration of digital processes into their making practice and conversely using craft skills to intervene in technology-based production. They have insight into the utilization of both craft and high-technological methods, and balance them with various textiles specialisms and approaches, to continue developing and pushing the boundaries of traditional skills or to provide new creative opportunities. Due to their pervasive nature and presence in our lives, textiles cannot exist without material outcomes and can never exist solely in a digital space. They must be made material and tangible, and so knowledge and understanding of making are critical to the future; most practitioners demonstrate a duality of approach, fusing, blending, and merging skills either as individual practitioners or as collaborators with other experts.

Change defines the modern world and textile designers and makers have always adapted and ultimately thrived in response to the adaption of new technologies. With wide knowledge and understanding of materials and their behaviour, textile designers and makers are inventive and highly adaptable, exemplified in the approach to craft and digital practice as a convergent and ever-evolving activity. The craft and material base undeniably remains, but is enhanced and supported by digital process.

Recently, although there appears to be emerging acceptance of a digital aesthetic, there is still an audience perception of a quality hierarchy, with digital outputs being associated with mass production and a lower quality threshold. Craftsmanship in its traditional sense appears to have developed a higher degree of value, and if this is the case, then diminishing training and knowledge breeds a kind of craft elite: those highly skilled practitioners with the deepest knowledge and experience, the keepers of the skills whose role might be to encourage and educate future practitioners. The emerging generation of makers might have digital skills ingrained from early years, but the traditional skill base of hand and craft skills is diminishing as they have less familiarity with time-consuming and labor-intensive processes.

Lidewij Edelkoort, the influential trend forecaster, curator, publisher, and educator, is of the view that:

> We are on a quest to save textiles—to honor and promote them and take them to new dimensions. It is important to take notice of textiles because they are an

endangered species. Mills and factories around the world are vanishing one by one and educational institutions are downsizing their departments or replacing looms with computers, therefore soon young talent may have no place to go.[32]

From a more global perspective, according to UNESCO, weaving, for example, is one of many crafts listed as a skill fast being lost in the increasingly technological Western world, despite its ancestry. Indeed, weaving has become recognized by UNESCO as one of the "intangibles" of cultural heritage:

> The term "cultural heritage" has changed content considerably in recent decades, partially owing to the instruments developed by UNESCO. Cultural heritage does not end at monuments and collections of objects. It also includes traditions or living expressions inherited from our ancestors and passed on to our descendants, such as oral traditions, performing arts, social practices, rituals, festive events, knowledge and practices concerning nature and the universe or the knowledge and skills to produce traditional crafts.[33]

Given these underlying trends and their potential impact on future generations' knowledge and understanding, there is undoubtedly much ongoing discussion around the complexities of developing skills and educating designers and makers within the craft/digital context, mindful of the need to retain knowledge of hand production while managing and integrating technology. Contemporary textiles practice requires the designer/maker to identify and negotiate a path between both hand and digital processes. We must consider different training and the development of new skill sets, while compensating for the loss of traditional skills and knowledge. This means promoting an integration of approaches to making, combining mastery of tools and materials with contemporary digital processes that enable communication, collaboration, and exchange.

Further challenges for education lie in the definition of key areas of knowledge and establishment of parameters which may look very different from the traditionally stranded approach, such as print, weave, and embroidery, where digital process may have been approached as a kind of add-on, so that taught skills are relevant to the current context; digital process can blur the boundaries and distinctiveness between specialisms in a number of ways that allow for multiple interdisciplinary outputs. You might be using hand methods to design for digital production; you might be using digital processes to enable hand production, by yourself or another; or you might be combining a series of processes juggling multiple approaches. You may never physically engage directly with the material. We must be mindful of developing this set of intertwined skills for the next generation, and supporting collaboration.

Being a good craftsperson, maker, or designer is underpinned by a deep understanding of tools and materials, whether digital or traditional. But as the world becomes increasingly complex, it becomes more important for individuals with broader experiences and differing areas of expertise to work together to motivate and manage change, and to challenge convention to develop new forms of practice. Underpinning this and enhanced by digital means is communication; we can readily access information, data and research, online communities of practice, share knowledge, and collaborate in a virtual environment. These multiple resources are required to continue making advances in the ways in which we work, both as independent practitioners and with others, including scientists and experts from industry.

As Jessica Hemming points out, "The knowledge that first created what we consider today to be complex woven structures is far from new. While weavers can now work with the assistance of Computer Aided Design, the advent of this technology has not made woven cloth fundamentally any more complex."[34] Digital applications are becoming ever more sophisticated, responsive, intuitive, and reactive, but however well the computer modeling functions are designed, achieving innovative and creative new work relies on experience and a deep understanding of materials and process.

Notes

1. Glenn Adamson, "Introduction," in *The Craft Reader*, ed. Glenn Adamson (Oxford: Berg, 2010), 2.
2. Adamson, "Introduction," 3.
3. Sarah E. Braddock Clarke and Jane Harris, *Digital Visions for Fashion and Textiles: Made in Code* (London: Thames and Hudson, 2012), 33.
4. Braddock Clarke and Harris, *Digital Visions for Fashion and Textiles*, 33.
5. Julie Holyoke, *Digital Jacquard Design* (London: Bloomsbury Academic, 2013).
6. Nigel Cross's "designerly way of knowing" describes a synthesizing and iterative process that carries knowledge embodied in the design activity and the design products. See Nigel Cross, *Designerly Ways of Knowing* (Basel: Birkhäuser, 2007).
7. Glenn Adamson, *Thinking through Craft* (Oxford: Berg, 2007), 7.
8. Carole Gray and Gordon Burnett, "Making Sense: An Exploration of Ways of Knowing Generated Through Practice and Reflection in Craft," in *Proceedings of the Craftticulation and Education Conference*, ed. Leena K. Kaukinen (Helsinki: NordFo, 2009), 51. https://helda.helsinki.fi/bitstream/handle/10224/4810/Kaukinen_verkko.pdf?sequence=2 [accessed July 13, 2015].
9. Achim Menges and Sean Ahlquist, *Computational Design Thinking: Computation Design Thinking* (Hoboken, NJ: Wiley, 2011), 19.
10. See Chapter 7: "Maintaining the Human Touch—Exploring 'Crafted Control' Within an Advanced Textile Production Interface," 91–102.
11. Braddock Clarke and Harris, *Digital Vision for Fashion and Textiles,* 126.
12. Ibid., 119.
13. Kerstin Kraft, "Textile Patterns and Their Epistemological Functions," *Textile: The Journal of Cloth and Culture* 2, no. 3 (2004): 274–89.
14. Daina Taimina, *Crocheting Adventures with Hyperbolic Planes* (Wellesley, MA: A. K. Peters, 2009). For a crocheted model, see Plate 17.
15. Howard Risatti, *A Theory of Craft: Function and Aesthetic Expression* (Chapel Hill, NC: University of North Carolina Press, 2007), 51.

16. Malcolm McCullough, *Abstracting Craft: The Practiced Digital Hand* (Cambridge, MA: MIT Press, 1996), 59.
17. McCullough, *Abstracting Craft*, 60.
18. See Chapter 6: "The Digital Print Room—A Bespoke Approach to Print Technology," 77.
19. See e.g. McCullough, *Abstracting Craft*.
20. Ibid., 63.
21. See Chapter: "Maintaining the Human Touch," 96.
22. Rachel Philpott, "Entwined Approaches: Integrating Design, Art and Science in Design Research-by-Practice," in *Proceedings of Design Research Society Conference—Re:Search: Uncertainty, Contradiction and Value* (Bangkok: Chulalongkorn University, 2012), 1496–511.
23. See Chapter 8: "*Garment ID*: Textile Patterning Techniques for Hybrid Functional Clothing," 107.
24. Malcolm Barnard, *Fashion as Communication* (London: Routledge, 2002), 72–9.
25. Braddock Clarke and Harris, *Digital Visions for Fashion and Textiles*, 19–29.
26. Helen Rees, "Patterns of Making: Thinking and Making in Industrial Design," in *The Culture of Craft*, ed. Peter Dormer (Manchester: Manchester University Press, 1996), 122–3.
27. Tim Ingold, *Lines: A Brief History* (Abingdon: Routledge, 2007), 2.
28. See Foreword, xx.
29. Angharad Thomas, "Knitting Gloves" https://knittinggloves.wordpress.com/about/ [accessed July 27, 2015].
30. Ellen Dissanayake, *Homo Aestheticus: Where Art Comes From and Why* (Séattle, WA: University of Washington Press, 1995), 51.
31. Anon 2010 in Faith Kane, "Digital Embroidery and Expression: A Review of Closely Held Secrets," *Craft Research* 2 (1) (2011): 161–8.
32. Lidewij Edelkoort and Philip Fimmano, "Talking Textiles Waxman Textile Prize—The Finalists #2015." http://www.trendtablet.com/4155-talking-textiles/ [accessed July 30, 2015].
33. UNESCO, "Intangible Heritage Domains in the 2003 Convention." http://www.unesco.org/culture/ich/index.php?lg=en&pg=00052 [accessed July 30 2015].
34. Jessica Hemmings, "A Certain Kind of Judgement." http://jessicahemmings.com/?s=a+certain+kind+of+judgement [accessed July 30, 2015].

Bibliography

Adamson, Glenn, *Thinking Through Craft* (Oxford: Berg, 2007).
Adamson, Glenn, "Introduction," in *The Craft Reader*, ed. Glenn Adamson (Oxford: Berg, 2010).
Barnard, Malcolm, *Fashion as Communication* (London: Routledge, 2002).
Braddock Clarke, Sarah E. and Jane Harris, *Digital Visions for Fashion and Textiles: Made in Code* (London: Thames and Hudson, 2012).
Dissanayake, Ellen, *Homo Aestheticus: Where Art Comes From and Why* (Seattle, WA: University of Washington Press, 1995).
Gray, Carole and Gordon Burnett, "Making Sense: An Exploration of Ways of Knowing Generated Through Practice and Reflection in Craft," in *Proceedings of the Crafticulation and Education Conference*, ed. Leena K. Kaukinen (Helsinki: NordFo, 2009), 44–51. https://helda.

helsinki.fi/bitstream/handle/10224/4810/Kaukinen_verkko.pdf?sequence=2 [accessed July 13, 2015].

Holyoke, Julie, *Digital Jacquard Design* (London: Bloomsbury Academic, 2013).

Ingold, Tim, *Lines: A Brief History* (Abingdon: Routledge, 2007).

Kane, Faith, "Digital Embroidery and Expression: A Review of Closely Held Secrets," *Craft Research* 2 (1) (2011): 161–8.

McCullough, Malcolm, *Abstracting Craft: The Practiced Digital Hand* (Cambridge, MA: MIT Press, 1996).

Menges, Achim and Sean Ahlquist, *Computational Design Thinking: Computation Design Thinking* (Hoboken, NJ: Wiley, 2011).

Rachel Philpott, "Entwined Approaches: Integrating Design, Art and Science in Design Research-by-Practice," in *Proceedings of Design Research Society Conference—Re:Search: Uncertainty, Contradiction and Value* (Bangkok: Chulalongkorn University, 2012), 1496–511.

Rees, Helen, "Patterns of Making: Thinking and Making in Industrial Design," in *The Culture of Craft*, ed. Peter Dormer (Manchester: Manchester University Press, 1996).

Risatti, Howard, *A Theory of Craft: Function and Aesthetic Expression* (Chapel Hill, NC: University of North Carolina Press, 2007).

Taimina, Daina, *Crocheting Adventures with Hyperbolic Planes* (Wellesley, MA: A. K. Peters, 2009).

PART ONE
DIGITAL TECHNOLOGIES INFORMING CRAFT

2
CRAFTING TEXTILES IN THE DIGITAL AGE: PRINTED TEXTILES

Cathy Treadaway

Introduction

This chapter explores what it means to craft printed textiles in the digital age. The first section documents ways in which digital imaging and print technologies have changed the practice of printed textile design over the last thirty years. Digital design processes are now ubiquitous and many textile practitioners today employ a hybrid digital practice in which a diverse range of technological and traditional handcrafts are combined. Practitioners engage with digital processes such as digital print, laser cutting and etching, digital stitch, and embedded electronics to pattern textiles.[1] The precision, speed, and flexibility of digital tools are frequently combined with the serendipity and creative unpredictability of handcraft, adding value and significance to the printed artifact.[2] This chapter presents examples of different approaches taken by artists and designers who exploit digital crafting strategies within their printed textile practice.

Crafting printed textiles

Making by hand is an innate human capacity; we are embodied beings and our creative and cognitive agility is deeply connected to the ways in which we use our hands.[3] In our highly cephalocentric society,[4] which prioritizes mind over body knowledge, we often lose sight of the importance of the ways in which our manual experience shapes who we are and how we think. Our hands are our interface with the world—reaching to draw in sensory experience to the body and then reshaping our world through manipulative activity.[5] This iterative cycle of experience and interaction is at the heart of hand making and enables personal expression and intimate human connection to be communicated in the artifacts we make.[6]

For centuries textile crafts have provided everyday creative opportunities for people, not only to fabricate useful artifacts but also to convey personal stories and cultural narratives through pattern and decoration.[7] We elaborate artifacts as a way of imbuing them with economic and cultural value. Our engagement with craft practice enhances personal well-being; it helps sustain social relationships and provides self-worth.[8] Tacit knowledge, developed over many hours of making, imbues the hands with tactile sensibilities and procedural knowledge crucial for craft skill.[9] This *body knowledge* enables us to enter the state of creative *flow* we can experience when we are lost in the joyful moment of making.[10] Our personal touch becomes evident in the artifacts we create and the marks we make when we draw.[11] Handwriting is a perfect example of this and reveals how our personal expression is visually unique in character: shaped by life experience, tool use, personality, and emotion.

Our hands will continue to be crucial in the process of crafting textiles in the digital age despite technical developments that have automated many of the analog manual design skills.[12] Some of the most laborious hand processes, essential in the preparation of design work for printed textiles in the past, are now executed with speed and accuracy using computer-aided design (CAD) software.[13] Digital inkjet printing has changed the types of designs that it is possible to reproduce. Millions of colors can be printed with ease and there is no longer a technical necessity for developing repeating patterns and color separations in order to create printed textile lengths.[14]

Textile practitioners today routinely embrace digital technologies in most aspects of design and fabrication.[15] But how is the creative potential of hand making capitalized in digital processes? How is technology extending creative possibilities for printed textile practitioners now and how will it do so in the future? The following section explores the evolution and development of digital imaging technology for printed textiles.

Printing as process

From the earliest times, man has used textiles and non-woven cloth to keep warm and to make dwellings comfortable. Our human desire to add cultural and economic value or to personalize the things we make has resulted in a rich heritage of embellishment, evident both in the construction techniques used and the surface decoration of these artifacts. Printing is one of the earliest forms of pattern making due to the relative simplicity of the processes required to replicate a motif on a surface. The craft of printing on textiles most likely evolved from simply using fingers and hands to mark surfaces; prehistoric handprints found in cave paintings are evidence of this. Simple artifacts were probably dipped in pigment to make the earliest examples of printed cloth. Carved materials, such as wood, bone, and stone, were used later to generate more complex surface pattern imagery, leading to the development of woodblock printing, which continued as a form of commercial textile printing until the twentieth century. Today highly detailed photogravure roller printing enables textile substrates to be enriched with color, texture, and pattern economically and at vast speeds. Digital print processes are now widely used to produce fabrics in millions of colors in economically viable short runs and as bespoke or personalized designs for both the fashion and furnishing industries. Although the process remains slower than that used in analog mass production textile roller printing, it is likely that digital printing processes will play an increasingly important role in the manufacture of printed textiles globally in the future.[16]

The *design* of printed textiles has always been closely aligned to the technical advances in the processes used to manufacture patterned cloth.[17] The technologies deployed help to define the characteristics of what is deemed by society to be appropriate, fashionable, or *on-trend* as a surface pattern design.

Textile repeating patterns, their scale and format, were originally developed to accommodate the constraints of industrial roller printing for mass production.[18] Consequently, designs that conform to the technical requirements of the manufacturing process have

Figure 2.1 Visual characteristics of printed textile process. Top left: engraved roller printing. Top right: silkscreen printing. Bottom left: block printing. Bottom right: digital inkjet printing. Photograph: Cathy Treadaway.

become the visual language of printed textile imagery.[19] The block and screen-printing processes require that colors be separated out from the original artwork and printed in different layers. This leads to the creation of patterns that include limited numbers of colors, flat areas of blocked color, and defined edges of pattern motifs. As the production methods have evolved, so too have the visual characteristics of surface pattern designs that predominate in the market (Figure 2.1). This is evident today in textile designs found in high street stores that exhibit the characteristics of digital inkjet printing, such as tonal gradation, millions of colors, photographic representation, placement, and engineered prints.

Digital tools

Digital imaging is now an integral part of the textile design process and many textile designers working in industry today rely heavily on their digital rather than hand-crafting skills. The use of computer-aided design (CAD) reduces lead times in production, enabling companies to respond with speed to the rapid changes demanded by the ever-increasing time-to-market spiral.[20] Internet-based print-on-demand bureaux and large format digital inkjet printing in industry make outputs quick to produce, short runs feasible, and strike offs unnecessary. Without competency in using a range of design software, however, it is difficult to access the digital processes and techniques that are now available to pattern cloth.

It could be argued that any designer who is fluent with the software could develop designs for digitally printed textiles. Currently many design studios include graphics and product designers who have had little training in textile design. However, a good textile designer understands the flow and drape of cloth; the ways in which pattern can be composed to add interest to a surface as well as to bring rest to the eye. Good repeating patterns provide flow and harmony on a surface. Uncomfortable spaces, tilts, and skews in a design can be identified as flaws and are visually difficult to live with. Understanding how to place an image on a garment or on the face of a piece of cloth requires a sensitivity to composition and an appreciation of balance and scale within the parameters of the fabric selvedge. Good textile designers do this intuitively; they understand; they feel it—it is an embodied understanding of how pattern works. Digitally printed textiles may no longer require the structural conventions of textile repeat pattern making, but an understanding and sensitivity for balance, flow, and composition is essential in digital print textile craft.

Developments in digital printing

Textile design practice has evolved dramatically over the last thirty years as a result of technological change in the textile printing industry. Digital imaging tools have been available for use by textile designers since the 1970s,[21] although, even at the turn of the millennium, the majority of textile designers were using paint and paper to originate and supply design work to industry. Early computer systems were hugely expensive; however, the advent of the microcomputer in the 1980s enabled more designers to engage with the technology. The Quantel Paintbox and the Pluto graphics system, developed in the early 1980s for the film, TV, and games industries, influenced early software used creatively by designers. Wider adoption of technology by graphics and textile designers in the early 1990s led to the development of software such as Adobe Photoshop and Illustrator® and Corel Draw and Corel Paint®. Digital inkjet printing emerged in the late 1990s and stimulated wider interest in CAD by printed textile designers who were now able to render their digital images (on-screen) directly onto cloth.

Digital inkjet print technology began to re-characterize the visual characteristics of printed textile design at the beginning of the twenty-first century, breaking the design conventions rooted in engraved roller and silkscreen printing where repeating pattern was an economic and technical necessity of the process. Textile practitioners such as Hitoshi Ujiie, J. R. Campbell, and Jean Parsons in the USA and Vibeke Riisberg and Hil Driessen in Europe pioneered digital processes in the early years of the new century, creating innovative designs that exploited digital print as a new medium with its own unique visual qualities including photographic representation, unrestricted numbers of colors, engineered designs, and non-repeating pattern. These practitioners worked in universities where they had access to the latest computer and print technology and opportunity to experiment. Ujiie developed ground-breaking work in digital print at Philadelphia University, and Campbell and Parsons explored engineered printed apparel design and mass customization at Iowa State University.[22] Danish designer Vibeke Riisberg was an early exponent of CAD and, before access to digital printing, had developed a four-color separation process in order to translate her designs onto fabric using silkscreen printing. Hil Driessen experimented using photographic imagery digitally printed onto fabric to create trompe l'oeil effects that have been used for interior furnishings and large-scale internal and external wall coverings for commercial and industrial buildings in the Netherlands. In the UK, textile artist Norma Starszakowna developed hybrid digital textile craft processes combining handcraft and technology. Her *Hinterland* textiles produced for the Scottish Parliament building in Edinburgh in 2004 were produced via layers of printed, heat-reactive and metallic colors that exploit coloration produced through oxidization and patination.

Fashion designers have been quick to exploit the creative possibilities of digital inkjet printing.[23] The potential of the process to produce fabric for one-of-a-kind garments in which pattern, garment shape, and fabric drape are engineered to work together has resulted in highly innovative outputs and rich collaborations with textile designers and technologists.[24] Fashion designers Issey Miyake, Basso and Brooke, Hussein Chalayan, Alexander McQueen, Hamish Morrow, Eley Kishimoto, and Jonathan Saunders integrated digitally printed textiles into their catwalk collections during the first decade of the millennium. Basso and Brooke were the first fashion partnership to use digital inkjet printing extensively throughout an entire collection. In 2002 they developed printed fabrics engineered to work in harmony with the garment shape. Hussein Chalayan's Spring/Summer 1996 collection contained pixelated floral textile designs by Wakako Kishimoto.

Her later work for the Eley Kishimoto partnership involved the production of intricate photorealistic designs that would have been difficult to replicate using analog printing processes. Jonathan Saunders, who worked initially for Alexander McQueen, uses a print process that combines digital print with hand silkscreen printing. In 2003 he produced a collection of designs that were an innovative mix of hand drawing with digitally rendered imagery, printed directly onto flat garment pattern pieces prior to garment construction.

Software has influenced the kinds of designs that have been created; in the late 1990s Eros Tang worked with sophisticated 3D computer graphic software developed for the film industry to create 3D floral imagery for printed textile motifs. Philip Delamore produced a collection of textile designs for Hamish Morrow's Spring/Summer 2004 collection using a combination of 2D and 3D software. Other designers such as Rory Chrichton and Casey Reas have exploited video, moving image, and generative software to develop surface pattern designs for printed textiles.

Hybrid craft: A personal case study

Over the last three decades I have explored and used digital technology within my creative practice as a designer. I have always considered it to be just one of a number of tools, media, and processes that inform and support the surface pattern work that I create. I began to integrate digital imaging into my practice in 1983 using an Apple IIe computer with a Robocom joystick developed for early computer games (Figure 2.2). Mice, scanners, and printers were in their infancy and not widely used at this time, and the output from my system was via a simple pen plotter, which was able to translate the black-and-white screen image into a single line on paper.

The design work I produced was largely geometric and comprised simple geometric pattern forms and grids that would have been laborious to draw by hand. The computer was able to speed up the process, rescale imagery, and provide a degree of accuracy that was difficult to replicate by hand. The plotter drew the structure onto paper, to

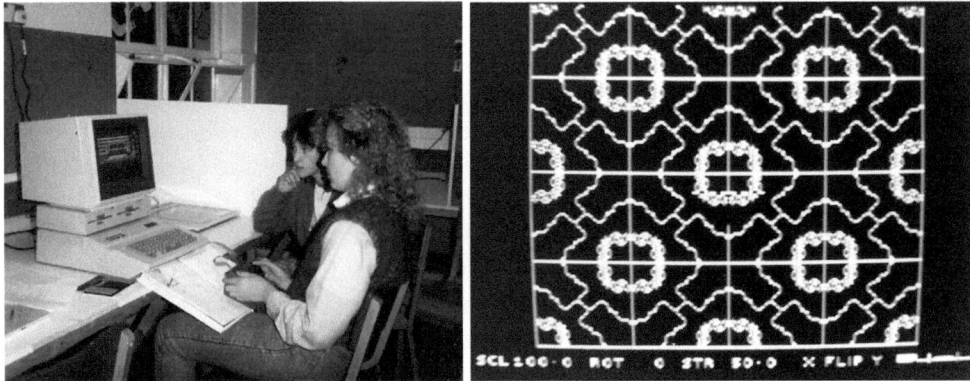

Figure 2.2 Left: designing on an Apple IIe microcomputer, 1983. Right: CAD design, 1983. Photograph: Cathy Treadaway.

Figure 2.3 CAD-generated printed design with hand-rendered watercolor and gold pigment, designed for Precision Studios, 1984. Photograph: Cathy Treadaway.

which I added watercolor, gouache, and metallic pigments (Figure 2.3). Designs from this collection were sold to companies to embellish a variety of products including fashion fabrics, paper products, ceramic tableware, and glass.

In 1986 I began working with an IO Research Pluto graphics system and PC; this was considered sophisticated digital imaging technology at this point in time. The system had been developed as a cheaper competitor to the Quantel Paintbox used in the TV and film industries. Drawings were created using a graphics tablet and digitizing pen and, for the first time, video input enabled photographic image capture. Digital scanners were not widely available, so I mounted a video camera on a photographic enlarger stand in order to create a device to input imagery to integrate within the designs I was creating. I began using the system to develop patterns that were much more sophisticated than had been possible using the previous system I had worked with in the early 1980s (Figure 2.4).

I was intrigued by the possibilities of integrating scanned imagery within my work, but the lack of color printed output was frustrating. I wanted to capture and print the full-color graphic representation on the monitor in order to manipulate it further with hand processes and materials. This led me to develop a photographic color separation process using film to create positives for silkscreen and litho printing. As in my earlier work, digital imaging was an integral part of the creative process but it was not able

Figure 2.4 CAD repeating pattern designed on the Pluto Designer system, Cathy Treadaway, 1987. Photograph: Cathy Treadaway.

to provide the visual characteristics I was striving for. I always felt that the aesthetic of the digital output was lacking something and I worked to extend it further through the addition of hand-rendered or applied color. The motifs I created at this time inevitably exhibited the pixilation of the early low-resolution computer graphics (Plate 1). Screen images were digitally color separated and then printed in up to six colors and often further embellished by hand.

In the late 1980s and 1990s there were great advances in graphics processing speed, screen resolution, increased memory for data storage, and new peripheral devices, largely driven by the demands of TV, film, and the computer games industry. During this period I devised a method of outputting vector-based graphics onto paper using an A3 flatbed inkjet printer. This enabled me to exploit digital accuracy when creating repeating structures and motifs and change scale with ease. The process saved time and enabled me to focus on the creative application of layers of color and texture by hand to create design work for textiles, paper products, and ceramic surfaces. By printing onto good quality watercolor paper I could apply layers of paint and dyes, achieving a sensitivity that could be replicated by manufacturing processes used in industry. It also provided the satisfaction of combining hand and machine in a truly integrated hybrid digital craft practice.

Developments in inkjet paper and textile printers began to make possible the replication of full-color digital imagery by the late 1990s; digital cameras and flatbed scanners were more widely available and used as input devices for photographic imagery. These developments greatly influenced the work I was creating. With access to a Mimaki TX2 inkjet textile printer in 2003, I was able to print images I was creating on screen with ease onto different fabric substrates. I continued to explore ways in which hand-rendered work could be integrated within digital imagery to capture the human touch within the machine-generated precision. This included using an early tablet computer and pen and combining hand-rendered work with digital photographs and video stills (Plate 2). My creative intention was always to try to craft with my digital toolbox, not to simply accept the "digital aesthetic" that was so often evident in computer-generated design work at the time but rather to fuse the best of both hand and machine.

My interest in the role of hand use within digital creative practice led me to develop a new body of work in 2008 exploring surface and texture, using three-dimensional printing.[25] The artworks were created using a haptic tool and Freeform software and were printed in starch and plastic using both Z Corp and FDM (Fused Deposition Modeling) printers. The haptic tool provided force feedback to emulate the tactile experience of working with physical media; in this body of work the computer simulated working with clay. Although I found the interface relatively crude, it enabled me to generate the STL

Figure 2.5 "Cape Cornwall," digitally printed starch with pigment and metallic foil embellishment, Cathy Treadaway, 2009. Photograph: Dirk Dahmer.

(STereoLithography) files required to access 3D printers for the first time. As with previous digital print exploration, I found that I wanted to reintroduce physical handcraft and so some of the printed pieces were embellished further using metallic foils and pigments (Figure 2.5).

One of the joys of combining hand with digital craft is the opportunity to develop multiple solutions from the digital file. Each printed artifact is a unique rendition of the digital code and can replicate exactly or contain subtle variations of the original digital file. The final hybrid work, combining digital and handcraft, reintroduces the element of risk and serendipity that the precision and replication of the machine code denies. It is this workmanship of risk[26] that seems to add humanity and emotional connection in the way the resulting artwork is perceived.[27] Throughout this digital journey I have resisted suggestions from others in the field to learn computer programming in order to develop my own software, preferring to work with off-the-shelf packages. In my own practice, digital crafting means working with the available tools rather than spending time developing code from scratch.

Crafting with code

Digital data is stored as numeric code: zeros and ones. It can be argued that the true original artwork resides in the code, not the on-screen visualization, or the printed artifact.[28] The code remains virtual and without intrinsic meaning until it is "performed" as a visual image or a physical print. The same code can produce a variety of performances with very different visual and material characteristics depending on *how* it is performed or by what technologies or materials it is represented.[29] This has led to two conceptual approaches to creative digital craft practice: those who interact directly with the machine through crafting their own code, and others who craft with the software developers' code. Both are valid approaches and have their advantages and limitations.

Digital practitioners who advocate crafting code as their creative practice seek to maintain a greater intimacy over the machine and what it can do. Pioneers in this approach to software crafting include Casey Reas and Ben Fry, who developed "Processing", an open source programming language, in 2001. Reas's printed textile designs developed using this approach involve digitally constructed kinetic systems.[30] Reas perceives the software he develops as having its own attributes that he compares to being like a physical material, which offers him creative access to infinite types of mark and structure. Like Reas, Hilary Carlisle developed an innovative approach to designing non-repeating patterns for digital inkjet printing through developing her own software algorithms in the first decade of the century. Gail Kenning developed code based on textile crafting in which she explores the theme of perfect repetition in machine code compared to the irregularity of the handmade (Figure 2.6).

Most designers however do not have the skills, time, or inclination to craft directly with the code, but choose to manipulate it through commercial software packages.[31] Although this constrains the designer to the logic of the software engineer and removes some of the control (desired by the digital code crafters), it does help speed up engagement with

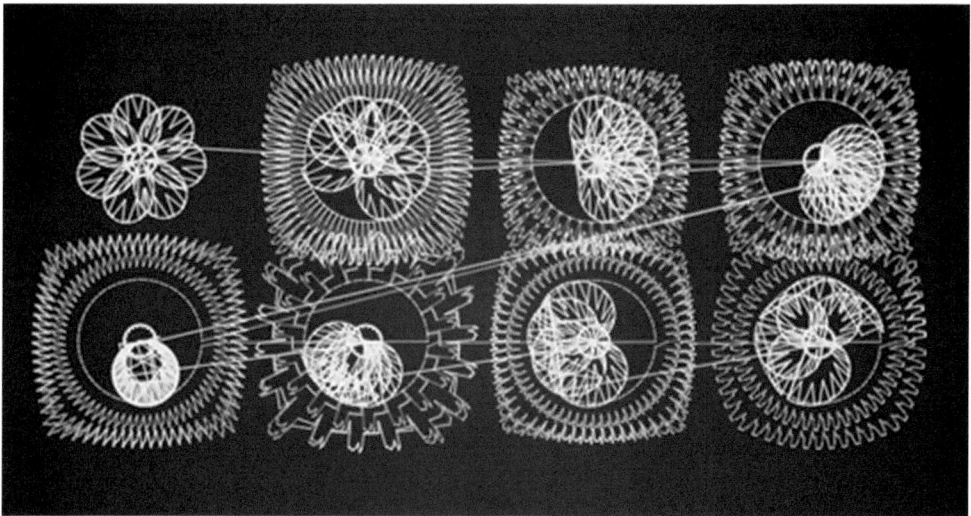

Figure 2.6 Digital code: "Evolving Lace," Gail Kenning, 2010. Photograph: Gail Kenning.

the technology. Any manipulation of digital imagery with software changes the code and so it can be argued that exploiting established software is an equally valid approach to digital practice.[32] The most important aspect of creative crafting concerns gaining mastery and fluency with the tools; it is the artistic intention, visual interest, and aesthetic result that has the most perceived value in the resulting design. Interfaces that are quick to learn and easy to use enable designers to concentrate on the process of achieving their creative goals.[33] Data gloves, haptic tools, and organic interfaces[34] are used by designers who wish to exploit code in ways that make use of gestural and haptic sensibilities of handcraft within their digital practice. Tavs Jorgensen, for example, has explored the use of data gloves and motion-capture software as gestural interfaces for design, and

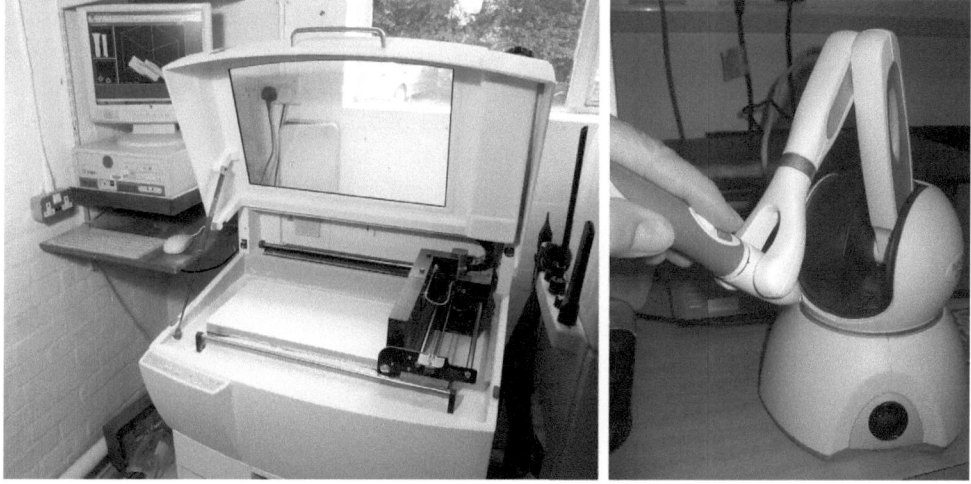

Figure 2.7 Left: Z Corp 3D printer. Right: haptic tool. Photograph: Cathy Treadaway.

Ann Marie Shillito has developed new haptic tools and software for 3D-generated forms (Figure 2.7).[35]

Developments in printed textiles embellished with electronics (sensors, light-emitting diodes, actuators, RFID, etc.) suggest that, in the future, crafting code will affect not only the appearance of printed textiles but also their functionality. It is already possible to program the performance of a textile pattern using simple electronic microprocessors such as Arduino[36] and Adafruit.[37] This, along with open source code, has already taken the potential of code crafting to a wider, less technically savvy community through Hackspaces[38] and online craft communities. The Maker Movement, DIY communities, and social media have made new approaches to crafting with code more democratic and accessible.[39]

Future

Printed textiles in the future are likely to include not only *embedded* electronics but also printed circuitry on their surface, to add functionality. Nano technological developments in the printing and coating industry are leading to new types of conductive pigments and sensors that can be printed onto textiles. Designers are already exploiting the potential of combining conductive textiles with digital inkjet printing to create innovative fabrics that can react to environment and emotion. In 2006 Philips Design in the Netherlands launched its Skin Probe series,[40] combining intelligent materials with interactive and ambient sensing properties linked to the body. Interest in emotional and affective computing is encouraging designers to consider integrating interactive properties, embedded sensors, and actuators within their printed designs. Amy Winters is a designer who is reimagining printed textiles as intelligent soft surfaces. Her work is exploring the interactive quality of print to create "emotional functionality" through environment-changing inks that react to sunlight and water, as well as sound-activated printed electronics. Winters's "Thunderstorm" dress (Figure 2.8), created for the *Made in Future* exhibition in Milan in 2012, was a collaboration with EL International,[41] a producer of electroluminescent technology. The designer's intention behind integrating this type of playful interaction into the design is to initiate a deeper emotional relationship between the wearer and the garment. Her designs have been used as showpieces in advertisements, for live events, and are available commercially through retail boutiques.

Developments in 3D printing are proposing completely new paradigms for future textiles in which it will be possible to print whole garments in three dimensions.[42] In the first decade of the century Philip Delamore pioneered the use of 3D print technology to prototype innovative designs for shoes.[43] Working with Janne Kyttänen and Jiri Evenhuis from Freedom of Creation, Delamore contributed to a reimagining of textile fabric structure using 3D print technology; the result was a new kind of 3D printed chain-mail type material. More recently, Iris van Herpen[44] has created designs using 3D print technology for couture fashion. Her collaboration with the architects Daniel Widnig in 2011 and Philip Beesley in 2014 has resulted in innovative garments only realizable using the 3D print process. Her sculptural garments are made from 3D printed laser-fused

Figure 2.8 "Thunderstorm" dress, Amy Winters for Rainbow Winters, 2012. Photograph: Rainbow Winters.

polyamide and she also employs injection molding and laser cutting to give her garments dynamic shape.

Work investigating the potential of 4D printing by researchers at MIT in the USA is exploring the development of more resilient, lighter printed structures that can respond to the world around them. Four-dimensional printing adds the potential for dynamic materials that can change over time and adapt to specific uses or to the surrounding environment.[45]

Summary

This chapter has provided an overview of the ways in which the practice of crafting designs for printed textiles has been influenced by developments in digital technology. The current generation of textile practitioners are digital natives; acceptance and use of technology in creative processes are second nature to them. Although traditional and digital media are converging through the development of increasingly sensitive and sophisticated interfaces, the importance of hand skill and physical craft is unlikely to be replaced entirely.[46] Our hands help us think and physical making provides opportunities for serendipitous and accidental creative insights that the logic and control of the machine can often inhibit. By combining traditional textile handcraft, such as hand embroidery, screen printing, and hand painting, digitally printed surfaces can be embellished and enriched, providing qualities that complement the digital output and imbue the work with the touch of the maker. Digital print processes are still relatively new and textile print techniques such as devoré, discharge, flocking, and metallic printed colors are not yet achievable using the current generation of digital inkjet printing machines.[47] Nevertheless, practitioners are able to develop rich surfaces by combining digital print with these traditional hand-printed processes. The resulting visual aesthetic reflects this hybridization of traditional and digital processes.

Digital inkjet printing has its own particular visual characteristics. Designs with millions of colors, fine detail, precise lines, and graded tonal qualities that would be impossible via analog methods can be produced easily and at less cost to the environment. Engineered, one-of-a-kind, and bespoke designs can be replicated cost-effectively and with ease. The economic viability of digital inkjet printing for short runs reduces time to market, warehousing and transportation costs, enabling a more personalized and sustainable model of production.

New types of textiles are currently being developed that will require a more interdisciplinary and collaborative approach to design. Textiles that are interactive and responsive will require the skills of a variety of practitioners including technologists, engineers, and designers with expertise in electronics, computing, and nanotechnology.[48] Future digital craft for printed textiles will inevitably be more democratic, agile, easily communicated, shared, manipulated, downloadable, and replicable in 2D, 3D and ultimately, with shape-changing potential, in 4D.

Notes

1. Sarah E. Braddock Clarke and Jane Harris, *Digital Visions for Fashion + Textiles: Made in Code* (London: Thames & Hudson, 2012).
2. Cathy Treadaway, "Digital Imaging: Its Current and Future Influence upon the Creative Practice of Textile and Surface Pattern Designers" (PhD Thesis, University of Wales Institute Cardiff, 2006).
3. Richard Sennett, *The Craftsman* (London: Allen Lane, 2008).
4. The cephalocentric thesis of Plato and Hippocrates was that the brain was the seat of all thought. Jean-Pierre Changeux, *Neuronal Man: The Biology of Mind* (New York: Pantheon Books, 1985).
5. Raymond Tallis, *The Hand: A Philosophical Inquiry into Human Being* (Edinburgh: Edinburgh University Press, 2003).
6. Cathy Treadaway, "Materiality, Memory, and Imagination: Using Empathy to Research Creativity," *Leonardo* 42 (2009): 231–7.
7. Ellen Dissanayake, *Art and Intimacy: How the Arts Began* (Seattle, WA: University of Washington Press, 2000).
8. Cathy Treadaway, Gail Kenning, and Steve Coleman, "Designing for Positive Emotion," in *The Colors of Care: 9th International Conference on Design and Emotion*, ed. Pieter Desmet, Juan Salamanca, Geke Ludden, Andrés Burbano, and Jorge Maya (Bogota, Colombia: Design and Emotion Society and Universidad de Los Andes, 2014), 545–51.
9. Peter Dormer, *The Art of the Maker: Skill and its Meaning in Art, Craft and Design* (London: Thames and Hudson, 1994).
10. Mihaly Csikszentmihalyi, *Creativity: Flow and the Psychology of Discovery and Invention* (New York: HarperCollins Publishers, 1996).
11. Tallis, *The Hand*.
12. Treadaway, "Materiality, Memory, and Imagination."
13. Hitoshi Ujiie, *Digital Printing of Textiles* (Cambridge: Woodhead Publishing, 2006).
14. Melanie Bowles and Ceri Isaac, *Digital Textile Design*, 2nd edn (London: Laurence King, 2012).
15. Simon Clarke, *Textile Design* (London: Laurence King, 2011).
16. Ujiie, *Digital Printing of Textiles*.
17. Amanda Briggs and Gillian E. Bunce, "Breaking the Rules: Innovatory Uses of CAD in Printed Textiles," *Ars Textrina* 24 (1995): 185–203.
18. Ujiie, *Digital Printing of Textiles*.
19. Briggs and Bunce, "Breaking the Rules."
20. Ujiie, *Digital Printing of Textiles*.
21. Millitron Printing System by Milliken in the mid-1970s made use of early digital imaging and print technologies.
22. J. R. Campbell and Jean Parsons, "Taking Advantage of the Design Potential of Digital Printing Technology for Apparel," *Journal of Textile and Apparel, Technology and Management* 4 (3) (2005): 1–10.
23. Braddock Clarke and Harris, *Digital Visions for Fashion + Textiles*.
24. Cathy Treadaway, "Digital Printing," in *Smart Clothes and Wearable Technology*, ed. Jane McCann and David Bryson (Cambridge: Woodhead Publishing, 2009), 300–18.

25. Cathy Treadaway, "Creative Momentum in the Information Age," in *Momentum* [exhibition catalog], ed. Craft in the Bay C (Cardiff: Makers Guild in Wales, 2011), 4–7.
26. David Pye, *The Nature of Design* (London: Studio Vista, 1964).
27. Cathy Treadaway, "Digital Imagination: The Impact of Digital Imaging on Printed Textiles," *Textile: The Journal of Cloth and Culture* 2 (3) (2004): 256–73.
28. Boris Grois, *Art Power* (Cambridge, MA: MIT Press, 2008).
29. Lev Manovich, "Database as Symbolic Form," in *Museums in a Digital Age*, ed. Ross Perry (London: Routledge, 2010), 64–71.
30. Braddock Clarke and Harris, *Digital Visions for Fashion + Textiles*.
31. Ibid.
32. It can be argued that exploiting established software is an equally valid approach to digital practice since most designers work with accessible, readily available physical tools and materials and rarely make their own paintbrushes and paper.
33. Malcolm McCullough, *Abstracting Craft: The Practiced Digital Hand* (Cambridge, MA: MIT Press, 1996).
34. OUIs are interfaces with a non-flat display where users control an object by manipulating an actual physical shape.
35. Ann Marie Shillito, *Digital Crafts: Industrial Technologies for Applied Artists and Designer Makers* (London: Bloomsbury, 2013).
36. http://www.arduino.cc/ [accessed November 25, 2014].
37. http://www.adafruit.com/ [accessed November 25, 2014].
38. http://www.hackspace.org.uk/view/Main_Page [accessed November 25, 2014].
39. Faythe Levine and Cortney Heimerl, *Handmade Nation: The Rise of DIY, Art, Craft, and Design* (New York: Princeton Architectural Press, 2008).
40. http://www.design.philips.com/philips/sites/philipsdesign/about/design/designportfolio/design_futures/dresses.page [accessed November 25, 2014].
41. http://www.el-international.co.uk/ [accessed November 25, 2014].
42. Braddock Clarke and Harris, *Digital Visions for Fashion + Textiles*.
43. Treadaway, "Digital Printing."
44. http://www.irisvanherpen.com/ [accessed November 25, 2014].
45. http://sjet.us/MIT_4D%20PRINTING.html [accessed November 25, 2014].
46. Braddock Clarke and Harris, *Digital Visions for Fashion + Textiles*.
47. Bowles and Isaac, *Digital Textile Design*.
48. Xiaoming Tao, *Wearable Electronics and Photonics* (Cambridge: Woodhead Publishing, 2005).

Bibliography

Bowles, Melanie, and Ceri Isaac, *Digital Textile Design*, 2nd edn (London: Laurence King, 2012).
Braddock Clarke, Sarah E., and Jane Harris, *Digital Visions for Fashion + Textiles: Made in Code* (London: Thames and Hudson, 2012).
Briggs, Amanda, and Gillian E. Bunce, "Breaking the Rules: Innovatory Uses of CAD in Printed Textiles," *Ars Textrina* 24 (1995): 185–203.

Campbell, J. R., and Jean Parsons, "Taking Advantage of the Design Potential of Digital Printing Technology for Apparel," *Journal of Textile and Apparel, Technology and Management* 4 (3) (2005): 1–10.

Clarke, Simon, *Textile Design* (London: Laurence King, 2011).

Csikszentmihalyi, Mihaly, *Creativity: Flow and the Psychology of Discovery and Invention* (New York: HarperCollins Publishers, 1996).

Dissanayake, Ellen, *Art and Intimacy: How the Arts Began* (Seattle, WA: University of Washington Press, 2000).

Dormer, Peter, *The Art of the Maker: Skill and its Meaning in Art, Craft and Design* (London: Thames and Hudson, 1994).

Grois, Boris, *Art Power* (Cambridge, MA: MIT Press, 2008).

Manovich, Lev, "Database as Symbolic Form," in *Museums in a Digital Age*, ed. Ross Perry (London: Routledge, 2010), 64–71.

McCullough, Malcolm, *Abstracting Craft: The Practiced Digital Hand* (Cambridge, MA: MIT Press, 1996).

Pye, David, *The Nature of Design* (London: Studio Vista, 1964).

Sennett, Richard, *The Craftsman* (London: Allen Lane, 2008).

Levine, Faythe, and Cortney Heimerl, *Handmade Nation: The Rise of DIY, Art, Craft, and Design* (New York: Princeton Architectural Press, 2008).

Tallis, Raymond, *The Hand: A Philosophical Inquiry into Human Being* (Edinburgh: Edinburgh University Press, 2003).

Treadaway, Cathy, "Digital Imagination: The Impact of Digital Imaging on Printed Textiles," *Textile: The Journal of Cloth and Culture* 2 (3) (2004): 256–73.

Treadaway, Cathy, "Digital Imaging: Its Current and Future Influence upon the Creative Practice of Textile and Surface Pattern Designers" (PhD Thesis, University of Wales Institute Cardiff, 2006).

Treadaway, Cathy, "Digital Printing," in *Smart Clothes and Wearable Technology*, ed. Jane McCann and David Bryson (Cambridge: Woodhead Publishing, 2009), 300–18.

Treadaway, Cathy, "Materiality, Memory, and Imagination: Using Empathy to Research Creativity," *Leonardo* 42 (2009): 231–7.

Treadaway, Cathy, "Creative Momentum in the Information Age," in *Momentum* [exhibition catalog], ed. Craft in the Bay C (Cardiff: Makers Guild in Wales, 2011), 4–7.

Treadaway, Cathy, Gail Kenning, and Steve Coleman, "Designing for Positive Emotion," in *The Colors of Care: 9th International Conference on Design and Emotion*, ed. Pieter Desmet, Juan Salamanca, Geke Ludden, Andrés Burbano, and Jorge Maya (Bogota, Colombia: Design and Emotion Society and Universidad de Los Andes, 2014), 545–51.

Shillito, Ann Marie, *Digital Crafts: Industrial Technologies for Applied Artists and Designer Makers* (London: Bloomsbury, 2013).

Tao, Xiaoming, *Wearable Electronics and Photonics* (Cambridge: Woodhead Publishing, 2005).

Ujiie, Hitoshi, *Digital Printing of Textiles* (Cambridge: Woodhead Publishing, 2006).

3
DIGITAL EMBROIDERY PRACTICE

Tina Downes, Tessa Acti, and Donna Rumble-Smith

Introduction

Over the past thirty years computer technology has transformed the process of translating embroidery designs from beautifully executed, large-scale, paper drafts held in manufacturer archives to digital design files that can be emailed anywhere in the world within seconds. These technological advances have made it possible to geographically separate the process of embroidery designing from manufacturing, frequently losing the tacit, human-held knowledge base in the process. As much large-scale embroidery manufacturing relocated to areas of the world with cheaper labor costs, digitizing houses have been set up in independent locations, selling a design digitizing service worldwide.

Further democratization of design[1] occurred when software manufacturers, capitalizing on increased access to home computers, marketed embroidery software packages to untrained hobbyists.[2] Thus, the early 1990s saw a rise in the "garage" industry, where novice enterprises set up small embroidery businesses producing licensed products with a multi-head embroidery machine and some embroidery software in their own homes. Consequently, a plethora of poor designs was produced and software manufacturers found it necessary to provide libraries of pre-digitized designs or online technical support to increase embroidery stitch-out quality.

Software manufacturers, embroidery designers, and educators agree that the quality of commercial multi-head embroidery for fashion and interior applications has greatly improved in the last decade. Still, the creative parameters of a technology might be more easily tested by artists and researchers unconfined by commercial restraints.[3] The multi-head embroidery machine is a lock stitch machine capable of at least the same stitch effects as, and potentially far more than, the Irish and domestic machines can achieve. The difference lies in its input process that is digital rather than manual, but how this affects artistic expression has not been studied. On the one hand, manually handled machines are capable of capturing the sweeping, gestural speed of a paintbrush.[4] On the other hand, the digitizing process, defined here as the computerized translation of a design into digital stitch, is carried out with the computer's mouse accessory in a careful tracing and clicking process. It in fact applies methodical thought more akin to that required for hand stitching than one might imagine.

It has been demonstrated that even within subdisciplines of textiles, approaches to digital design can vary substantially. Briggs-Goode describes the digital printing process as essentially a reproductive tool for CAD design, where it is hoped that imagery will be printed exactly as planned.[5] Print-based CAD programs have enabled the development of a new visual language, creating marks that are not possible to make using physical studio media and releasing print from the limitations of traditional processes.[6] By contrast, digital embroidery is still confined by the parameters of the embroidery machine and the reality of material production. In other words, it may be possible to design something digitally in an embroidery program that is impossible to stitch out. It is also possible to intervene during the production process to manually add elements that are not included in the digital aspect of its creation.

The advent of digital design has caused educational managers to ask whether it is possible to bypass the time-consuming and expensive investment of learning through hands-on engagement with materials and processes. This is a strong challenge for textile design pedagogy, which has a tradition of learning through practical experience, building up material knowledge through creative experimentation in the workshop, alongside tutors who are also practitioners. Knowledge that is passed on through demonstration, gesture, and practice is often hard to classify. Instinctively, we know its value. It is important for textile designers to define the unspoken, tacit elements of what they have come to know through this embodied experience.[7] This chapter presents five case studies exploring a diversity of scenarios and perspectives to draw out the nature of embroidery knowledge within a digital context. All case studies were conducted through interviews and practitioners' documented reflections.

Case Study 1: On boundaries and limitations, tools and conventions

Tessa Acti is an artist, research assistant, and technician exploring the multi-head digital embroidery machine as an artistic and innovative tool. Acti subverts the machine's original intentions through mechanical exploration to produce playful and tactile surfaces. Her methodology questions the pioneering value of what is essentially a machine utilized for mass production. Acti first exploited traditional embroidery stitches to create extreme-scale stitch work, including drapery and 3D cutwork, and employing the digitizing process as a "hand" process. Then she turned this medium into a mechanical conversation between artist, machine, and material (Figure 3.1). This investigative approach to digital embroidery, machinery, and material play has led to Acti's fascination with the relationships that evolve during the exploration of the digital embroidery machine; this is to say that tool usage, even when machine powered, can remain very much human.[8] By documenting reflections on her practice, Acti defines three relationships that enable a personal narrative to develop:

Human and machine

Acti defines the primary relationship between *human* and *machine* as foundational to two subsequent relationships. As an operative of the machinery, Acti has the luxury of uninterrupted interaction with the digitizing process through to material outcome. Knowledge of embroidery, digital embroidery, and the machine's limitations allows spontaneous intervention and the opportunity to re-work materials during the stitching out process. An artist's personal intention can be lost if they hand work over to be interpreted by another hand, eye, and mind. Being an operative of the machinery gives Acti insight into its demanding and somewhat sensitive nature. She has the opportunity to observe, question, intervene, and reflect from within the process: "Is the tension too tight? Am I using the right needle? That stitch density is too heavy! What is that sound? The machine does not sound right!"[9]

Materials and machine

The selection of materials and their interaction with the machine is underpinned by Acti's textile design experience. When exploring Bernina, Cornely, Irish machines and hand embroidery, her wealth of knowledge is built up regarding material, stitch, and techniques. This in turn leads to an awareness of how selected materials may react during the production process, and whether the fabrics are right for the outcome required. Reflection on the embroidery takes place as soon as the machine starts. Digitization, selected threads, and fabric are no longer separate entities; they connect each other as if they were paintbrushes to paper. Acti's reflection in the act of embroidering includes, for example: "That color is not quite right, let's stop the machine! That fabric is too delicate! Oops! There's a hole … but I like it, how can I exploit this now?"[10]

Human and material

The most exciting relationship takes place when ideas are stitching out, watching with anticipation as the stitch number increases to a resolve. With a final "bleep," the artist/operative is eager to pull the material out of the clamps and feel the work. This presents the opportunity to further explore any additions to be made and assess developments to take forward; the use of a digital tool does not guarantee accurate results. Acti feels tacit knowledge is essential to fully understand the boundaries that can be pushed while exploring limitations of the machinery. The awareness of hand, domestic, and industrial embroidery altogether underpins her practice, enabling challenges to be solved through the knowledge of alternative techniques and the awareness of the material and mechanical limitations of the multi-head embroidery machine. This knowledge, in turn, enables the creative spontaneity and innovation in the design process that is thought to be lost with digital practice.

Figure 3.1 "Closely Held Secret," "Extreme Scale Stitches," Tessa Acti, 2010. Photograph: Tessa Acti.

Case Study 2: On materials and tacit embroidery knowledge

In the series "Signatures Exchanged for Passwords," Donna Rumble-Smith's art textile practice explored precious exchanges in the form of personal handwritten letters. She considered the intimacy and physicality that has been lost in the digital age of emails and text messages. Working with the process of free machine embroidery, she painstakingly transcribed handwritten sentiments into stitch, selecting fabric and thread weights as carefully as one might select a good quality paper and pen. The pace and versatility of the domestic machine allowed her to make decisions about thread, fabric, and embroidery techniques as she worked, enabling a deeply embodied and responsive relationship between concepts, materials, and process.

When commissioned with a large-scale installation, Rumble-Smith realized that the textile would require more strength and manufacturing speed than her usual freehand

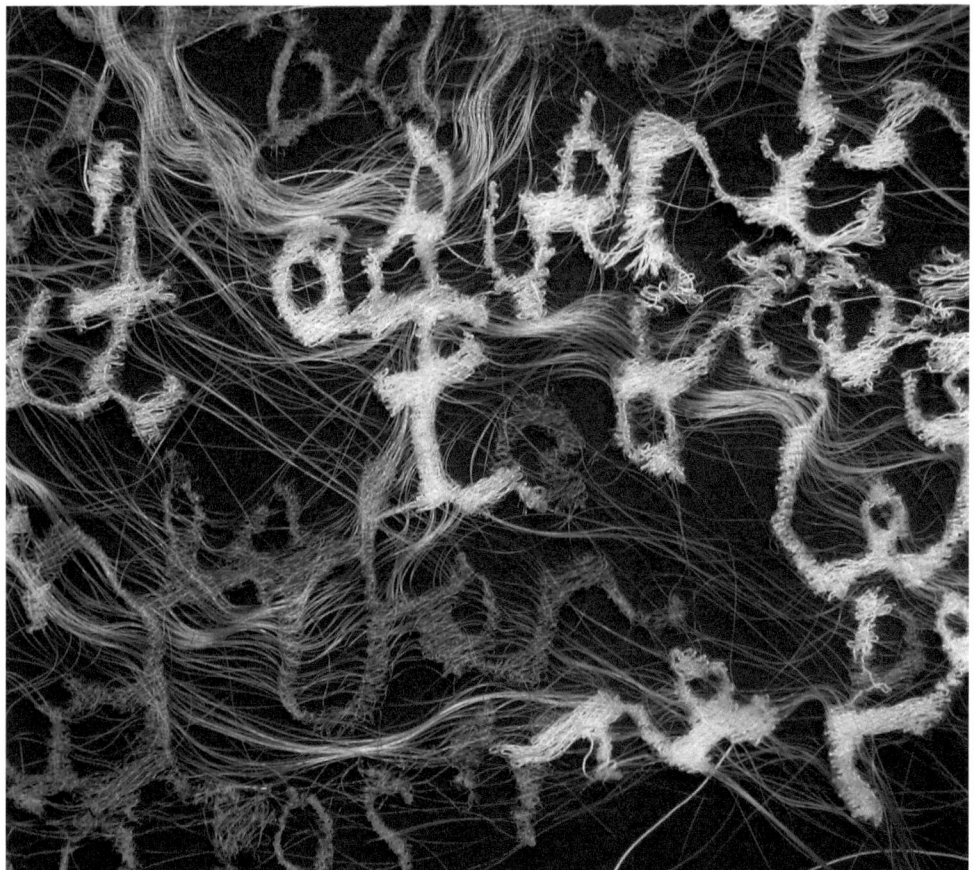

Figure 3.2 "Signatures Exchanged for Passwords," Donna Rumble-Smith, 2009. Photograph: Donna Rumble-Smith.

processes allowed. Working digitally with the multi-head embroidery machine challenged the very core of the concepts that Rumble-Smith was exploring and disconnected her from the immediate materiality of her practice. In an interview, she described her fear: she felt that applying this approach would produce work that "was too planned for exciting incidentals, where stitching was too perfect and lacked a 'by-hand' quality."[11] Although the speed of the stitching process was required for Rumble-Smith to produce work of a large scale, her attitude became one of uneasy compromise.

Nevertheless, what Rumble-Smith brought to this digital venture was a wealth of fabric and embroidery knowledge. She purposefully selected materials that would create opportunities for chance as they came off the machine. Using a water-soluble substrate, Rumble-Smith trapped invisible strands of monofilament to support the abstracted digitized text. She knew that when the substrate dissolved some of the letters would be unsupported and would start to unravel in random areas (Figure 3.2). To increase the random factor, she intervened in the production process in earlier trials by: (1) stopping and restarting the stitch program; (2) disguising the repeat within the text by manually moving the machine head into various positions; and (3) continually changing the threads so that no two areas of repeated design used the same textured thread. The final installation exceeded the bed size of the machine several times without any repeats. This was made possible with the support of a knowledgeable technician who was able to help realign stitched-out sections of the fabric in the frame while maintaining the flow of the design. In this way Rumble-Smith used the digital process to "exploit the time-saving characteristics of machine production but applied a craft aesthetic to the process of making."[12]

Case Study 3: On no prior textile knowledge

Luisa Gil, an international student from Colombia, started the one-year Master's program in Textile Design Innovation at Nottingham Trent University, UK with no prior experience of textiles. As an industrial designer, her skills lay with hard materials and related processes such as wood, metal, ceramics, plastics, forming, and molding. In terms of manufacturing and production, she was used to thinking in industrial terms, working with CAD and CAM for mass production rather than through hand processes. With no understanding of even the fundamental differences in structure between woven or knitted cloth and no experience of yarn/fiber properties, her audacious project proposal was to construct 3D smart fabrics with enhanced functionality to improve lifestyle and well-being.

While the student spent much of the first term voraciously researching the smart textile sector, medical and well-being applications, and the healing properties of yarns, the supervisor was keen to see a balance of practical application to build up textile experience and hands-on knowledge of fabric and process responses. It became clear early on that results from the domestic or small industrial embroidery machines were hampered by lack of hand skills and there was insufficient time to build these up. Gil wanted a very precise outcome. This goal was better matched when working digitally

Figure 3.3 3D digital embroidery structures, Luisa Gil, 2011. Photograph: Luisa Gil.

through CAD processes and mapped onto her prior experience of working with industrial manufacturing systems. Scanning in unfolded paper models of 3D tessellating structures, Gil translated geometric patterns into digital stitch, initially with guided support from her supervisor, but increasingly on an independent basis. Through systematic trial and error, she came to realize the complexity of stitch structures, stitch densities, fabric stability, and the importance of designing an effective route for the multi-head to stitch out the embroidery. The production process and how the digital design transformed into a material outcome that was not predicted from the computer screen fascinated Gil. She became attuned to the impact that minute changes between thread, fabric, and stitch density could have on the embroidered outcome and started to manipulate these to her advantage. Finally, she devised methods to heat set the embroidered cloth into intriguing 3D forms, connecting her industrial design experience of molding to textiles (Figure 3.3).

Case Study 4: A pedagogical perspective

While Gil's acceptance on the Master's program for Textile Design Innovation at Nottingham Trent University, UK with no prior knowledge of textiles is unusual, there is certainly more call from Master's students who want to expand their skills profile beyond their previous area of knowledge in order to enhance their employability. Employers frequently seek CAD skills and the desire to work across discipline boundaries in new employees. Postgraduate students come with diverse backgrounds, and there is high potential for innovation by connecting their prior expertise with cross-disciplinary aspirations for future learning. Their background defines their approaches to embroidered textiles, and they are able to enrich the subject with new methods. One example of this is the work of creative pattern cutter Yuri Nakamatsu, who learnt to use simple linear stitches and one input method on the embroidery software. She developed flowing linear designs and integrated them into garment forms through an iterative process of draping embroidered pattern segments on the mannequin and redrafting the embroidery design and pattern piece until they were engineered to fit perfectly (Plate 3). Thus, a very simple embroidery process was applied with a pattern cutter's intelligence.

As a newly qualified lecturer in the mid-1990s, it took Tina Downes some time to realize that what she saw on the computer screen when digitizing embroidery designs was not the same as the second-year undergraduate textile design students with limited prior knowledge of embroidery production or fabric. What the novice students saw was a glass screen with a grid as backdrop and a bewildering array of icons and input methods. In their hand they held a mouse rather than a needle or a pencil to translate sections of their design into digital stitch. In the virtual realm of CAD, scale and color were variable and areas of the design shifted on and off the screen as students zoomed in to add stitch detail. There was no sense of materiality or immediacy—the process removed for the time being from thread and cloth. The students initially worked with a scanned drawing from their sketchbooks as a backdrop on the screen; they had much to think about when mapping spontaneous marks with vector points that would have taken seconds with a pencil. Where to start? Where to finish? What order to digitize the design so that it would stitch out effectively on the multi-head embroidery machine? What stitch would most represent this mark? How long, short, dense, variable should the stitches be? How many colors to use? Which effects would be created by stitch and which by pre-treating or finishing the fabric post-embroidery production? The screen told part of the story, but Downes realized from the students' questions in the early stages that she was making multiple adjustments in her mind's eye to the on-screen, digital view. This was possible because of her hands-on experience of the reality that would materialize during the production process.

Case Study 5: Technician and translator

Working as a technician leads to a completely different relationship with the software and machinery. As a facilitator, Acti has the advantage of operating the machinery as well as digitizing, giving a deeper insight into material realization. An understanding of yarn/thread weight, materials, stitch types, embroidery as a process, and how all of these separate elements will interact with the machine, is vital for full exploration. When working as a facilitator, one is also working as an interpreter of ideas. The potential for the exploration of human error through decisions regarding color choice, placement, and scale are greater.

The *Closely Held Secrets* Exhibition[13] led by Nottingham Trent University's Bonington Gallery featured nine visual artists working alongside skilled digital embroidery technicians. Using original images, paintings, or ideas from the artists, Acti explored the capacity of the multi-head machine to best transform these works into embroidered reinterpretations.

Fine artist and painter Geoff Diego Litherland wanted to subvert embroidery motifs via the traditional use of the multi-head for repetition, which he chose to exploit through selected rules and parameters. As a consequence the pieces created were influenced not only by the limits of the machine but also by intuition, communication, miscommunication, and error. Litherland also explored repetition through the use of dense areas of stitch, parts of which were so thick that the materials started to warp. He wanted to see how far he could push the machine before it would *break*, thus exploring the physical fragility of the machine as opposed to investigating the software.

Fine artist and senior lecturer Danica Maier wanted to incorporate the meticulous, minute-scale handwriting, which appears throughout her practice, into embroidered pieces. Due to scale limitations of the multi-head, Maier had to reevaluate this theme and hence had the opportunity to learn how to use the software herself, selecting, editing, and layering up tactile stitched surfaces in one color (Plate 4). This limitation gave Maier the chance to ask different questions of textiles and stitch. Artists need collaborators who understand or are empathetic to their need to exercise control for themselves.[14] Therefore, Maier called upon the knowledge of the technician when required during the production process, but the technician played a much more peripheral role when digitizing.

As a technician working with artists, much of Acti's time was spent prior to production in addressing the perception of the machinery and software. This required highlighting the mechanical and material limitations. Conversations establishing whether the work was led by the artist's practice or the technology identified the level of support necessary. Acti's investigation during collaborative projects gave her the opportunity to identify a recurring theme evident in the exploration of digital embroidery within practice: the search for the *human* element of the machine. Her reflections suggest that there is a need to explore error, limitations, and physicality of the machinery as part of creative practice. By pushing the boundaries of a machine typically intended for commercial manufacture, new ways of working with the machine as an artistic tool have been devised. The artists acquired a hunger for further exploration as time went by. This suggests "that we can only relate to machines by investing them with a degree of humanity—by translating their gestures into an idiom of human emotion—while simultaneously merging with them and becoming mechanical subjects."[15]

Conclusion

The process of digital embroidery is less immediate than that of hands-on, free machine embroidery on a domestic or Irish machine. There are disruptions, interventions, and delays between the origination of an idea and the production of a material outcome. The process of digitizing a drawing as a scanned backdrop on the computer screen involves the digitizer in multiple technical and aesthetic decisions about stitch type, length, width, density, and interpretation of style. When considering whether knowledge and practical experience of traditional embroidery processes are necessary in the practice of digital embroidery, one has to consider that ultimately digital embroidery cannot remain separated from the reality of its material outcome. The case studies reveal that students and collaborative artists who have little prior embroidery knowledge find it difficult to visualize the difference between the virtual digital design on the computer screen and the physical reality of the cloth yet to be produced. Downes draws attention to the multiple adjustments that must be made in the mind's eye to interpret the on-screen design into reality. The time delay between creation and production is a stumbling block for novices who have little sense of the scale, density, handle, and mark-making qualities of stitch that will be revealed from their digitized designs.

In contrast, embroidery designers with a wealth of stitch and fabric knowledge, although with no digital skills, are better placed initially to direct the digital interface towards a material outcome that they have some control over, with a small amount of digitizing instruction. Rumble-Smith was able to overcome her initial preconceptions of the digital interface to employ the production capacity of the multi-head machine as an artistic tool. She brought desirable human qualities, elements of chance and imperfection, which she mediated skillfully through her textile knowledge. Lack of digital awareness did not interrupt envisioning the material outcome.

Acti notes that the idea that digitizing is not a creative process is to disregard the human element. As digital technology has advanced, there has been a shift away from the conception of computers and automation as a replacement for human skills, to a more collaborative view that considers what skills a human being can bring to the computer.[16] Acti is able to draw upon her embroidery experience, both hand and digital, to ask intelligent and demanding questions of the software and machinery. She carefully inputs stitch data, co-ordinating hand, eye, and mind; the use of a digital tool does not guarantee accurate results. Her reflections on process point towards indefinable tacit skills, such as: (1) understanding the limits and breaking points in the interactions between fabric and machine; (2) noting minute changes in sound as a design is stitched; (3) understanding different relationships between *human and machine*, *materials and machine*, and *human and material*. The computer is outside of her awareness, subsumed as a tool for her work.[17]

This kind of tacit knowledge is deeply embedded in the experience and action of making, and often seems so obvious to the practitioner that it remains unarticulated. Yet this knowledge is revealed as valuable to the uninitiated.[18] From earlier discussions, it would be easy to draw the conclusion that traditional embroidery skills are certainly a requirement for developing successful digital embroidery. Yet, the innovation that the fine artists Litherland and Maier, and cross-disciplinary Master's students Nakamatsu and Gil, bring to the subject contradicts this notion. The cultural knowledge they bring from their own disciplines causes them to ask questions that a textile designer might not think of, so that they become catalysts for new ways of thinking.[19] While all of these collaborators require support from supervisors or technicians to translate their ideas into practice and may need to compromise when faced with real limitations, both sides leave enriched by new ideas, processes, and approaches.

In the end, when considering digital processes, the human element cannot be ignored. Tacit, hand skills enhance the digital dialogue. The computer is a tool in human hands and, in the words of McCullough, it would be "absurd to ignore the role of talent, of inarticulable knowledge, of contextual understanding and of dedicated practice"[20] in the development of innovative digital embroidery practice.

Notes

1   Democratization of design, in this instance, refers to increased accessibility to knowledge and technology previously retained by specialists. These specialists acted as "gatekeepers" ensuring a particular approach and quality. Advances in digital software, computerized technology, and the internet have removed traditional barriers, creating access and affordability to the masses with no specific design training. This phenomenon is discussed in Briggs's thesis. Amanda Briggs, "A Study of Photographic Images, Processes and Computer Aided Textile Design" (PhD thesis, Nottingham Trent University, 1997).
2   Melanie Miller, "Embroidered Textile Design," in *Textile Design: Principles, Advances and Applications*, ed. Amanda Briggs-Goode and Katherine Townsend (Oxford: The Textile Institute with Woodhead Publishing, 2011), 129–44.
3   Cathy Treadaway, "Digital Imagination: The Impact of Digital Imaging on Printed Textiles," *Textile* 2 (3) (2004): 256–73.
4   Alice Kettle and Jane McKeating, *Machine Stitch Perspectives* (London: A&C Black Publishers, 2010).
5   Amanda Briggs-Goode, Tina Downes, and Nigel Marshall, "Digital Textile Futures: Integration of New Technologies," in *Proceedings of 11th Annual Conference for the International Foundation of Fashion Technology Institutes: Fashion and Well-being?*, ed. Elizabeth Rouse (London: Centre for Learning and Teaching in Art and Design [CLTAD], 2009), 505–16.
6   Treadaway, "Digital Imagination: The Impact of Digital Imaging on Printed Textiles".
7   Sarah Kettley and Tina Downes, "Revealing Textile Knowledge Through Interdisciplinary Research," in *Proceedings of Re-Defining Research Conference* (Nottingham: Nottingham Trent University, 2010).
8   Malcolm McCullough, *Abstracting Craft: The Practiced Digital Hand* (Cambridge, MA: MIT Press, 1998).
9   Tessa Acti worked as a digital embroidery technician for the *Closely Held Secrets* exhibition held in the Bonington Gallery at Nottingham Trent University, UK, October–November 2010. The aim of the exhibition was to explore the relationship between the artist and the technician, revealing the hidden dialogue between the originator of an idea and the agent of interpretation. Acti collaborated with several visual artists to reinterpret their work in stitch.

Comments from her reflective journal capture Acti's reflection-in-action (as knowledge was actually becoming embodied) in the lead-up to the exhibition.

10   See Note 9.
11   Tina Downes conducted an interview with Donna Rumble-Smith on June 14, 2011. The purpose of the interview was to explore the attitudes and experience of a knowledgeable hand and machine embroiderer working with digital embroidery processes for the first time.
12   Jennifer Harris, "The 'Craft' of Machine Embroidery," in *Machine Stitch: Perspectives*, ed. Alice Kettle and Jane McKeating (London: A&C Black Publishers, 2010), 13.
13   Katherine Townsend, Geoff Litherland, and Tony Taylor, *Closely Held Secrets* [exhibition catalog] (Nottingham: Nottingham Trent University, Bonington Gallery, 2010).
14   Linda Candy and Ernest Edmonds, *Explorations in Art and Technology* (London: Springer, 2002).
15   Nuit Banai, "Pia Lindman," *Art Papers* 30 (4) (2006): 56.
16   McCullough, *Abstracting Craft; The Practiced Digital Hand*.
17   Banai, "Pia Lindman."
18   Kettley and Downes, "Revealing Textile Knowledge Through Interdisciplinary Research."
19   Candy and Edmonds, *Explorations in Art and Technology*.
20   McCullough, *Abstracting Craft: The Practiced Digital Hand*, ix.

Bibliography

Banai, Nuit, "Pia Lindman," *Art Papers* 30 (4) (2006): 56.
Briggs, Amanda, "A Study of Photographic Images, Processes and Computer Aided Textile Design" (PhD thesis, Nottingham: Nottingham Trent University, 1997).
Briggs-Goode, Amanda, Tina Downes, and Nigel Marshall, "Digital Textile Futures: Integration of New Technologies," in *Proceedings of IFFTI 2009: Fashion and Well-being? 11th Annual Conference for the International Foundation of Fashion Technology Institutes*, ed. Elizabeth Rouse (London: Centre for Learning and Teaching in Art and Design [CLTAD], 2009), 505–16.
Candy, Linda, and Ernest Edmonds, *Explorations in Art and Technology* (London: Springer, 2000).
Harris, Jane, "The 'Craft' of Machine Embroidery," in *Machine Stitch Perspectives*, ed. Alice Kettle and Jane McKeating (London: A&C Black Publishers, 2011), 10–3.
Kettley, Sarah, and Tina Downes, "Revealing Textile Knowledge Through Interdisciplinary Research," in *Proceedings Re-Defining Research Conference*, College of Art & Design and the Built Environment (Nottingham: Nottingham Trent University, 2010), 1–17.
McCullough, Malcolm, *Abstracting Craft; The Practiced Digital Hand* (Cambridge, MA: MIT Press, 1998).
Miller, Melanie, "Embroidered Textile Design," in *Textile Design: Principles, Advances and Applications*, ed. Amanda Briggs-Goode and Katherine Townsend (Cambridge: The Textile Institute with Woodhead Publishing, 2011), 129–44.
Treadaway, Cathy, "Digital Imagination: The Impact of Digital Imaging on Printed Textiles," *Textile* 2 (3) (2004): 256–73.

4
TEXTILE ILLUSIONS— PATTERNS OF LIGHT AND THE WOVEN WHITE SCREEN

Anne Louise Bang, Helle Trolle, and Anne Mette Larsen

Introduction

How are knowledge and the practical experience of traditional processes, specifically hand skills, applied in the context of digital jacquard handloom weaving? Interestingly, the Design School Kolding in Denmark has offered weavers and artists with an interest in weaving residencies access to a digital jacquard handloom since 1998. This chapter discusses ways in which the craft and practice of hand weaving have undergone changes in Denmark due to the introduction of the digital jacquard handloom at the Design School Kolding.

The "Textile Illusions" group was established in 2003 by the authors of this chapter, Anne Louise Bang, Helle Trolle, and Anne Mette Larsen, all trained as textile designers and artists specialized in weaving. The cogwheel of our collaboration is a keen interest in exploring and challenging the craft of weaving in various ways. This chapter pays particular attention to the exhibition project TWEEN, which was specifically crafted for and exhibited in the Design Museum Denmark in Copenhagen in 2006–7. The project serves as a case study to exemplify and discuss the potential for professional and creative development that lies in the use of a digital jacquard handloom. To provide a framework and context for our discussion, the chapter begins with a short historical background to digital jacquard handlooms, followed by an introduction to a selection of experienced Danish weavers' varied use of a digital jacquard handloom to demonstrate the impact the tool has had on the textile thinking of weavers in Denmark. The chapter concludes by reflecting on the importance of the development of the textile profession with regard to access to technological tools such as digital jacquard handlooms.

The digital jacquard handloom

In recent decades, textile art and design faculties within higher education worldwide have acquired advanced digital jacquard handlooms. A number of independent textile artists and designers have also purchased these tools.[1] A variety of exhibitions, books, journals, and websites offer diverse insight into the exploration of the loom. The "Banishing Boundaries" exhibition in 2006 displayed the work of eleven American weavers.[2] This was probably one of the first exhibitions that dedicated itself to showing tapestries produced on digital jacquard handlooms. Books introducing the creation of weave patterns on digital jacquard handlooms have been published: *The Woven Pixel* by Alice Schlein and Bhakti Ziek (2006)[3] and *Digital Jacquard Design* by Julie Holyoke (2013)[4] are worth mentioning here. The authors of both books focus on the fact that we require new textbooks in order to make the most of the new digital weaving tools. Regarding journals, *Textile Forum*, published by the European Textile Network, has frequently included articles about the use of digital tools in textile design and textile art. In 2013 the journal dedicated a whole issue to "Jacquard Tapestries."[5] As for websites, the most important website is probably "Digital Weaving Norway."[6] Apart from promoting the digital jacquard handlooms TC-1 and TC-2, the website disseminates the newest practical knowledge about this specific area.

As early as 1968, at the HemisFair in San Antonio, Texas, IBM presented a jacquard loom which connected directly to a computer. Visitors could make a design on the computer and instantly see the design woven into a textile sample.[7] In the 1980s electronic jacquard equipment became available to the textile industry. The Italian company Bonas is widely recognized as the first company to introduce electronic jacquard equipment at the ITMA fair in 1983.[8] However, the tool did not become accessible to textile artists and designers until the 1990s, when the Norwegian lecturer in textiles, Vibeke Vestby initiated the development of an electronic loom which functioned as a jacquard weaving machine that the weaver could use like any other handloom. The result of her efforts and collaboration with the Norwegian company Tronrud Engineering resulted in the TC-1 loom launched in 1995.[9]

The TC-1 is a thread controller on which the weaver controls every single thread independently using a computer, which connects directly to the loom (Figure 4.1). The loom works with digital files, which are controlled by a relatively simple weaving program. A black pixel in the file indicates the lifting of a warp thread. The weaver has direct access to working with figured textiles using weave structures, such as shaded satins and weft-backed weaves. Weave structures normally used on dobby and countermarch looms can also be explored and challenged on the TC-1.[10] In principle, the TC-1 loom is accessible to weavers without prior weaving experience or technical knowledge.

In 1998 a group of Danish weavers raised regional and private funding which enabled the Design School Kolding to acquire a TC-1 loom.[11] Since then practitioners based externally to the school, both Danish and from other countries, have been offered access to the loom for half of the year. The students at the Design School Kolding have access to the loom for the remainder of the year. This agreement secures an arrangement whereby experienced textile artists and designers as well as future designers have access to exploring the potential that presumably lies in the digital jacquard handloom.

TEXTILE ILLUSIONS—PATTERNS OF LIGHT AND THE WOVEN WHITE SCREEN

Figure 4.1 Weaving on the TC-1. Photograph: Textile Illusions.

It is well recognized that there is an immediate interconnectedness between craft and technology in woven textiles.[12] In 1997 the British writer on visual arts, Peter Dormer pointed out that in weaving there is a strong link between the design process and the manufacturing process. He states in his essay about textiles and technology:

> There is a fluidity in the practice, design and art of woven textiles that enables textiles to fit easily with contemporary technology ... There is a natural affinity between weaving and mathematics, and the loom and the digital computer.[13]

In this light, it makes sense to ask how access to an advanced digital tool such as the digital jacquard handloom has influenced textile practice at the beginning of the 2000s. Therefore, we address the following question: How are knowledge and practical experience of traditional processes, hand skills in particular, applied in the context of digital jacquard handloom weaving? This is to determine how hand skills and professional expertise interact with new technology and how these skills are relevant to contemporary and cutting-edge textile art and design.

To emphasize the potential of the digital jacquard handloom, the next section will introduce four Danish textile artists specialized in weaving. Each of them has challenged their own practice using the TC-1 loom. This is of course not an exhaustive report of the international or even the Danish use and exploration of the loom. Nevertheless, we find that these artists' approaches illuminate the limitless possibilities of using the loom in the contemporary context while maintaining the importance of hand skills.

The potential of the digital jacquard handloom

Weavers are generally trained in systematic thinking, as they need to operate traditional looms that require a highly organized way of working, threading warp ends on a number of shafts and inserting weft picks in an accurate order. Regarding the organization of weft yarns, countermarch looms have a number of treadles connected to the shafts, whereas manual or computerized dobby looms work with lift plans. This means that the weaver must understand the interaction between shafts and treadles or lift plans in order to achieve the desired woven pattern. The experimentation of several experienced Danish weavers on the TC-1 loom has focused on uncovering and exploring the assumed potential of the tool. Through their weaving practices, the textile artists introduced in this section place emphasis on diverse issues such as dynamic pattern generation, optical color blending, figured textiles, and multiple-layered weaving. This section demonstrates how these artists and designers, who are trained and highly specialized in weaving, approach the digital jacquard handloom through craft expertise, skill, and knowledge.

In "Manual Work" (2004), the textile artist Kirsten Nissen worked with dynamic pattern generation based on real-life registrations, where the weaver's body measurements were continuously fed into a pattern generator.[14] The resulting pattern was translated to black and white pixels readable by the TC-1 loom. Nissen took advantage of the fact that each warp end is controlled independently on the loom. This gave her the potential to weave a dynamic pattern that is regularly fed with new information from the pattern generator and the real-life registrations. She used her hand skills and practical experience to combine the single thread controller with Chinese jin weaving, which is a warp-faced compound weave.[15] The weft was not visible and the black and white warp created a non-repetitive pattern. In the end, the eight lengths of fabric reflected the weaver's bodily reactions of weaving eight hours per day for eight days straight.

Grethe Sørensen recognized an advantage of the TC-1 loom that freed her weaving practice from the use of traditional weave structures.[16] Having mainly worked with the digital jacquard handloom since 2000, Sørensen has constantly challenged her practical experience and hand skills. One of the results of her efforts is the development of a weave structure that she calls "random weave."[17] This weave structure allows Sørensen to work with optical color blending, as shown in the 2012 exhibition "Traces of Light."[18] Using a weft system of eight colors on a black and white warp allowed her to create the basic colors and every shade between them in her woven pieces. The motifs for the wall hangings were based on still images of video recordings of light in different cities. From a close distance the weavings are "pixelated" into the eight thread colors, while from a greater distance the wall hangings depict delicate motifs of light.

Lise Frølund's weaving focuses on figured textiles based on photographic images.[19] In the "Women's Millennium" series produced around 2006, she explored coarse materials on warps with a maximum of six threads per centimeter. Working with a color system that in many ways resembled the CMYK system known from color printing, Frølund took advantage of the TC-1's thread controller to translate the photorealistic motifs into woven textiles. In one of the wall hangings, she used six colors in both the weft and the warp, enabling her to create numerous tones and shades.[20] She used her hand skills and practical experience to combine the weave structure with a variety of materials. In combination with the coarse materials and a multilayered weave structure that emphasized transparency, the result of this weaving, from a close distance, dissolved into colored dots and pure material. The motif itself was not recognizable until it was experienced from a certain distance.

For a textile artist trained in weaving and the logic of the vertical versus the horizontal, it is quite extraordinary to get access to create diagonal lines and vanishing points in woven textiles. For many years, Anne Mette Larsen has explored color combinations created by multiple-layered weaving, and her use of colored stripes in both warp and weft combined with the multilayered weaving technique has allowed her to create a subtle palette of colors.[21] In the "Under Construction" series, Larsen utilized the TC-1 loom to combine the multilayered weaving technique with diagonal lines.[22] Not only can she create even more colors and color combinations due to the unlimited thread control of the TC-1 loom, she can also use diagonal lines instead of vertical and horizontal lines to separate the different layers.

This section has exemplified a selection of Danish weavers' different approaches to the TC-1 loom. In order to get a more detailed understanding of the influence from practical experience and hand skills in digital jacquard hand weaving, the next section will introduce the motivation and engagement that lies behind the authors' collaboration within the group "Textile Illusions." The next section will also describe how we have applied our knowledge of materials, yarns, dyeing, color, weaving, and other hand skills gained through years of working with the TC-1 loom.

Textile Illusions

When we founded the group "Textile Illusions" in 2003, each of us had occasionally experienced feedback on exhibition events, from artists within other disciplines or domains and from the audience, taking a view on woven textile art and design as "slow" and even "old-school." These statements provoked us, as trained and proud weavers, in a way that forced us to take action. Our collaboration in "Textile Illusions" is therefore rooted in a shared interest in contributing to contemporary art using weaving as the driving force.

We have chosen to challenge the traditional and meticulous world of weaving through a digital lens. It is crucial for our work that there is a clear connection between the physical material and the digital bits and bytes, so that our work benefits from the potentials inherited from both worlds. We often use animated pattern sequences of light to focus on and emphasize the woven and braided material. The purpose is to bring attention to the immanent dynamics of the static textile. Through these means we aim to draw the attention to the sublime craft of weaving and the opportunities that lie in that world. For us, weaving is a thoughtful and complicated process, which is heavily influenced by the logic of the chosen structure: the weave pattern. In that respect we can agree that it is a "slow" language in a "fast" world. By adapting digital tools and media focusing on animated pattern sequences, complex weave structures, surfaces, and rhythms, we intend to supply the laborious and rule-bound craft with a sense of freedom and unpredictability.

The TWEEN project

"Textile Illusions" crafted the TWEEN project specifically for the Design Museum Denmark in Copenhagen in 2006–7.[23] In the exhibition catalog, Master of Arts and curator at the museum Rikke Rosenberg reads the work as follows:

> TWEEN is a system of cross-fading patterns whose open, uncompleted character discards all conception of integral wholes and closure. TEXTILE ILLUSIONS wants to create patterns founded on new procedures that rock the old founding principles of good proportions, harmony, singularity, technique and choice of materials etc. Patterns are created on the basis of new principles such as displacement, shifts and transformation and therefore the works become a symbol of our age, characterized by open networks and structures in transformation.[24]

TEXTILE ILLUSIONS—PATTERNS OF LIGHT AND THE WOVEN WHITE SCREEN

This section uses the exhibition project TWEEN to further exemplify and discuss ways in which digital tools can be challenged and explored through traditional craft skills. The TWEEN screen particularly demonstrates how we access the digital jacquard handloom and our work with the relationship between the woven white screen and patterns of light projected onto it. While developing the project, we had access to the TC-1 loom at the Design School Kolding several times over a period of two years. In the beginning we used it for sample weaving and later for weaving the final pieces for the TWEEN screen.

As trained weavers, we are used to thinking through materials and the ways in which different materials contrast with each other. When working with light projection, it was obvious to explore the contrast between matt and shiny. The gloss level of materials varies, which means that materials can reflect or absorb light in a number of different ways. As shown in Plate 5, the digital patterns of light appeared to have a physical surface texture when they were projected onto a woven screen. This effect could be so intense that it appeared that the projected patterns were integrated as luminous threads in the woven screen. However, it was almost instantly revealed as an illusion because the patterns were constantly changing. This added an extra dimension of "materiality" to the projected light, which we had earlier explored in various projects.[25]

Basically—and this would go for the digital animations as well as the woven textiles— "Textile Illusions" worked with the flow of patterns and weave structures that were created when the weft met the warp, i.e. the horizontal and the vertical threads in the fabric. The woven piece had a double function. It served as a screen for projection and when the projection was turned off, either intentionally or by accident, it functioned as a piece in its own right. In the TWEEN project, white and transparent materials were combined into a monochrome "screen," where the motif or the pattern is built into the surface texture.

The TWEEN exhibition project consisted of three pieces. On arrival at the exhibition, visitors experienced the first piece in the yard in front of the museum. In the exhibition hall, the two remaining pieces mirrored each other on opposite walls. Showing part of the project outside and part of it inside the museum allowed us to tell the story in stages.

The outdoor piece was simply a pattern animation projected on a raw wall (Figure 4.2). In the animation, two block patterns were transformed from one to the other and back again in a fast continuous loop of yellow light, which was relatively simple to read. Exhibiting one piece in the museum yard gave us an opportunity to offer visitors a hint of the textile world they would experience inside the museum. If they only recognized the animation on the way out, they had a chance to reflect on their experience while leaving the exhibition.

The pieces inside the museum were more complex and difficult to read. On one wall hung the white-on-white TWEEN screen consisting of four woven lengths 2.85 meters tall and mounted side by side in a 3-meter-wide composition (Plate 6). The weave pattern on the TWEEN screen told the same transformation story as the outdoor animation, but in four static steps. An animation showing various transformations of the two basic block patterns was projected on this screen. The pattern sequences in this animation were multicolored. On the opposite wall a composition of 24 smaller weavings represented "cut-outs" from the four lengths. These were mounted in a way that mirrored both the dimension and the weave pattern of the TWEEN screen. On top of that, each of the

Figure 4.2 The outdoor piece in the TWEEN exhibition at the Design Museum Denmark is simply a pattern animation projected on a raw wall in the museum yard. In the animation two block patterns are transformed from one to the other and back again in a fast continuous loop of yellow light. Photograph: Ole Akhøj.

24 pieces was interwoven with colored yarns simulating different moments from the animation.

For the TWEEN screen, a weave pattern was developed based on a "block double weave."[26] The surface design was basically a deconstructed block pattern with no repeats in the weft order or across the fabric. This caused a surface consisting of numerous blocks horizontally and vertically, and therefore requiring a jacquard loom for production. The TC-1 loom allowed the construction of a non-repetitive weave pattern based on the deconstructed block pattern. Furthermore, we could combine our weaving skills with the use of the TC-1 loom to explore different combinations of weave patterns and materials in an intuitive and direct way before we settled on the final pieces. The efforts resulted in a complex surface pattern with clear references to traditional white-on-white and checkered damask tablecloth construction.

Basically, the practical work with the TWEEN screen took its starting point in an animation transforming one traditional block pattern into another. We used the computer program Adobe Flash to morph one block pattern into the other in a seamless transition. This resulted in an animation consisting of more than 200 frames composed by different mixes of the original patterns.

TEXTILE ILLUSIONS—PATTERNS OF LIGHT AND THE WOVEN WHITE SCREEN

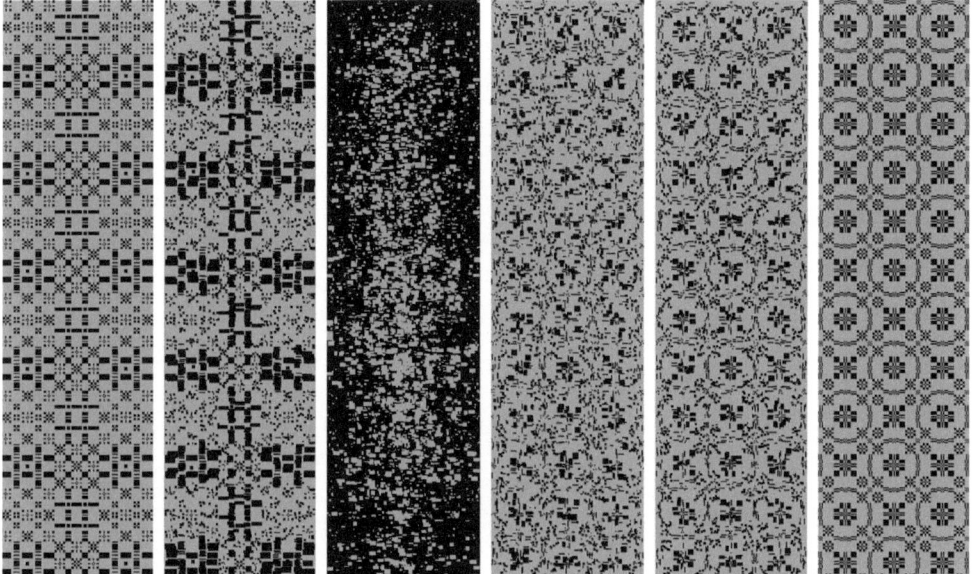

Figure 4.3 Each of the four pieces of the TWEEN screen built on a still image from a morph animation between two block patterns. The four still images represent the continuum between the two original patterns and are used as the "block pattern" for the woven TWEEN screen. Artwork: Textile Illusions.

In the end, the large TWEEN screen was built of four white-on-white woven screens, each based on a still image from the morph animation. The four screens thus represented the continuum between the two original patterns (Figure 4.3). The woven lengths are white-on-white consisting of two materials: a matt Japanese paper tape, and a shiny transparent polyester monofilament. A double-layered structure was used since it allowed us to keep the two materials separate and thereby create a surface with the largest possible contrast between shiny and matt. The paper tape was woven in a satin structure, while a plain weave was used for the monofilament. The satin structure enhanced the soft texture of the paper tape, while the plain weave caused the harder monofilament to sparkle as much as possible due to the dense structure of the plain weave.

Several sequences of patterns inspired by the two original block patterns and the various transitions between them were subsequently designed and combined into a five-minute animation. The animation was composed of a rich variety of colors with many subtle nuances. During the exhibition it was projected on the TWEEN screen in order to enhance the weave structure and the compositions of mixed block patterns (Figure 4.4). The two matt and shiny materials reflect and/or absorb the light from the projection, which produces new patterns combination on the screen. Over and over again, the combination of the woven white screen and the patterns of light told the story of transformation and deconstruction of the weave tradition of block patterns.

For a decade, the "Textile Illusions" group has challenged and explored the weaving tradition in various ways, often embracing textile basics such as stripes, circles, and

Figure 4.4 Detail of the TWEEN screen. During the exhibition at the Design Museum Denmark, an animation composed of a rich variety of colors with many subtle nuances was projected on the screen. Two basic block patterns served as inspiration for the pattern sequences. Photograph: Ole Akhøj.

rectangles and the concept of the twill weave. In the TWEEN project it was the traditional hand-woven damask tablecloth, which is characterized by a white-on-white checkered satin or twill pattern, that served as our basic inspiration for both weaving and pattern animation. Thus, the basic idea was to challenge the tradition but keep the logic of the white-on-white block patterns. The limit of dobby weaving generally lies in the number of shafts on the loom, and though it is possible to break the block structure to a certain extent and thereby make quite complicated block patterns, it is not possible to deconstruct the block structure altogether. With the TC-1 loom, we had access to an unlimited and complex world of weave structures. Our aim was therefore to challenge the traditional way of thinking about block patterns and at the same time to use some of the principles from block patterns as constraints.

Reflections

The previous sections have exemplified and discussed different approaches to the digital jacquard handloom. First, we investigated the approaches of four experienced textile artists to the tool exploring varied subjects such as dynamic pattern generation, optical color blending, figurative textiles, and multiple layers. Then the TWEEN project was used as a case to explore in detail how the group "Textile Illusions" used the TC-1 loom to develop a series of deconstructed block patterns based on a traditional block double weave. Throughout the chapter, the overall emphasis has been on clarifying ways in which experienced textile artists and designers trained in weaving invest their existing knowledge and skills in the exploration of the digital jacquard handloom, capturing the new tool in order to investigate and benefit from the presumed potential.

This review of the "Danish" approach to the digital jacquard handloom indicates two interesting aspects that may contribute to answering the question: How are knowledge and practical experience of traditional processes and specifically hand skills applied in the context of digital jacquard handlooms? First, it can be argued that the textile artists referred to in this chapter are very much able to transform and use their already acquired technical expertise and knowledge of weaving structures and patterns when they approach a new digital tool such as the TC-1 loom. Second, it is clearly demonstrated that when artists and designers trained in weaving explore the tool to create their work, they not only use and benefit from their already achieved skills and knowledge, but also develop them further in the weaving process.

For example, we have seen how Nissen uses her knowledge about weaving patterns to choose a warp-faced compound weave working with dynamic pattern generation based on real-life registrations in order to reach the preferred aesthetic expression. It can also be argued that she contributes to the textile profession's further development, since the tool allows her to apply the chosen technique in a new and surprising way.

Frølund's interest in figurative weaving in combination with coarse and heavy yarns has taken her on a journey where she used the material to challenge the typical expression of figurative weaving. Figurative weaving is often characterized by fine details and a relatively fine and smooth surface structure. Thus, it can be argued that Frølund uses her knowledge about materials and color blending to add to the tradition of figurative weaving.

Sørensen has utilized her thorough weaving experience to consider weave patterns in a completely different way, taking the starting point from the colored pixels instead of an existing weave structure. In contrast to Frølund, Sørensen has used this new way of thinking weaving patterns to refine and develop the surface structure of the woven pieces into a very smooth and fine surface, which allows the optical blending of thread colors.

Larsen has employed the digital jacquard handloom to refine her already acquired knowledge of, for instance, multiple-layered weaving through the exploration of diagonal lines and the further development of traditional weaving patterns. She takes advantage of the freedom that the loom offers in terms of access to unlimited combinations of weave structures and block patterns, and this allows her to develop further the tradition of multiple-layered weave structures.

The TWEEN project takes its inspiration from the traditional hand-woven damask tablecloth. As members of the "Textile Illusions" group, we have used our knowledge about weaving to turn the traditional block pattern into a double-layered structure with multiple blocks. The TC-1 loom, in combination with appropriate materials, serves as a tool to develop a weave structure that allows us to turn the complex block pattern into a screen suitable for reflecting projected light in different ways. By completing a project that combines animation and weaving, we contribute to the development of contemporary textile art.

The examples show that experienced textile designers and weavers who approach and employ the digital jacquard handloom can activate and further develop a variety of their professional skills and knowledge of weave patterns, materials and surface texture, color and other media. Each example illustrates how the digital jacquard handloom has contributed to the artists' continuous professional development within the field of textiles, allowing them to contribute to cutting-edge textile art.

Concluding remarks

This chapter has examined how a selection of Danish textile artists trained as weavers challenge and explore the traditions of weaving, combining the digital jacquard handloom with their craft skills and knowledge. Examples show how each of them takes their starting point in well-known mindsets, techniques, and skills, and in doing so understands how to challenge their own knowledge and enhance already achieved skills. Furthermore, the chapter has demonstrated that the digital tools represent a great potential for professional development. In conclusion, it can be argued that craft skills and expertise matter when artists challenge the tools for digital crafting, hence contributing to contemporary and cutting-edge textile art.

More generally, when accessing a digital jacquard handloom such as the TC-1, it is fascinating for a weaver to think that there are no limitations in terms of the number of shafts and treadles or other dobby or draw systems. With a digital jacquard handloom, the weaver receives a privilege to control the weaving process in a way that any other handloom will not permit. It is fairly simple to adapt and adjust the loom, and it can be used for sample weaving in an intuitive and explorative way. In that way, digital jacquard handlooms provide direct access for "everybody" to weave (complex) patterns and techniques. However, the study of the TWEEN screen, together with the other examples given in this chapter, demonstrates that it is mainly the knowledge, skills, and practice of the artist that make it possible to further advance skills and artistic expression. In a future study, it might be interesting to explore ways in which textile students, including novice textile artists, designers, and artists without prior experience of weaving, approach the digital jacquard handloom, in comparison to professionally trained textile artists.

Notes

1. Alice Schlein and Bhakti Ziek, *The Woven Pixel: Designing for Jacquard and Dobby Looms Using Photoshop®* (Greenville: Bridgewater Press, 2006), 347–51.
2. Patrice F. George (ed.), *Banishing Boundaries—Weaving Digitally* (Grand Rapids: Grand Rapids Art Museum, 2006).
3. Schlein and Ziek, *The Woven Pixel: Designing for Jacquard and Dobby Looms Using Photoshop®*.
4. Julie Holyoke, *Digital Jacquard Design* (London: Bloomsbury Academic, 2013).
5. Dietmar Laue (ed.), *Textile Forum—Special Issue: Digital Tapestries* 2 (2013).
6. Digital Weaving Norway, http://www.digitalweaving.no/en/home [accessed September 24, 2014].
7. Janice Lourie, *Textile Graphics/Computer-Aided* (New York: Fairchild Publications, 1973), 239.
8. Sabit Adanur, *Handbook of Weaving* (Florida: CRC Press, 2000), 159.
9. Vibeke Vestby, "The TC-1," in *Banishing Boundaries—Weaving Digitally*, ed. Patrice F. George (Grand Rapids: Grand Rapids Art Museum, 2006), 30–1.
10. Schlein and Ziek, *The Woven Pixel*, 7–10
11. Lise Frølund, "A Handweaver's Jacquard Experiments," *Textile Forum* 2 (2013): 32.
12. Peter Dormer, "Textiles and Technology," in *The Culture of Craft*, ed. Peter Dormer (Manchester: Manchester University Press, 1997), 170.
13. Dormer, "Textiles and Technology," 168.
14. Kirsten Nissen, "Pattern Generation in Dynamic Systems: An Approach to Textile Design," in *Proceedings of Ambience 08*, ed. Lars Hallnäs and Pernilla Walkenström (Borås: University College of Borås, 2008), 131–8.
15. John Becker, *Pattern and Loom: A Practical Study of the Development of Weaving Techniques in China, Western Asia and Europe* (Copenhagen: Rhodos, 1986), 55–79.
16. http://www.grethesorensen.dk [accessed June 26, 2015].
17. Grethe Sørensen, "From Traditional to Digital Tools," in *Textile Society of America Symposium Proceedings 2010*, Paper 51:3. http://digitalcommons.unl.edu/tsaconf/51 [accessed September 24, 2014].

18 Grethe Sørensen, *Spor af Lys—Traces of Light* (Copenhagen: Rundetaarn, 2012).
19 http://www.lisefrolund.dk [accessed June 26, 2015].
20 Frølund, *A Handweaver's Jacquard Experiments*, 32–3.
21 http://www.annemettelarsen.dk [accessed June 26, 2015].
22 Anne Mette Larsen (ed.), *Auf der Anderen Seite #2* (Silkeborg: Silkeborg Bad, 2012).
23 Textile Illusions (eds), *Tween—Tekstile Illusioner* [exhibition catalog] (Copenhagen: Design Museum Denmark, 2006).
24 Rikke Rosenberg, "Textile Illusions," in *Tween—Tekstile Illusioner*, ed. Textile Illusions (Copenhagen: Design Museum Denmark, 2006), n.p.
25 Textile Illusions, http://www.tekstile-illusioner.dk [accessed 24 September 2014].
26 Carol Strickler, *A Weaver's Book of 8-Shaft Patterns: From the Friends of Handwoven* (Loveland, CO: Interweave Press, 1991), 208.

Bibliography

Adanur, Sabit, *Handbook of Weaving* (Florida: CRC Press, 2000).
Becker, John, *Pattern and Loom: A Practical Study of the Development of Weaving Techniques in China, Western Asia and Europe* (Copenhagen: Rhodos, 1986).
Dormer, Peter, "Textiles and Technology," in *The Culture of Craft*, ed. Peter Dormer (Manchester: Manchester University Press, 1997), 168–75.
Frølund, Lise, "A Handweaver's Jacquard Experiments," *Textile Forum* 2 (2013): 32–3.
George, Patrice F. (ed.), *Banishing Boundaries—Weaving Digitally* (Grand Rapids: Grand Rapids Art Museum, 2006).
Holyoke, Julie, *Digital Jacquard Design* (London: Bloomsbury Academic, 2013).
Larsen, Anne Mette (ed.), *Auf der Anderen Seite #2* (Silkeborg: Silkeborg Bad, 2012).
Laue, Dietmar (ed.), *Textile Forum—Special Issue: Digital Tapestries* 2 (2013).
Lourie, Janice, *Textile Graphics/Computer-Aided* (New York: Fairchild Publications, 1973).
Nissen, Kirsten, "Pattern Generation in Dynamic Systems: An Approach to Textile Design," in *Proceedings of Ambience 08,* ed. Lars Hallnäs and Pernilla Walkenström (Borås: University College of Borås, 2008), 131–8.
Rosenberg, Rikke, "Textile Illusions," in *Tween—Tekstile Illusioner*, ed. Textile Illusions (Copenhagen: Design Museum Denmark, 2006), n.p.
Schlein, Alice, and Bhakti Ziek, *The Woven Pixel: Designing for Jacquard and Dobby Looms Using Photoshop®* (Greenville: Bridgewater Press, 2006).
Sørensen, Grethe, "From Traditional to Digital Tools," *Textile Society of America Symposium Proceedings 2010,* Paper 51. http://digitalcommons.unl.edu/tsaconf/51 [accessed 24 September 2014].
Sørensen, Grethe, *Spor af Lys—Traces of Light* (Copenhagen: Rundetaarn, 2012).
Strickler, Carol, *A Weaver's Book of 8-Shaft Patterns: From the Friends of Handwoven* (Loveland, Colorado: Interweave Press, 1991).
Textile Illusions (eds), *Tween—Tekstile Illusioner* (Copenhagen: Design Museum Denmark, 2006).
Vestby, Vibeke, "The TC-1," in *Banishing Boundaries—Weaving Digitally,* ed. Patrice F. George (Grand Rapids: Grand Rapids Art Museum, 2006), 30–1.

5
THE INTELLIGENCE OF THE HAND

Monika Auch

Introduction

In this chapter I set out to explore the introduction of digital tools into traditional crafting with a focus on weaving. It is informed by my personal development as an artist with a background in the worlds of both arts and medical science, and by interviews with designer-makers. The worlds of science and arts are each governed by their own rules. Valid scientific research is bound by the rigors of scientific parameters and statistics, whereas arts research thrives through out-of-the-box thinking. In this chapter I discuss the intelligence of the hand, the development of a sensibility for materials, the importance

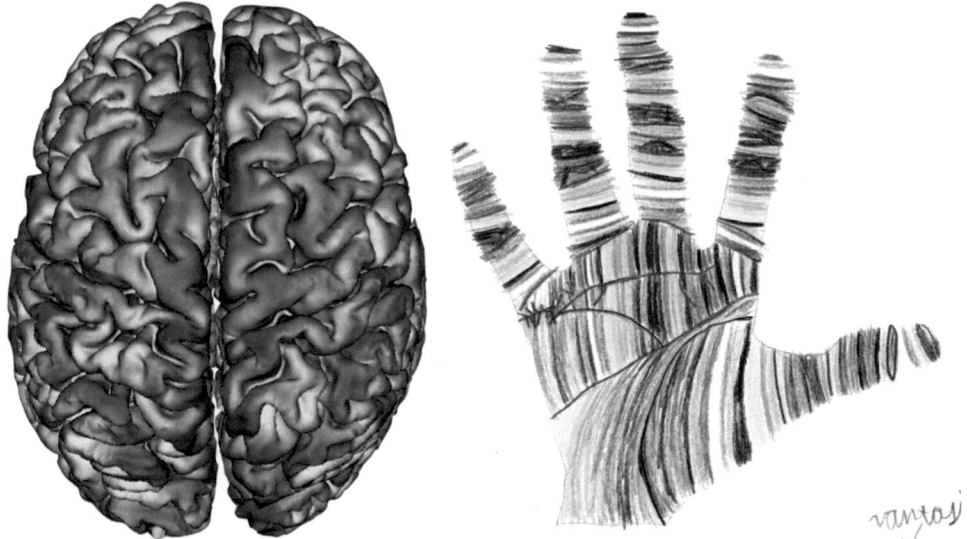

Figure 5.1 A collage of rendered MRI-scan imagery of the author's brain and a drawing by her daughter Nora at the age of five. © Monika Auch.

of cognition, and the use of algorithms, all in relation to the current use of digital tools in weaving and in other disciplines of arts. I conclude by describing my own project, "Stitch_ Your_Brain," in order to offer a wider perspective on the use of digital tools in crafting.

Anatomy and weaving

I became a weaver because I studied medicine. During the required five years of theoretical studies I missed working with my hands so badly that I attended private weaving lessons in order to engage in creative making. After learning the basics from a Finnish traditional weaver, I worked in the studio of Margot Rolf, a Dutch weaver and Bauhaus descendant, between the hospital internships.

Combined with the wealth of materials, the mathematical structure of weaving with its endless possibilities appealed to me. However, looking at weaving as a visual artist, I really wanted to explore it as a 3D construction technique. In order to widen my horizons, I attended a course for Computer Aided Design and Computer Aided Manufacturing (CAD/CAM) for weaving soon after such courses became available. Weaving is the oldest binary technique and can be easily translated into computer programs. Working on a computer-controlled loom ever since, I have taken weaving out of its traditional context and used it as a contemporary, autonomous construction technique in order to create woven sculptures. It was critical feedback about the obvious but unintended anatomical qualities of the sculptures that opened my eyes to the analogy between anatomy and weaving in terms of construction, for example, in the microscopic growth patterns and the multilayered embryologic shapes of the 3D woven objects. On another level, practicing as a medical doctor and as an artist needed the same hands-on skills, inquisitiveness, and problem-solving approach. This perception initiated my research about the intelligence of the hand and the fascinating axis between hand and brain in the creative process (Plate 7).

In contemporary artists' studios, the combination of craft and digital processes has become common practice. In regard to weaving, it takes time to master a technique using CAD/CAM tools that allow a freedom of expression that is not restricted by technical problems. Apart from learning applicable techniques, other indispensable skills are dexterity, hands-on experience with any specific materials and, finally, a good amount of curiosity to solve any problems and nurture innovative developments at the same time.

The hand

The human hand is central to this discussion on crafting in digital times. Frank Wilson, an American neurologist, researched the importance of the hand for musicians, jugglers, and visual artists alike. In his book *The Hand*, he wrote about the evolution of the hand, from the important grasping function of thumbs and fingers to the subtle and mysterious interaction of the hand and the brain during a creative process, be it open heart surgery or the

THE INTELLIGENCE OF THE HAND

Figure 5.2 Engraving on paper by Henricus Wilhelmus Couwenberg, 1830–45, shows postures and gestures of the thumb and other fingers. Dimensions: 150 x 108 mm. Photograph: Rijksmuseum, Amsterdam.

making of a sculpture.¹ Wilson describes the work of jewelry maker George McLean, who lost the four fingers of his right hand in an accident but taught himself to work with the remaining grasping function of the right thumb and the intact left hand. McLean explains the sensual pleasure of working with tools and materials:

> When you're filing or hammering there's also the sound. Hammering on a piece of metal is like ringing a bell. A person needs to have feeling for all of those things. You know, tools are very sensual things, and using them can be.²

In this quote, he refers to a visual vocabulary, stating how materials have an inherent meaning for him and an emotion attached, which in turn gives his pieces a unique personal stamp. Based on this and other cases in the book, Wilson considers that, through material knowledge and skill, the hand can be transformed into an articulate organ of expression.

Margot Rolf, a former professor of weaving and a Bauhaus descendant, looks at the warp–weft combination in a hand-woven piece with a magnifying glass and can see exactly where the weaver stopped for a break, because the rhythm of the cloth has changed. In weaving by hand, even the slightest, most minimal differences in positioning a weft thread or how the woven thread is pushed into place by the beater changes the expression of the woven piece. A high degree of critical observation and motor skill practice is needed in order to develop such sensibility.

In medical practice, we use our fingertips as eyes to explore and interpret palpable tissue matter and its position when visual information is hidden beneath the skin or inside a body cavity. Is a lump fixed to the surrounding tissue, is it mobile and soft or hard as stone, suggesting either the head of a baby or a tumour? Tactile sensibility and good visuospatial orientation are crucial in medical practice even with available modern image-making techniques such as scans and X-rays.

The sum of these sensitivities could be expressed as a material sense, which appears to be important to weaving and medical practice alike. How does a material sense develop?

Material sense through seeing and touching materials

> Quality, light, color, depth, which are there before us, are there only because they awaken an echo in our bodies and because the body welcomes them.³

As soon as we are born, we explore our environment with our mouths and hands. Touching or being touched is an essential sensation. Textiles touch and envelop us from birth to death. Once we consciously make the connection between the different sensations evoked by the haptic and visual perception of different sorts of textiles, we are able to experience textiles as warm but itchy wool, cool linen, soft velvet, caressing silk that feels like water flowing over you, electrostatic synthetic fiber, or clammy nylon. These sensations can be associated with feelings such as security, desire, or revulsion. Sometimes these feelings are so intense that they make the hairs on your arms stand on end or give you the shivers when you just think about a particular material.

When we look at textiles, memories of previous experiences are activated within our brains. This can lead to an automatic reaction like reaching out towards the fabric in front of us to check if our association matches the reality. The well-worn maxim "you look with your eyes and not with your hands" forbids the instinctive urge to touch something that is visually attractive. Meant as a warning for children to neither touch everything they see nor grab what tempts them, the saying implies that touching is less important than looking or, in fact, a second-rate impulse. This is certainly not the case for blind people, who experience the world to a great extent through touch.

In Denis Diderot's famous "Letter on the blind" from 1749, a blind man answers the question whether he would like to see:

> I would just as soon have long arms: it seems to me my hands would tell me more of what happens in the moon than your eyes and your telescopes; and besides, eyes cease to see sooner than hands to touch. I would be as well off if I perfected the organ I possess, as if I obtained the organ which I am deprived of.[4]

This man, blind from birth, concludes the sense of touch to be a more reliable source of understanding and states that seeing with the eyes is equal to feeling with the hands. Ultimately, it is proof of the intelligence of our hands. In conjunction with tactile memory, our hands allow us to experience the softness of velvet, the animal sturdiness of horsehair, the warmth of wool, the fluidity of silk, the roughness of jute, and the artificiality of Tyvek, by just looking at such materials. We do, indeed, see with our hands and instantaneously feel—even if we do not touch. Experiences and memories we have collected through our hands provide us with an understanding of materials.

Knowing and valuing the behavior, properties, and emotional meaning of materials can only be acquired by touching them and, in weaving, by using yarns in unusual ways. However, will computers, laser machines, 3D printers, and other innovative tools place a barrier between us and the material world, and limit us to touching a screen or mouse pad? Or does this limitation in turn cause a craving for touching materials in order to establish a physical link with the world?

Hand and cognition

Bearing these questions in mind, the important cognitive steps of seeing, understanding, and representing an object visually through drawing by hand or by computer needs to be discussed. Drawing is still one of the basic skills taught in art school programs. It is of particular importance to artists working with digital methods in order to implement a "natural" touch into computer-generated designs. Since 1999, renowned jewelry artist

Ted Noten has been working with 3D printing. The first task for interns in his studio is to draw an apple. Competent in computer skills, the interns usually work with an image from the internet. Noten sends them to the greengrocers to buy an apple and to draw by hand the shape of the fruit, complete with texture and light reflection. By executing this elemental cognitive step they learn how to add tactile qualities to software designs, like Noten does for his 3D printed jewelry pieces.

In medicine, drawing has a long tradition going back to Leonardo da Vinci, but it has sadly been struck off the curriculum in medical faculties. Before technical means like photography and scans were available to visualize anatomy, drawing was a basic skill for a career in science.

Jan Swammerdam (1637–80), a famous Dutch anatomist, was an astute observer, taxidermist, and skilled draughtsman. He fully understood the cognitive steps of observing, understanding what he saw, and reproducing it as realistically as possible on paper, in order to communicate the findings to a greater audience and lay personal claims to any profound discoveries. Through the powerful single-lens microscope of his fellow countryman Antonie van Leeuwenhoek, Swammerdam observed and documented virtually unexplored territory using specimens of frogs and lice to see structures whose functions he could only guess at because nobody had ever looked at them before. In his work, he fused the scientific with the artistic view, and even described his findings in terms borrowed from the arts, thus reflecting also the rich art world of his times. "Repeatedly he spoke of the astonishing 'handiwork' or 'embroidery' of the tiniest creatures."[5]

Material making and time

The current idea that the use of digital tools will speed up any time-consuming learning and making processes begs critical consideration. In interviews with designer-makers, it is obvious that the time factor has to be regarded in relation to the quality of work. Ted Noten, for example, made hundreds of material samples before he reached the exquisite balance between materials, form, and content in his 3D printed pieces. In weaving, making samples is essential preparatory work in order to explore the qualities of weft–warp tension, the special qualities of materials, and structure of any cloth or sculpture. There are no shortcuts or time-saving procedures in this necessary step. CAD/CAM machines do not speed up the process but, quite contrarily, can slow it down because of the increased number of possibilities in designing and manufacturing.

During their residency period at the European Ceramic Working Centre in the Netherlands, the design duo Minale and Maeda were creating a porcelain dining set and using a 3D printing machine for the arduous production of molds. Unexpectedly, the water-attracting qualities of the printing material defeated their attempts to produce an evenly surfaced mold and a smooth, industrial-looking product. The cast porcelain showed random irregularities, and numerous test runs with different materials were necessary until a satisfactory flawless result had been achieved. The designers stated that digital techniques like rapid prototyping are, in fact, a new time-consuming craft with its own rules that can only be applied creatively after mastering them.[6]

Freedom in algorithms

In an interview, Swiss architect Michael Hansmeyer points out that computers and software are tools to realize what would not otherwise be possible. Hansmeyer creates columns with an amazing aesthetic appeal by using a computational method and laser technology for designing and manufacturing the pieces. He says: "Modern software simplifies the drawing of very complicated forms. There are hardly any limits for complexity in design and production processes."[7] He uses a computational method whereby information is fed into the software which then draws a design autonomously in a repetitive loop with playful variations. A relatively simple input results in complex forms. The process is not totally controlled, but has a calculated freedom of expression—a moment of surprise. This is comparable to the human or natural touch that other designer-makers introduce in their 3D printed or CAD/CAM engineered work. The maker defines the variable parameters and conditions, not the design of the final object itself.

In the weaving process, I develop my work using a collage of materials, with the blueprint of the multilayered embryonic growth in the back of my mind. My working method of alternating slow manual weaving with planning the next step on the computer interface leaves room for playfulness and serendipity. The physical contact with the material and loom is crucial for the process. The final shape of the woven sculptures depends on the barely controllable interaction of the materials and is only revealed

Figure 5.3 Morphology studies, three objects from the "Ludens" series, 2011. Left: "Incompleta." Middle: "Spina Aperta." Right: "Spina Occlusive." Materials: plastic yarn, surgical drains, horsehair, paper yarn, and heat-reactive yarn. Dimensions: approximately 13 x 5 cm each. Photograph: Ilse Schrama. © Monika Auch.

when the tension of the warp is released. The unfolding of the 3D form happens at that very moment which I documented in the video "Weaving Proxyclones."[8] In contrast to weaving with industrial CAD/CAM machines that require control of all parameters, the manual interweaving of materials on a computer-controlled loom offers creative freedom during the construction process. In this "laboratory" of forms, I create series of objects that are not intended to be true-to-life copies of existing forms, but rather additions to what nature had not yet thought of, even with construction defects, such as mutations and aberrations. All woven objects in a series are of equal value. There are no failures as such, only new and unexpected forms. The freedom in creating with a unique and highly personal technique is the basis for my artistic grammar—a morphology of woven forms.

Digital technology has been with us now for some time and it has been followed by a renaissance in crafting. The contradiction that seemed to sit between craft and digital technology has been resolved. Parallel to the discovery and implementation of digital technologies, a reevaluation of craft and making by hand is taking place. The transfer of the sensibility of the hand into digital tools is a logical and often-applied step in the process. A combination of traditional, time-consuming methods and contemporary, instantaneous technology, i.e. a visible clash of digital and tactile methods, can strengthen the material impact of the viewing experience.

Ann Marie Shillito's book *Digital Crafts: Industrial Technologies for Applied Artists and Designer Makers* (2013), about the use of industrial technologies for applied artists and designers, fuses a craft-minded approach with 2D and 3D digital technologies.[9] In Shillito's design of a haptic device, this way of designing has come within the reach of every artist and designer.

A theoretical consideration of working with digital technology must address the definition of authenticity. Public opinion regards the replica of an artwork as possessing less value than the original work. In digitally produced work, however, there are only perfect replicas—or to use a more appropriate word, clones. A copy in the sense of a less valuable product does not exist any longer. Artists who create using CAD/CAM production are, in fact, redefining authenticity.

"Stitch_My_Brain"

I set up the project entitled "Stitch_Your_Brain" in order to introduce a wider perspective on the use of digital tools in crafting. Where does creativity—the fundamental aspect in the process of making—originate, and what are the influences of digital tools on creative making by hand, i.e. crafting? Creativity is after all the cornerstone of what makes us human. Can creativity be traced and measured? Is it possible to jump the Cartesian void dividing mind and hand by using science in order to trace artistic creativity?

In an attempt to measure creativity I set up two experiments. In the first one—"Stitch_My_Brain"—I measured my own brain activity during a defined creative action with the help of innovative brain technology. The second on-going experiment—"Stitch_Your_Brain"—is open to the public and documents the engagement of participants in a crafting task and their reflections on it in a questionnaire.

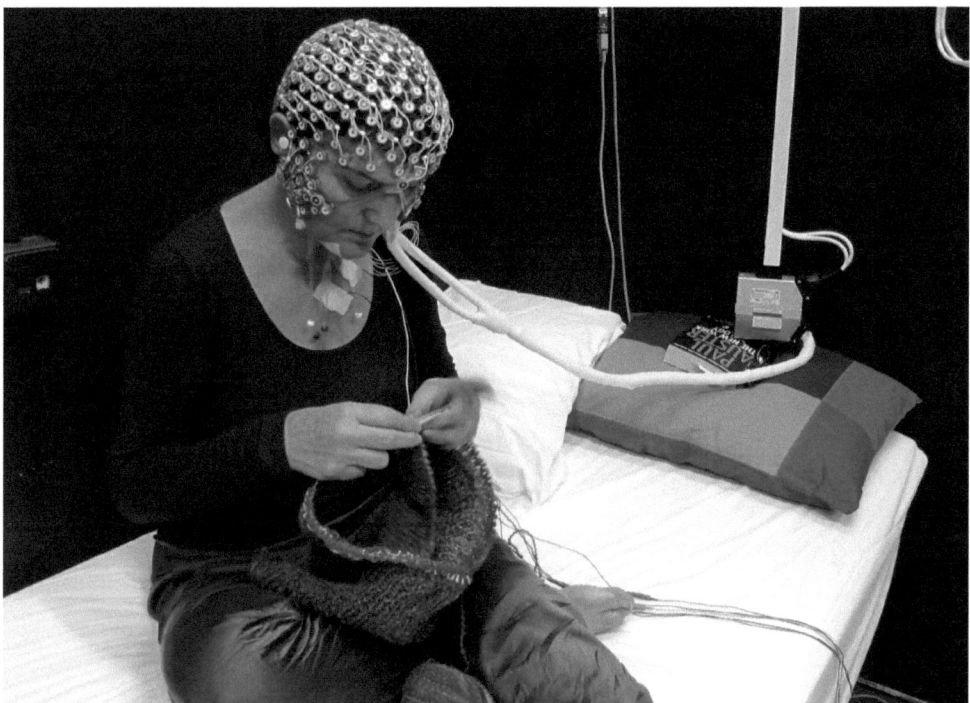

Figure 5.4 The author is wired up while knitting at the Netherlands Institute for Neuroscience for EEG registrations, mapping dexterity through scientific data. Photograph: Jennifer Ramautar. © Monika Auch.

In the "Stitch_My_Brain" project, creativity is defined as the interruption of a repetitive automatic movement (i.e. knitting) by making a mistake (i.e. dropping a stitch) which initiates the learning of a new action in the brain. This definition of creativity is based on the observation that innovation very often occurs in studio practice as a happy accident—a moment of serendipity or a "Eureka" moment. This happens when a maker incidentally changes the usual placement of a tool in the hand, or when a skilled hand fumbles, or when a material behaves differently. At the Netherlands Institute of Neuroscience in Amsterdam, I registered the execution of a new motor skill action with medical technology using functional Magnetic Resonance Imaging (fMRI)[10] scanning and Electroencephalographic (EEG)[11] registrations. The registrations yielded slight, expected variations in brain patterns, mapping the change from the automatic to non-automatic movement, but gave no clue as to the origins of creativity.

In framing the origins of creativity in combination with the influence of digital tools, the net has to be cast wider, involving a larger and more varied group of people and different research methods. Why, after all, do humans enjoy and even crave creative making? What motivates them to put so much effort into learning a skill in order to make objects? And—returning to the original question—how does digital technology influence crafting?

"Stitch_Your_Brain"

The "Stitch_Your_Brain" (SYB) project and website were launched at the Impact International Printmaking Conference in Dundee, Scotland.[12] SYB is a textile-related project which consists of an embroidery kit with the schematic representation of a brain to embellish. The project aims to engage participants in making work by hand, while at the same time reflecting on a visual representation of their brain (Plates 8 and 9). Participants are asked to send an image of their stitched brain for the SYB website. Additionally, they are asked to complete a questionnaire with twenty questions covering the developmental and cognitive aspects of individual creativity and dexterity, such as social environment, education, the use of digital tools in everyday life, emotions during crafting, and peer group-related goals. They are asked about their experience of crafting and to comment freely on the subject. With the involvement of international participants of all ages and their different ways of approaching the task, the project is expected to give answers to queries about possible changes in manual skills and generally about the changed experience of crafting since the arrival of digital tools. Once a representative number of submissions have been received, the stitched brains and questionnaires will be analyzed.

A surprising new angle on crafting has appeared in discussions as to its contribution to the improvement of health and well-being. Artists and healthcare workers have discovered the positive effects of crafting on mental health. Physiotherapist Betsan Corkhill established the stress-reducing effects of knitting in her study involving more than 3,500 participants. This has gained the interest of healthcare workers and medical specialists alike.[13] Corkhill's findings and the statement of many women that a knitting, crochet, quilting, or other craft project has kept them in a stable mental state in times of crisis can be used as a concept towards the prevention of rising healthcare costs. It also strengthens the point that creative making is a fundamental and necessary human activity. The idea that crafting can actually contribute to well-being is supported by healthcare institutions and funded Arts projects in Great Britain.[14] It is an interesting theme to be discussed at another place and in the context of healthcare policies.

Conclusion

The conclusion of this discussion about the influence of digital tools on crafting and its parameters, i.e. the hand, cognition, and creativity with a focus on embroidery and weaving, is an interpretation of the early results of the SYB project, interviews with designers/makers, and my studio practice of weaving on a digital loom. A preliminary analysis of about forty admitted works of the SYB project shows that participants under the age of fifty who regularly work with digital tools, i.e. a computer, and are not professional designer-makers have a very different approach to crafting in general and less detailed skills in performing a manual creative task than the fifty+ generation. It is necessary to continue the study in order to gain more data before further conclusions can be made. Interviews with designer-makers show that digital tools have become yet another skill that has to be mastered—a new craft. By now designer-makers working at the cutting edge of innovative technology have implemented digital tools in their work and adapted them, fitting their individual signature and style. Weaving has been the ideal playground for experimenting with software and CAD/CAM technology, because it is the ultimate and original binary technique. The technical aspects are easily learned. The challenge is to combine new materials in a meaningful way with the infinite possibilities of the CAD/CAM loom. Groundbreaking discoveries in smart materials will add more possibilities for constructing woven artwork or applied woven structures, e.g. body prostheses, in the field of medicine. There has never been a more exciting time for weavers than now.

The developments of working with digital tools in crafting and especially weaving can be summarized by Tim Ingold's observations on livelihood, dwelling, and weaving as a dynamic process:

> First, the practitioner operates within a field of forces set up through his or her engagement with the material; secondly, the work does not merely involve the mechanical application of external forces but calls for care, judgement and dexterity;

Figure 5.5 Two objects of the morphology series, "Neurotubes." Dimensions: approximately 20 x 25 x 10 cm each. Materials: fishing line, horse hair, and heat-reactive yarn. Technique: 3D weaving on a computerized loom. Photograph: Ilse Schrama. © Monika Auch.

and thirdly, the action has a narrative quality, in the sense that every movement, like every line in a story, grows rhythmically out of the one before and lays the groundwork for the next.[15]

Where making (like building) comes to an end with the completion of a work in its final form, weaving (like dwelling) continues for as long as life goes on—punctuated but not terminated by the appearance of the pieces that it successively brings into being. Dwelling in the world, in short, is tantamount to the ongoing, temporal interweaving of our lives with one another and with the manifold constituents of our environment.[16]

Notes

1. Frank R. Wilson, *The Hand* (New York: Pantheon Books, 1998).
2. Wilson, *The Hand*, 142.
3. Maurice Merleau-Ponty, "Eye and Mind," in *The Merleau-Ponty Aesthetics Reader: Philosophy and Painting*, ed. Galen A. Johnson, trans. Michael B. Smith (Evanston, IL: Northwestern University Press, 1993), 125.
4. Margaret Jourdain (ed.), *Diderot's Early Philosophical Works* (Chicago and London: The Open Court Publishing Company, 1916), 77.
5. Eric Jorink and Bart Ramakers (eds), *Art and Science in the Early Modern Netherlands* (Zwolle: Waanders, 2011), 169.
6. Monika Auch, "3D printen: het nieuwe ambacht?" [3D printing: The new craft?], *kM tijdschrift* 79 (2011): 20–3.
7. Monika Auch, "Antieke pilaren en algoritmische zuilen, de computational method van Michael Hansmeyer" [Antique pillars and algorithmic columns, the computational method of Michael Hansmeyer], *kM tijdschrift* 85 (2013): 16–9.
8. For the video "Weaving Proxyclones." http://www.monikaauch.nl/agenda [accessed June 22, 2015].
9. Ann Marie Shillito, *Digital Crafts: Industrial Technologies for Applied Artists and Designer Makers* (London: Bloomsbury, 2013).
10. Functional MRI (fMRI) is "a non-invasive tool for studying brain function, both in healthy volunteers and clinical patients." http://www.ed.ac.uk/clinical-sciences/neuroimaging-sciences/about-us/imaging-techniques/functional-mri [accessed November 17, 2015].
11. Electroencephalography (EEG) is "the recording of electrical activity along the scalp." It "measures voltage fluctuations resulting from ionic current flows within the neurons of the brain." http://www.ed.ac.uk/clinical-sciences/neuroimaging-sciences/about-us/imaging-techniques/electroencephalography [accessed November 17, 2015].
12. Monika Auch, "STITCH_MY_BRAIN," paper presented at Impact 8 International Printmaking Conference "Borders and Crossings: The Artist as Explorer," University of Dundee, August 28–30, 2013. http://www.conf.dundee.ac.uk/impact8/people/biographies-2/monika-auch/ [accessed February 7, 2015].
13. Betsan Corkhill, *Knit for Health & Wellness* (Bath: FlatBear Publishing, 2014).
14. Monika Auch, "The Intelligent Hand," keynote presented at symposium "Beyond the Toolkit: Understanding and Evaluating Crafts Practice for Health and Wellbeing," Falmouth University

and Arts for Health Cornwall, February 19, 2014. http://www.falmouth.ac.uk/content/beyond-toolkit-keynote-speakers [accessed June 21, 2015]

15 Tim Ingold, *The Perception of the Environment: Essays in Livelihood, Dwelling and Skill* (Oxon: Routledge, 2000), 347.

16 Ingold, *The Perception of the Environment*, 348.

Bibliography

Auch, Monika, "3D printen: het nieuwe ambacht?" [3D printing: The new craft?], *kM tijdschrift* 79 (2011): 20–3.

Auch, Monika, "Antiek pilaren en algoritmische zuilen, de computational method van Michael Hansmeyer" [Antique pillars and algorithmic columns, the computational method of Michael Hansmeyer], *kM tijdschrift* 85 (2013): 16–9.

Auch, Monika, "STITCH_MY_BRAIN", paper presented at Impact 8 International Printmaking Conference "Borders and Crossings: The Artist as Explorer," University of Dundee, UK, 28–30 August 2013. http://www.conf.dundee.ac.uk/impact8/people/biographies-2/monika-auch/ [accessed February 7, 2015].

Auch, Monika, "The Intelligent Hand", paper presented at symposium "Beyond the Toolkit: Understanding and Evaluating Crafts Praxis for Health and Wellbeing," Falmouth University, UK, February 19, 2014. http://www.falmouth.ac.uk/content/beyond-toolkit-keynote-speakers [accessed June 21, 2015].

Corkhill, Betsan, *Knit for Health & Wellness* (Bath: FlatBear Publishing, 2014).

Ingold, Tim, *The Perception of the Environment: Essays in Livelihood, Dwelling and Skill* (Oxon: Routledge, 2000).

Jorink, Erik, and Bart Ramakers (eds), *Art and Science in the Early Modern Netherlands* (Zwolle: Waanders, 2011).

Jourdain, Margaret (ed.), *Diderot's Early Philosophical Works* (Chicago and London: The Open Court Publishing Company, 1916). http://tems.umn.edu/pdf/Diderot-Letters-on-the-Blind-and-the-Deaf.pdf [accessed April 4, 2015].

Merleau-Ponty, Maurice, "Eye and Mind," in *The Merleau-Ponty Aesthetics Reader: Philosophy and Painting*, ed. Galen A. Johnson, trans. Michael B. Smith (Evanston, IL: Northwestern University Press, 1993).

Quinn, Bradley, *Contemporary Textiles* (London: Black Dog Publishing, 2008).

Shillito, Ann Marie, *Digital Crafts: Industrial Technologies for Applied Artists and Designer Makers* (London: Bloomsbury, 2013).

Wilson, Frank R., *The Hand* (New York: Pantheon Books, 1998).

PART TWO

CRAFT INTERVENTION IN DIGITAL PROCESS

6
THE DIGITAL PRINT ROOM—A BESPOKE APPROACH TO PRINT TECHNOLOGY

Helen Ryall and Penny Macbeth

Introduction

This chapter explores and expands the ideas that emerged during the development of a PhD research project titled *An Exploration of Digital Technology Over a Number of Manipulated Textile Surfaces* carried out by Helen Ryall, one of the authors.[1] The project aims to encourage designers to engage with traditional craft and design methods and apply these to digital technologies in the production of innovative textile surfaces. Within this project Ryall undertook the multiple roles of craftsperson, designer, and technician. This chapter reveals the creative collaboration of all three roles and their importance in the development of and the vision for the creative use of digital technology. It focuses on the exploration of the ideal studio scenario where the three roles collaborate and share their skills in experimenting with digital technologies as a creative design tool.

In the research, flexibility of mindset was vital for fully achieving the potential digital print technology had to offer the textile practitioner, involving a responsive approach to craft and technology. The way in which designers conceive digital technologies was fundamental. Confidence in the use of technology, a creative mindset, and an ambition to be experimental were also needed. The computer and printer became the palette, paintbrush, and dye vessel, while the print medium became the canvas on which the creativity could begin for Ryall. Recognition of this simple approach helped to bridge the gap between the craftsperson, designer, and technician.

The project set out to apply an experimental and innovative way of using digital textile printing. The main focus was to emulate the responsiveness of hand design production with a new digital application. The research explored the territory that digital print production had to offer during the period 2000–10. It combined the knowledge and expertise of the craftsperson, designer, and technician. While the designer usually provides the creative vision and ambition to develop new designs, the technician contributes the appreciation of the limitations and gaps in the performance and capability of the technology. Ryall had both the experience and skillset as a designer and a technician that played an essential role in the development of this project. The combination of knowledge, creativity, and skill was necessary to extend the printer's potential as a creative tool in order to develop innovative processes and introduce a new aesthetic for digitally printed textiles. The project resulted in a platform for practitioners to extend the possibilities of the design outcomes obtained within the project to develop the use of digital technology further.

The chapter outlines key factors regarding process, and also presents an aesthetic not normally associated or expected with digital design outcomes. It summarizes how design methods and print techniques can be individually developed and mastered, in order that each designer's personal handwriting will ensure original designs even when given the same constraints of material, dyestuff, software, and print technology.

The importance of a crafted approach to digital design

To fully appreciate the implications of this project, it is important to understand the emerging craft context to which it relates. As the use of digital processes has become more familiar and part of everyday practice, tacit approaches to textile making have emerged within a digital context. In *Thinking Through Craft*, Glenn Adamson explores David Pye's theories and expands the context of digital versus hand as an idea. He describes: "Pye's most well-known distinction is that between the workmanship of risk and the workmanship of certainty. This was a purposeful reframing of the dichotomy between craft and industry, or hand and machine."[2]

Pye's ideas developed during the 1960s enable us to consider and reflect upon the nuance and versatility of approaches to design and making required when executing a particular task. His ideas help us to understand the implications of the growing breadth of tools available in a digital age. This supports us in developing a more hybrid design methodology that harnesses the plethora of tools available, breaking through the mindset of either hand or machine made. In conclusion, one could argue that it is the way we interact with the tool and the creative mindset that is key to the production of innovative design work, not the tool itself.

This chapter explores the versatility of approaches adopted by the textile practitioner while sampling. For example, a range of processes come into play when textiles are constructed. Working with hands, the practitioner will make minute judgements about the texture, weight, and handle of the fabric. If dyeing a cloth, judgement and chance might well be harnessed within the process; many designer-makers use their "embodied knowledge" to make informed decisions about the color, the quantity of dyestuff needed, and the length of time the fabric should be left in the liquor. Textile designer-makers tend to utilize the qualities of their raw materials, working with the materials' properties and characteristics intuitively rather than rigidly imposing their ideas onto them. Flaws or unintended results can be assimilated into the overall design, if positive, and new methods and procedures are evolved as part of the reflective cycle. This was very much the approach adopted within this research to explore the territory of what digital technology could offer.

Japanese textile designers have been crafting with technology for years. Rather than the notional constraints of the technology, their overriding creativity comes to the fore, as McQuaid and McCarty comment: "These visionary designers incorporate both ancient methods and experimental technologies into their untypical ways of working with textiles."[3]

To master any process, digital or hand, the maker needs to become highly familiar with or obsessive about the technique and method used. Once mastered, a fluid, spontaneous and less conscious approach to making emerges. This approach is often termed "designing through making." With this approach in mind, the decision to work intuitively across technologies for Ryall's research project was made—an attempt to create new methods of digital design that were instinctive and responsive, rather than overly planned. McCullough explains the potential of this method:

> Instead of thinking the actions you feel the actions and actions stir your memory and give you a better sense of inhabiting your work. As an expert you sense what to try when, how far a medium can be pushed; when to check up on a process; which tool to use for what job.[4]

Inspiration for the collection of fabrics was gained through exploring the traditional handcraft processes of shibori and tie-dyeing on a trip to Zhoucheng, China; the use of physical resists were of particular interest. Through researching a range of resist printed cloths, an idea of developing a collection of "digital resists" emerged. The collection would apply the principles of resist through crafting an actual barrier during the printing process while utilizing the complexities and finely tuned technology that digital printing required. The aim was to apply the principles of "designing through making" to the collection, which would make the design process less reliant on the parameters of computer-generated artwork and establish a crafted aesthetic.

Physical resists, such as barrier methods, restraints, and manipulations, have been experimented with in a variety of ways. For example, lace and embroidery have been used to act as a barrier to the fabric, while a series of manipulation and pleating techniques have been utilized to enable restraint and resist effects. The aim of the experiments was to understand and embrace the limitations of the printer, as they could be the driver for the future generations of digital print technology.

Re-thinking digital print technology

Digital print technology has found its place in the textile industry and is seen as a reliable method of production for commercial markets. The technology is known for all its benefits in use of color, tonal printing, speed, and cost for short run productions. However, it is important to add a new focus or an alternative route to the use of this printing method that encourages the industry to view it as a highly creative design tool rather than simply an efficient means of production.

In Ryall's exploration of resist techniques with inkjet technology, it was vital to consider the surface of the print medium. The materials sent through the inkjet printer had a relatively even surface and were less than 5mm thick to enable the print heads to run smoothly above the printable medium and gain an evenly printed result, if desired.

The approaches to using digital print technology within this aspect of the work were to consider alternative possibilities from the industry norm. The digital print technology has not been used simply to print or decorate the cloth, but effectively been used like a dye bath or a paintbrush. It has been used to add splashes of color and simplistic pattern, allowing for the true pattern and decoration to occur from the physical resists. The benefit of using digital printing instead of traditional methods was the element of control that was achieved. Digital artwork was created to have many subtle gradient tones, which added sensitivity to the resist effects, when several colors were printed at one time, and the placement of the overprinting effect was measured and planned. The designer and craftsperson embraced these tools and used them to their advantage, permitting each design to be hand-crafted.

Making digital fluid

The physical resists that were experimented with were applied to the fabric grounds before printing over the print designs. The physical resists were applied singularly, various types of physical resist were applied, and fabrics were re-manipulated and re-printed to get the desired effect. Within the collection, materials such as lace fabrics and processes such as CAD embroidery and pleating were used to create pattern effects.

This research was designer-led, creating the printed designs by building up the complex patterns piece by piece. Placement, color, scale, direction, and printed effect were considered after each application. The challenge was to adapt, measure, and evaluate the outcome at each stage of the process, ensuring the pattern design remained consistent and well balanced, while appearing to be gestural and fluid. Key design influences for pattern came from Jonathan Saunders, Missoni, and Etro.

At times, the first manipulation had to be completely removed, or before building a new manipulation or adding a different resist, the fabric would need to be ironed flat for successful feeding through the printer. This enabled a change in direction for the manipulation to add further variation and experimentation to the design and research. Ryall would return to the digital software to generate a new print overlay responding to the pattern, texture, size, angle, and shape of the new additions needed. Basic color mixing principles were taken into consideration, as the true color outcome was not revealed until after post-treatment to the printed fabric.

The role of the designer and craftsperson is to focus on the creative process through the application of hand-developed and applied manipulations, and to perfect the overall design. The role of the technician is to concentrate on the capabilities of the printer, being experimental but achieving the highest quality outcome. Collaboration that combines the different perspectives of the designer, craftsperson, and technician is vital to achieve the results set out in this project and its approach to using digital technology.

In *Textiles Today: A Global Survey of Trends and Traditions*, Chloë Colchester reviews the work of the designer Tord Boontje and his collaboration with a computer programmer in the generation of random growing flower patterns from bud to decay. The process allowed the computer to adapt and randomly place the flowers for each design. Boontje recognized the importance of historical pattern design and that it should be embedded in current design inspiration. The flexibility and creative use of digital design applications allow the modern designer to move away from the standard form of quickly produced modern design outcomes to being influenced by seventeenth-, eighteenth-, and nineteenth-century hand-crafted decorative arts.[5]

Within the process intended for this project, the digital touch was essential for designing and achieving the variety of print qualities, yet the technology remained fluid and integrated into the overall design practice. The full focus was on the generation of the printed textile outcomes.

Lace

To obtain delicate resist patterns, lace fabrics were applied to the textile base, prior to digital printing. The forming of a resist pattern depended greatly on the lace fabric used. However, the design that was digitally printed had a major impact on the strength, location, and prominence of the resist marks made—Plate 10 demonstrates this clearly.

The resist pattern was controlled by two methods: (1) by accurately placing down a lace embellishment by hand; and (2) by using the creation of digital design and adjusting the starting point for the print heads (Figure 6.1). Once dry from the printing, the lace embellishment was removed to reveal the resist pattern created. Attaching a lace embellishment gave two benefits: (1) the printed resist result displayed delicate resist marks; and (2) the printed lace itself captured the residual color and pattern, leaving elusive traces of the print. A fine open lace was used for the experiment (Figure 6.2). The resist patterning provided real possibilities for an alternative fabric, produced by the designer or even upcycled, to be used to create samples, instead of a standard pre-treated fabric from the manufacturer for inkjet printing.

From the designer's perspective, there was a real sense of involvement and authority to the design aesthetic using this process. Typically in digital print technology, the designer creates the artwork and then passes it to the technician to be processed. This designer-led method allows the practitioner to fully reflect on the process and outcomes

Figure 6.1 Inkjet printing in action, demonstrating a lace fabric acting as a resist. Photograph: Helen Ryall.

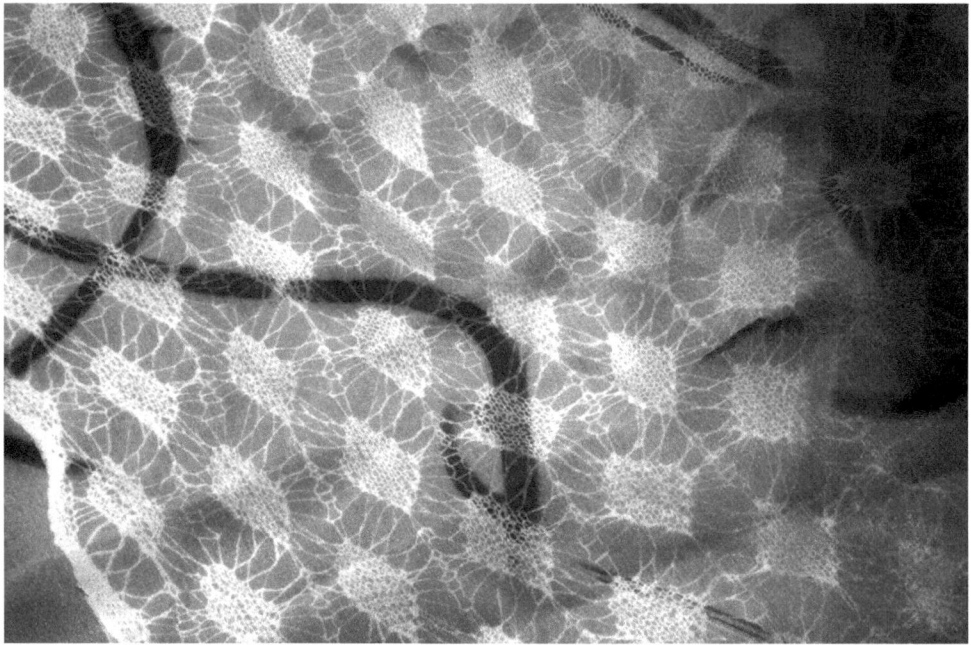

Figure 6.2 Lace resist print, silk habotai, Helen Ryall, 2009. Photograph: Helen Ryall.

and make additions/adjustments throughout the process to achieve the desired effect. The added element of surprise was generated when the lace was removed to reveal distinctive printed results, which could be anticipated but not fully determined—the process added its unique dimension to the overall visual appearance of the fabrics.

Embroidery

The use of embroidery produced highly detailed and delicate printed resist effects, almost creating the illusion of the embroidery itself. The embroidery techniques ranged from free machining onto a wash-away ground created using a domestic sewing machine to decorative hand stitch and computer-aided manufactured (CAM) embroidery. This method followed the same principles as the lace embellishment samples previously discussed, where the embroidery needed to remain relatively flat in order to pass through the digital printer heads. The designs were pre-planned as far as possible. However, unexpected enhancements to the design were anticipated, due to the nature of the process method. The resulting samples were an exciting collection of printed fabrics where the resists added character to the finished fabric, emulating the aesthetic of a hand-crafted design.

The results were very different to those using lace. With highly detailed resist effects, each stitch added left a resist mark. This is due to the fact that the amount of ink/dye used can be controlled on the digital printer, thus intensifying the sensitivity of the resist results. The digital overprint can have variety in the tonal qualities, and the placement can also be controlled to add unique and highly sensitive design results.

Pleats

Simple pleating and crushing of the fabric were used to create physical barriers for the digital resist effects to occur. The principles were to create a pattern by restricting the amount of dyestuff that could permeate through specific areas of the design by creating a resist. The beauty of this group of experiments was that the resists left evidence of some of the machine stitch work, which added the unique qualities of the design results (Figure 6.3). This had the potential to be initially planned as a design process, or alternatively the design could simply evolve with the placement of pleated effects. The accuracy of the pleated sections was not a prime concern; each stage of the design process would be reflected, reviewed, and redesigned where desired. With all of the knowledge gained, this only enhanced the design outcome and did not detract from the hands-on approach to using this technology.

Figure 6.3 Inkjet printed silk habotai, generated using pleating resist effects, Helen Ryall, 2009. Photograph: Helen Ryall.

The digital print room

The crafted approach to using digital technology gives the practitioner unique flexibility in the creation of designs. It is a process that to some extent can be planned, yet can be adjusted and manipulated to suit the practitioner and clients' needs. The printer is not looked upon as merely a production method, but as an integral part of design experimentation, key to both design innovation and small-scale production. Inventive thinking and experience in using the printer will expand the awareness and potential for using digital technology for the purpose of hands-on craft design. Once confidence has been built, the potential for directing the future commercial viability of these technologies is limitless. It will inform the next generation of technology, which will embed craft processes as an integral and iterative part of digital printing.

The chapter has explored the potential of a variety of physical resists that can be used with digital print technology. The resist and manipulation of the fabric will directly impact the design, but the results can only be truly reflected upon once all post-treatment is complete and the fabric returns to its original handle. Due to the physicality of sending the pre-manipulated fabric through the inkjet printer, some resist techniques present obvious restrictions when combined with digital print. In the majority of cases, the print heads have only a relatively small scope for adjustment; therefore, clearance is an issue. For example, most shibori techniques that create 3D fabric structures would not be compatible with the majority of widely available digital printers for this reason.

Figure 6.4 Silk habotai and chiffon (reactive dyes), Helen Ryall, 2010. Photograph: Andrew Farrington.

Each design created using these processes is unique, and therefore should be appreciated for its originality and visual complexity. While the process can be repeated, it is impossible to accurately reproduce the results. Figure 6.4 and Plate 11 demonstrate a fashion outcome that has been produced using hand-crafted digitally printed fabrics.

Commerciality and customer focus

After reflecting upon the processes and the results achieved above, the authors reviewed the markets that these outcomes could target. When considering the designs described above, the customer here would have full appreciation for the hand-crafted designs generated. The techniques and processes used are virtually impossible to reproduce accurately by hand alone. The process is complex and involves many stages to create one piece. In order to produce a particular design for a client, it would be essential to manage their expectations. As the results would vary, i.e. each design is original, the customer would be involved in the whole design process. These particular outcomes would be highly suitable for haute couture garments. Haute couture is a viable outcome for the processes explored here, but the techniques, if corralled, could have real potential to be used in a more commercial context. With this in mind, Ryall decided to explore an alternative angle.

The sampling continued and began to investigate whether the design results could be reproduced and targeted at the commercial designer ready-to-wear market and ultimately the high street. The challenge was to explore whether the delicate and detailed digital resists could be produced in larger batches, while retaining their visual aesthetic. However, for this to be achieved, a technical library compiling results and hand-crafted experimental samples would need to be created in order to provide resources for further developments of commercially viable products. It would also be essential to continue to develop this library to respond to trends and developments in print technology.

A process was therefore developed whereby the results achieved using the hand-crafted resist techniques were scanned back into the computer so that they could be reproduced digitally. This was a breakthrough in the project; it gave clear scope for further development and brought the results to a wider audience. It would not only give customers further alternatives and control of the design outcome, but would also mean the technique could have application for small-batch runs and ultimately the high street. An example of this was that elements of the crafted print effects could be extracted using the selection and mask functions in CAD programs. For the purposes of this project, many combinations of the resist techniques were collated together using textile CAD to create new designs. The designs in varying scale could now be intricately planned, providing the image quality was not affected. The placement of the design had the potential to be manipulated and to create repeat patterns, therefore generating instant colorways and greater scope to the amount printed. However, this did not allow for the same experimentation and spontaneity of design found when applying the resist techniques by hand. It is here that the digital printer returns to its traditional functionality;

these designs would be printed digitally to ensure that the same sensitivity and tonal effects could be reproduced. Not only did this give the designer the chance to reproduce some of the results, but it also allowed for further developments in the actual designs to be achieved, if desired, on-screen. The CAD programs with all their capabilities would come into play; these were not initially used to their full advantage in the generation of artwork for the digital resists. With this is mind, it was still essential to not detract from the delicate and detailed crafted results achieved. The reproduced results were an accurate representation of the original effect created.

A question that arose in the process of conducting this research was whether it is possible to pass on the hand-crafted results, produced in the digital resist experiments, to a commercial designer who has little knowledge of the origins and processes to achieve the design results. This could be possible. However, it is the opinion of both authors that it is essential to follow the process in full, from hand-crafted experiments through to reproducible digital prints suitable for the designer ready-to-wear and high street market. There must be full appreciation for the crafted resist effects, ensuring that the aesthetics remain realistic to the original outcome. They must also adopt a vision to adapt the scanned imagery appropriately and sensitively. This ensures no crafted aesthetics would be missed.

As innovative technology has become commonplace, customers are requiring it to do more, for example, to have an intuitive and nuanced aesthetic. "New technology is allowing a mass market to customise and create design."[6] Without the initial hand-responsive design work, the catalog of design information would be impossible to produce. The emphasis to explore the intersection between craft and technology facilitated the promise of an emerging digital aesthetic.

Research principles and embedding these into an educational context

Reflecting on the expertise and in-depth technical knowledge developed through this period of research, it is important to consider how adaptable the findings are. Could the methods and approaches to digital design established be utilized successfully within the teaching environment? If so, how could they contribute to an ongoing textile methodology? Rebecca Templeton, a final-year undergraduate on BA (Hons) Surface Design for Fashion and Interiors at the University of Huddersfield, was selected to test the findings. Rebecca was chosen because she had an excellent grounding in digital and hand approaches to printed and embroidered textiles. Her work utilized unique combinations of digital print together with hand embroidery. Her ideas on paper suggested that a fusion of these disciplines would be highly beneficial to her practice and would provide an excellent opportunity to test the viability of digital printing onto embroidered grounds.

To develop the research by working with a design student provided an insight into the potential of this bespoke approach to digital printing. The opportunity opened up the design potential for Rebecca both aesthetically and commercially. Her results are evidence of craftsmanship being vital when using new technologies. Hand and machine approaches can work coexistently or be fused to create a hybrid aesthetic; they are not mutually exclusive of each other. "The quality of the result is not predetermined, but depends on the judgement, care and dexterity which the maker exercises as he works."[7] This is the case whether the designer or craftsperson is working by hand, machine, or indeed adopting an interdisciplinary approach.

Conclusion and discussion for future research

By embracing this way of thinking and using digital technology as a key component in the design process, we are provided with a new perspective and a new set of creative design tools. This research has expanded the potential application of technology by incorporating it into the design process, rather than viewing it purely as a means of production. It has allowed the digital printer to become responsive to the practitioner. The chapter primarily focuses on the results gained from the development of digital resist techniques and the versatile approach to technology utilized throughout the design process.

It is vital to acquire a technical grounding in any technology for meaningful experimentation to occur. A designer needs to develop a level of confidence in their tools before embarking on a creative journey. Once this is achieved, exciting design opportunities become available. A creative and open mindset and a vision and desire to experiment will bridge the gap between traditional textiles and digital innovation. As McQuaid and McCarty say: "It is this type of intelligent playing that is forging original works, new discoveries and models of expression specific to our era."[8]

Given the fact that the subject matter of this chapter remains in its relative infancy, one will inevitably encounter technological limitations in the future. As in all walks of life, problems often inspire advancement. Any technological limitations should be viewed as opportunities, enabling the practitioner to be the driving force behind future technological development and ensuring the efficiency and effectiveness of the technology for both the practitioner and the industry as a whole.

While this research project recognizes that the method of digital crafting is effective from a design perspective, the process must also be efficient to ensure commercial viability. To enable these highly sensitive, innovative designs to reach a wider audience, Ryall has developed methods in which digital resists can be reproduced efficiently. This relies on the designer having full knowledge of, and the ability to utilize, digital technology. One must not allow the drive for efficiency and commerciality to detract from the effectiveness and creativity crafted into the digital designs that form the base for reproduction; a balanced approach in which creativity and inspiration are allowed to thrive should be sought.

Our future is one that almost certainly will embrace combined craft and digital approaches to designing and making which are mutually beneficial and reliant on each other. To move forward we must honor the past, prizing those traditional approaches that inform our technological futures.

Notes

1. Helen Ryall, "An Exploration of Digital Technology Over a Number of Manipulated Textile Surfaces" (PhD Thesis, University of Huddersfield, 2010).
2. Glenn Adamson, *Thinking Through Craft* (Oxford, New York: Berg, 2007), 73.
3. Matilda McQuaid and Cara McCarty, *Structure and Surface: Contemporary Japanese Textiles* (New York: Museum of Modern Art, 1998), 13.
4. Malcolm McCullough, "Abstracting Craft: The Practiced Digital Hand," in *The Craft Reader*, ed. Glenn Adamson (Oxford: Berg, 1997), 314–5.
5. Chloë Colchester, *Textiles Today: A Global Survey of Trends and Traditions* (London: Thames and Hudson, 2007), 157.
6. Martina Margetts, *Tord Boontje* (New York: Rizzoli, 2006), 192.
7. Adamson, *Thinking Through Craft*, 73.
8. McQuaid and McCarty, *Structure and Surface*, 13.

Bibliography

Adamson, Glenn, *Thinking Through Craft* (Oxford, New York: Berg, 2007).
Colchester, Chloë, *Textiles Today: A Global Survey of Trends and Traditions* (London: Thames and Hudson, 2007).
Margetts, Martina, *Tord Boontje* (New York: Rizzoli, 2006).
McCullough, Malcolm, "Abstracting Craft: The Practiced Digital Hand," in *The Craft Reader*, ed. Glenn Adamson (Oxford: Berg, 1997), 310–16.
McQuaid, Matilda, and Cara McCarty, *Structure and Surface: Contemporary Japanese Textiles* (New York: Museum of Modern Art, 1998).
Ryall, Helen, "An Exploration of Digital Technology Over a Number of Manipulated Textile Surfaces" (PhD thesis, University of Huddersfield, 2010).

7
MAINTAINING THE HUMAN TOUCH—EXPLORING "CRAFTED CONTROL" WITHIN AN ADVANCED TEXTILE PRODUCTION INTERFACE

Martin Woolley and Robert Huddleston

Introduction

Materials occupy a particular context in relation to contemporary and traditional crafts. Malleable materials, such as clay, react directly to the maker's skilled interventions with less physical resistance than more irregularly structured materials, such as timber. The focus of the crafts on material is reflected in the perception of the end product, as the crafts are largely defined by the materials used: for example "wood, metal, ceramics, and plastics" are standard descriptors for craft-based UK degree courses.

The notion of "passive" materials that offer little physical resistance and exist to be actively transformed also relates to the properties of the material in terms of their homogeneity or heterogeneity. Clay, for example, is a largely homogeneous material, while timber properties, determined by complex grain patterns, are heterogeneous. Where a material is physically uniform, or homogeneous, consistent workmanship is common because the material can be worked in predictable ways, as McCullough makes clear when commenting on Pye's workmanship theory:

> This kind of workmanship Pye contrasts with a "workmanship of certainty," which he presents as the basis of ordinary manufacturing. Certainty, particularly in the form of standardization, yields incontestable economies. But uncertainty, or diversity, can yield a wider range of practical endeavors and a more natural expression of material microstructure. By the latter is meant conditions where, like the wrinkles in finely tanned

leather, diverse irregularities in the medium, which might be eliminated in standardizing processes, instead become a source of beauty.[1]

Conversely, heterogeneous materials, as with timber, require adaptable workmanship, continuously responsive to the varying properties, with grain determining the tool selection, the techniques required, and the design approach. In this context, the purpose of workmanship is often to exploit the natural qualities of materials, for which an understanding of their underlying physical make-up is an important aspect of craft research and tacit knowledge. Even where highly processed materials have become remote from their natural state, plastics for example, a "craft ethos" can often be applied. This suggests a semi-natural order of related properties which exist to be exploited, subverted, or extended beyond the boundaries of their raw state.[2] Traditionally, craft skills engage with tacit knowledge of material properties and the related skills required to work with or overcome these properties. For example, the carpenter uses timber, either working with or against the grain, which partially determines the choice of tools, skills, and applications.

In the case of both synthetic and natural textiles, there are predetermined characteristics that the skilled maker understands and responds to. The constructed forms of these materials result in a wide range of potential craft options, with a high level of "crafted control." According to McCullough, the connection between the tool and the traditional medium is negotiable, but the medium remains essentially passive. He suggests that "[w]hen the tools are complex, when the artifacts produced are abstract, or when tools provide the only means of access to the medium (all common conditions in high technology), it can be difficult to say where a tool ends and a medium begins,"[3] and "[i]f a tool is kinetic, and under active human guidance, a medium is static, and passively presents limits to human control."[4] However, the passivity of some emerging intelligent materials, such as those currently in development for textile substrates that incorporate predetermined guidance systems for decorative laser treatments, can change markedly. Here the material might be considered active in the sense that it is continuously interacting with the tool and not just being acted upon. These substrates possess artificial parallels with natural structures (such as the visible growth patterns in timber) and respond to and are affected by the tool, in this case a laser beam, to generate original visual effects. As well as responding through the tool to the structures of the substrate, the craftsperson's or producer's intent via the tool is guided by a "smart grain" embedded within the substrate.

The ability to take calculated risks is considered a virtue in many aspects of human endeavor, from business and politics to medicine and horse racing. The reward for such behavior, if successful, can be purely financial and/or the personal satisfaction of a novel breakthrough or innovation. Conversely, risk is usually minimized in favor of certainty when outcomes are deliberately predefined, as in the case of traditional mass-manufactured goods for example. The downside of risk-taking is the potential for failure, varying from catastrophe to invaluable learning-through-failure experience. In the case of craft development activity, catastrophe is rarely encountered, whereas minor frustration, impaired reputation, delays, and lack of financial success are the more acceptable norms. This is also true in many aspects of the wider creative arts where risk tends to be relatively low. As a result, "uncalculated" risks are sometimes acted on—i.e. exploring risk for its own intrinsic value and without constraint. This kind of behavior is frequently associated with forms of contrived "chance" in which the creative process is deliberately engaged with accidental, unpredictable, and random influence.

Modern, digitally enabled design/production technologies are increasingly presenting new and flexible creative opportunities which blur the distinction between uniform and diverse product outcomes. In doing this, production processes have begun to offer a unique proposition in which creative risk-taking can be contrived, with much more emphasis placed on the calculation of risk. In other words, the "operator/crafter" has the possibility of determining the precise degree of predictable/unpredictable intervention possible in a given project. The notion of active materials with inbuilt digital characteristics is one example of how this can be achieved, whereby the operator/crafter can choose to operate through a chosen positioning within a spectrum ranging from predictable homogeneity to unpredictable irregularity. The Schlaepfer technologies discussed here provide an indicative example of how this might be developed in practice.

A conventional view of craft production emphasizes the importance of the physical proximity to the material from which the artifact is produced. The relationship between the practitioner and the material is highly variable when working directly with materials as opposed to mechanistically processing them and exploring the relationship between perception and the material at the same time. The use of hand and power tools, machines, and jigs inevitably introduces a distancing effect. However, digitization, in reducing physical phenomena to code, also reduces the potential for tactile proximity. This can take the form of simulation which is only an approximation of the multisensory complexity of a hand-crafted product, although visually it may closely mimic it. This dilemma is unlikely to change perception significantly in the foreseeable future, despite improvements in digital imaging with higher definition and more accurate color reproduction. The particular technological flexibility of textiles in simultaneously occupying craft and manufacturing contexts is emphasized by Dormer:

> There is a fluidity in the practice, design and art of woven textiles that enables textiles to fit easily with contemporary technology. A textile maker or designer who works at a small craft-shop level producing one-off pieces can, from the same conceptual base and using the same equipment, produce samples that industry can convert without fuss for factory production.[5]

For the craftsperson, the retention of some element of direct physical proximity is vital, because physical contact underpins the interplay between perception, skill, knowledge, and creativity on which practice depends. It can include advanced technological interventions (such as hand-controlled laser devices), but raises questions about the application of virtual technologies to designing and making. At one extreme may be a complete lack of hands-on engagement, even though the processes are entirely controlled by the practitioner. However, as with many automated production processes, there are opportunities to reverse-engineer systems and facilitate strategic craft interventions to imbue the product with unique qualities, as in the seminal ceramic work of Michael Eden, for example. The context within which craft interventions operate could take place at any point in the production process—from inception to end products. The hand/automation continuum of proximity in relation to crafted control is illustrated in Figure 7.1.

To understand the implications of emerging disruptive technologies for the crafts, the context within which they operate, and the dynamics of their application to the production process requires some analysis. At the "Cutting Edge: Lasers and Creativity" symposium held at Loughborough University in 2009, an industry report proposed: "Craft, design and technology can enable creativity and result in innovation if approached as interdependent methods and practices."[6] The evidence that supported this view described laser technology development within the Swiss company Jakob Schlaepfer's mixed-media setting of craft and industrial textiles. Schlaepfer's *Haute Couture* and *Prêt-à-Porter* clientele demand design exclusivity and depend upon the company for the creation, within ever-decreasing time scales, of unique, bespoke textiles. Schlaepfer, through successive technological developments, has achieved flexible manufacturing processes, facilitating wide-ranging fabric specification and digital pattern and structure origination, with applications in both two- and three-dimension formats. Effectively, the company is engaged in a strategy of "continuous innovation." Here the demands for constant change in high fashion and related textile contexts are addressed through the continuous adaptation of, and synergies between, design, flexible production technologies, specialized craft processes, and unique materials specification.

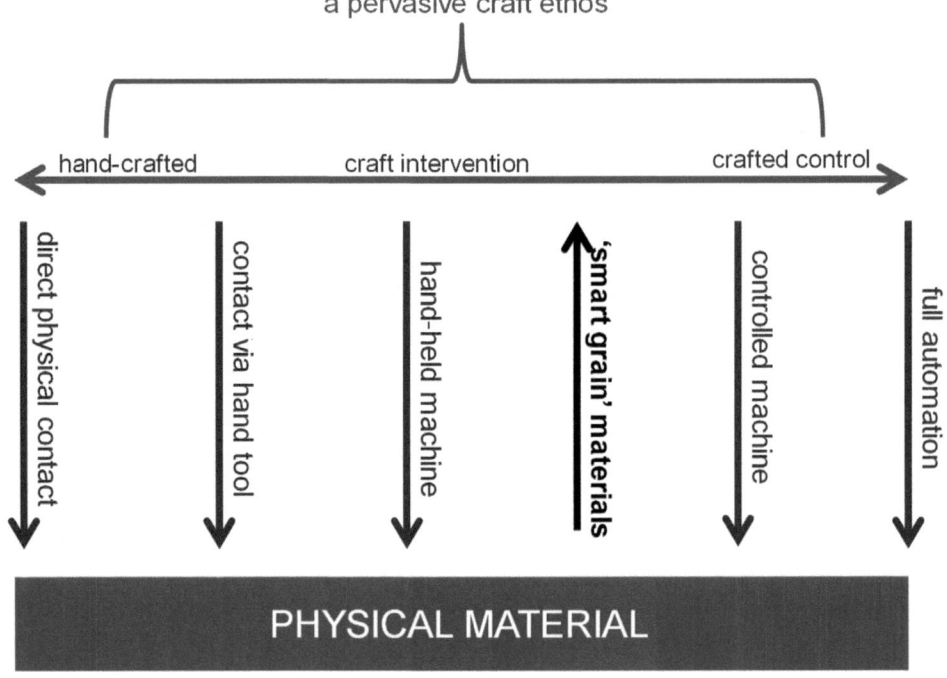

Figure 7.1 Hand/material proximity and "crafted control." © Martin Wooley.

For Schlaepfer, using advanced technology in the form of precision lasers provides a craft-sensitive means of accessing high-tech fabrics such as metal film-coated textiles, which because of their complex micro and nano scale structures make traditional techniques unsuitable. The lasers' precision often exceeds the resolution available via the textile machinery within which they operate, so laser textile processing is reliant upon tacit industrial/craft and engineering skills to guide the machine's interactions between the precision tool and flexible materials.

Extending craft control from the tool to the material may be the next major step within volume production. For example, a "smart grain" could be embedded within a substrate material, designed to guide the tool and selectively overriding the application of specified skills, while exercising others. Thus, a fully automated decorative laser pattern system interacting with textiles with embedded guidance systems, rather than devoid of craft opportunities, opens up new potentials for novel forms of skilled practice.

New craft interventions within this technological context could be envisaged, whereby the practitioner adopts a hands-on approach to the laser device either directly, by manipulating the laser tool, or indirectly, by designing new textile substrates that interact with the tool in unique ways. Such interventions thereby respond to the embedded guidance system through creative choice rather than automatically—i.e. a practice comparable to the carpenter choosing to work with, or across, the wood grain. A potential example would be to work with a precise geometric substrate pattern and deploy hands-on laser interaction to introduce irregularity into the pattern. On another level, the craft component could be an indirect intervention, in which hands-on experimental surface pattern treatments form the basis of the final automated production process. Rather as an industrial paint spray, a robot is programmed by mimicking the movements of a skilled operator. In both examples, the "workability" of the textile substrate has been partially predetermined during fabric production and in part by the settings applied to the laser tool. This differs from the inherent characteristics of heterogeneous materials, where natural material variations are simply responded to by hand, eye, and tool.

Decorative laser surface treatments are now common. Where their use was once largely confined to resistant materials, it now embraces malleable materials such as textiles, where the technology is still in its infancy and further refinements are envisaged. These generic processes set an important precedent, where the opportunities for interplay between brain/hand/eye and crafted outputs are negotiable. Equally they provide an example of craft-automated, or craft-embodied, production in which the precision of lasers interacting with intelligent materials parallels or extends human sensitivities and sensibilities.

Advanced textile companies such as Schlaepfer have already demonstrated that technologies such as "Emboscan,"[7] which integrates laser cutting with embroidery, can facilitate new kinds of craft-influenced automation. Led by Schlaepfer's creative director, Martin Leuthold, the development of this technology involved an interdisciplinary group of in-house and commissioned engineers, craft practitioners, designers, and material scientists. It resulted in an expanded range of laser techniques, including simultaneous two- and three-dimensional processes and a much greater variety of design formats. Recently a collaborative project has been proposed between Schlaepfer and university researchers in optoelectronics, materials science, applied design, and craft, to develop and refine these technologies around the design and manufacturing system at Schlaepfer. The project will address the strategic hybrid craft/production processes essential to the company's products, by developing a crafted control model. This will optimize the application of laser and textile technologies to the production process and fulfil the requirements of the company's niche clientele within a craft and design context.

The involvement of scientists will increase the group's knowledge of the performance potential of materials and their properties in relation to specific laser systems; the additional involvement of engineers, designers, and craft practitioners will boost creative innovation. Integrating these different approaches is also intended to inspire new interpretations of the processes, through the metaphor of their craft and industrial use and meaning. Metaphors such as "drawing with light," for example, create imaginative connections between the kinetic and tactile qualities of traditional techniques and the emerging technology.

From passive to active material characteristics

While *passive* characteristics are the fixed physical properties of materials that can be manipulated by hand, tool, and machine, *active* materials embed smart characteristics that respond directly to human, tool, or machine interventions. In the latter situation, an interactive digital data system links tool and material, in contrast to the traditional one-way encounter between tool and material or surface.

Embedding a digitally responsive map can enhance and widen the interactive capacity of passive materials, creating a partial or complete communication link between tool—either hand- or machine-controlled—and material. Constituting an augmented craft process, formal craft skills and knowledge are retained, operating within integrated virtual and physical realities. The "drawing with light" metaphor characterizes the tool as a surrogate graphic presence retaining physical, hand-held control, while dispensing with the traditional tactility of an implement such as a stylus. Direct physical contact is replaced by a beam of light in which digital interaction is two-way, merging practitioner intentions with direct haptic feedback. The complexities of integrating advanced design and production technologies with craft sensibilities require overarching strategic and operational capacities, defined in this model as crafted control.

The deployment of guidance systems in relation to craft is not new. There are analogies between the textile substrate laser map and traditional techniques where guides are employed for tools or hand-controlled machines such as jigs, templates, gauges, tracings, and stencils. These devices reside in an accepted craft genre of partial automation in which basic hand skills are retained, but the speed and precision of their operation are increased. Often this is to ensure that hands-on craft interventions are focused only on those parts of the process where added value is optimized—for example, hand-finished luxury goods where the bulk of the product is achieved through automated production and craft skills are only deployed in the final stages where the visible self-evident signifiers of craft skills are established. There is a parallel here with laser substrate

Plate 1 Printed motifs exhibiting the pixelated quality of early CAD, Cathy Treadaway, 1987. Photograph: Cathy Treadaway.

Plate 2 Digital inkjet print on silk crepe de chine, Debra Bernath and Cathy Treadaway, 2004. Photograph: Cathy Treadaway.

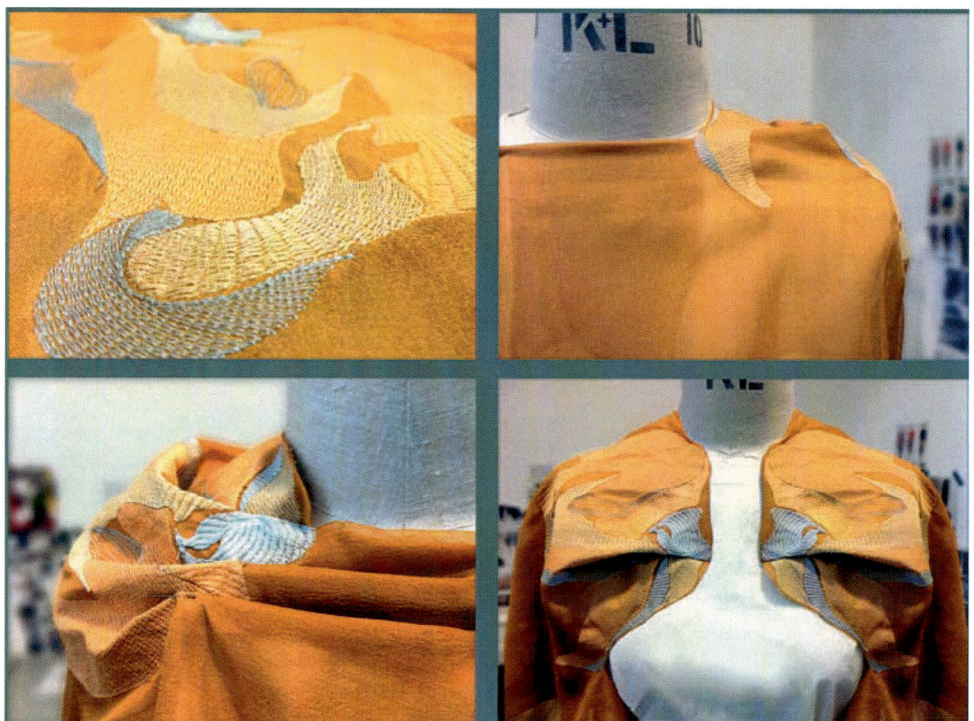

Plate 3 Integrating draped pattern cutting with embroidery design, Yuri Nakamatsu, 2011. Photograph: Yuri Nakamatsu.

Plate 4 "Harlequin Cloven Red," Danica Maier, 2010. Photograph: Danica Maier.

Plate 5 Detail of the TWEEN screen by "Textile Illusions." The digital patterns of light appear to have a physical surface texture when they are projected onto a woven screen consisting of matt and shiny areas. The effect can be so intense that it appears as if the projected patterns are integrated as luminous threads in the woven screen. Photograph: Ole Akhøj.

Plate 6 The white-on-white TWEEN screen consists of four woven lengths in a double-layered complex structure of matt and shiny areas. An animation showing various transformations of the two basic block patterns is continuously projected on the screen. Photograph: Ole Akhøj.

Plate 7 An Installation at the Museum Vrolik for Anatomy and Embryology in Amsterdam in 2011. It shows a 3D woven object of the embryologic series together with a fetus in the museum's collection. Photograph: Monika Auch.

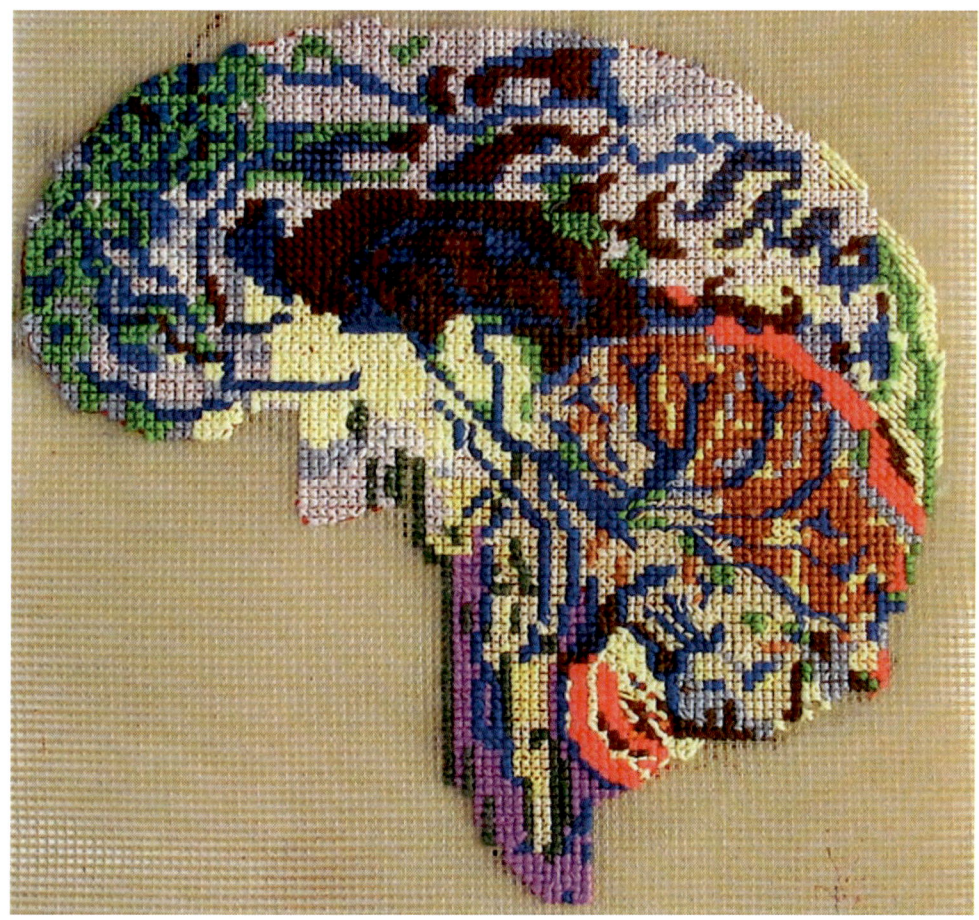

Plate 8 Stitched brain. The needlework of printmaker Jo Ganter from Glasgow, reflecting her very subtle graphic work. Photograph: Monika Auch.

Plate 9 Stitched brain. The interpretation of a brain by a Dutch high school student during a workshop. Photograph: Monika Auch.

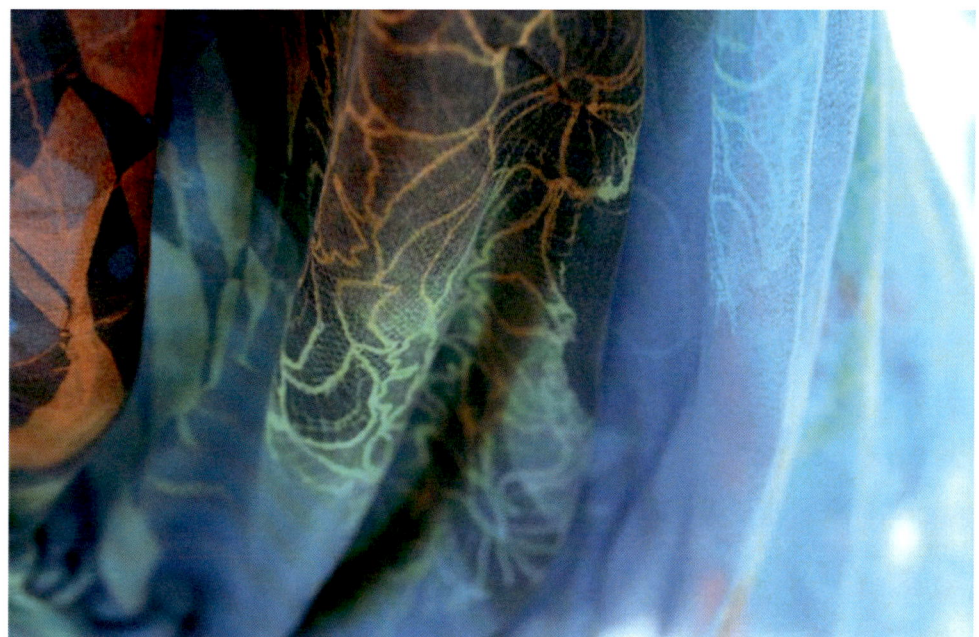

Plate 10 Inkjet printed silk chiffon, generated using lace resist effects, Helen Ryall, 2009. Photograph: Helen Ryall.

Plate 11 Silk habotai and chiffon (reactive dyes), Helen Ryall, 2010. Photograph: Andrew Farrington.

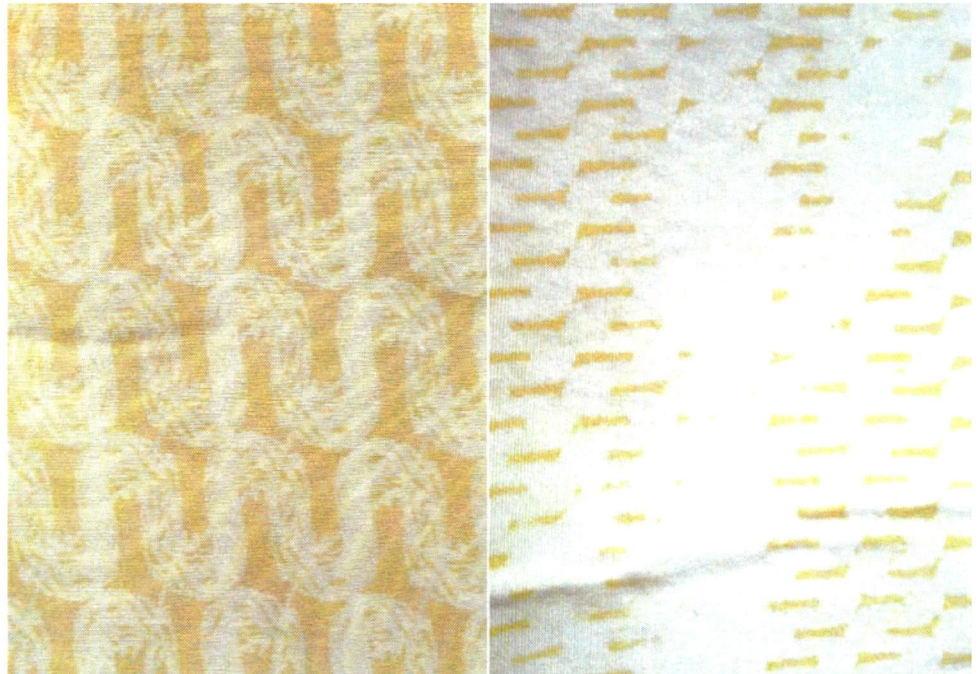

Plate 12 Screen printed knit patterns onto neoprene using discharge print paste, 2008. Photograph: Kerri Akiwowo.

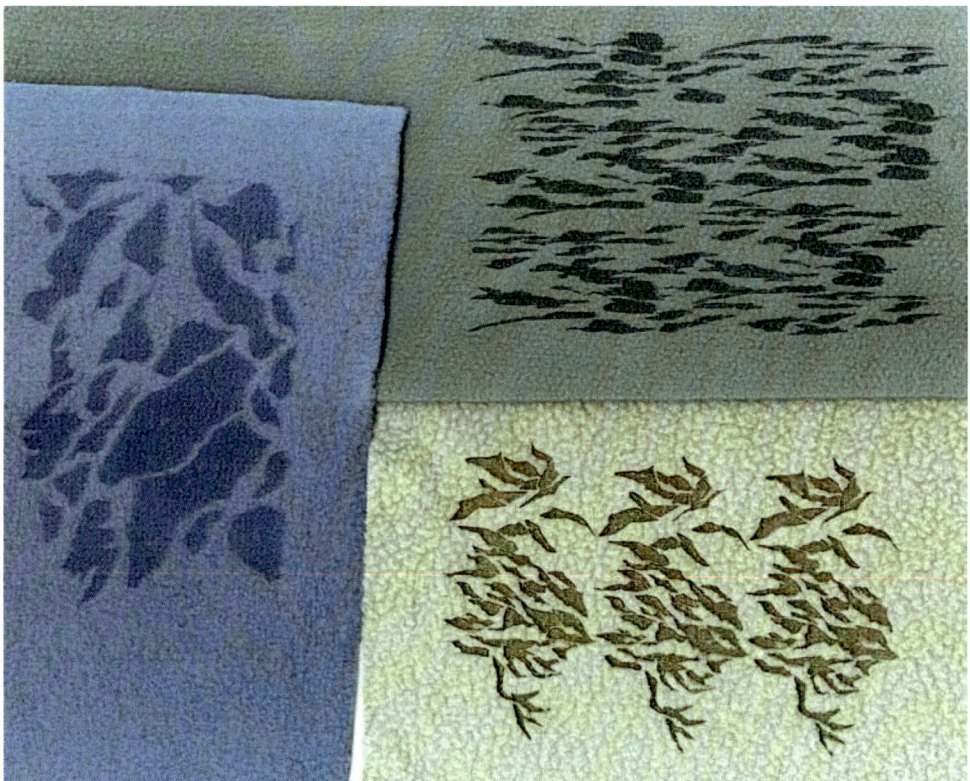

Plate 13 Laser etched Polartec® fleece fabrics: fragmented digital patterns, 2008. Photograph: Kerri Akiwowo.

Plate 14 Digitally printed and hand-crafted silk sample, randomly textured textile with cooling properties, 2010. Photograph: Susan Carden.

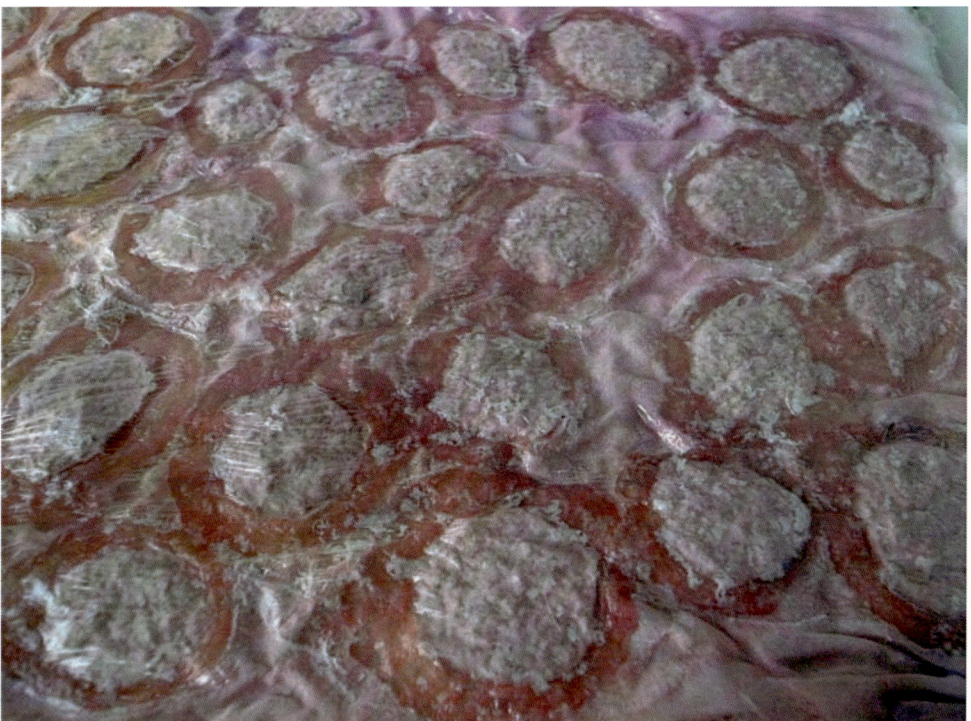

Plate 15 Digitally printed silk chiffon, silk with discrete cool areas, 2011. Photograph: Susan Carden.

Plate 16 "Anchor and Crown" tea cozy, Andrea Williamson, 2011. Photograph: Andrea Williamson.

Plate 17 Crocheted model of a geometric manifold, Daina Taimina, 2004. Photograph: Daina Taimina.

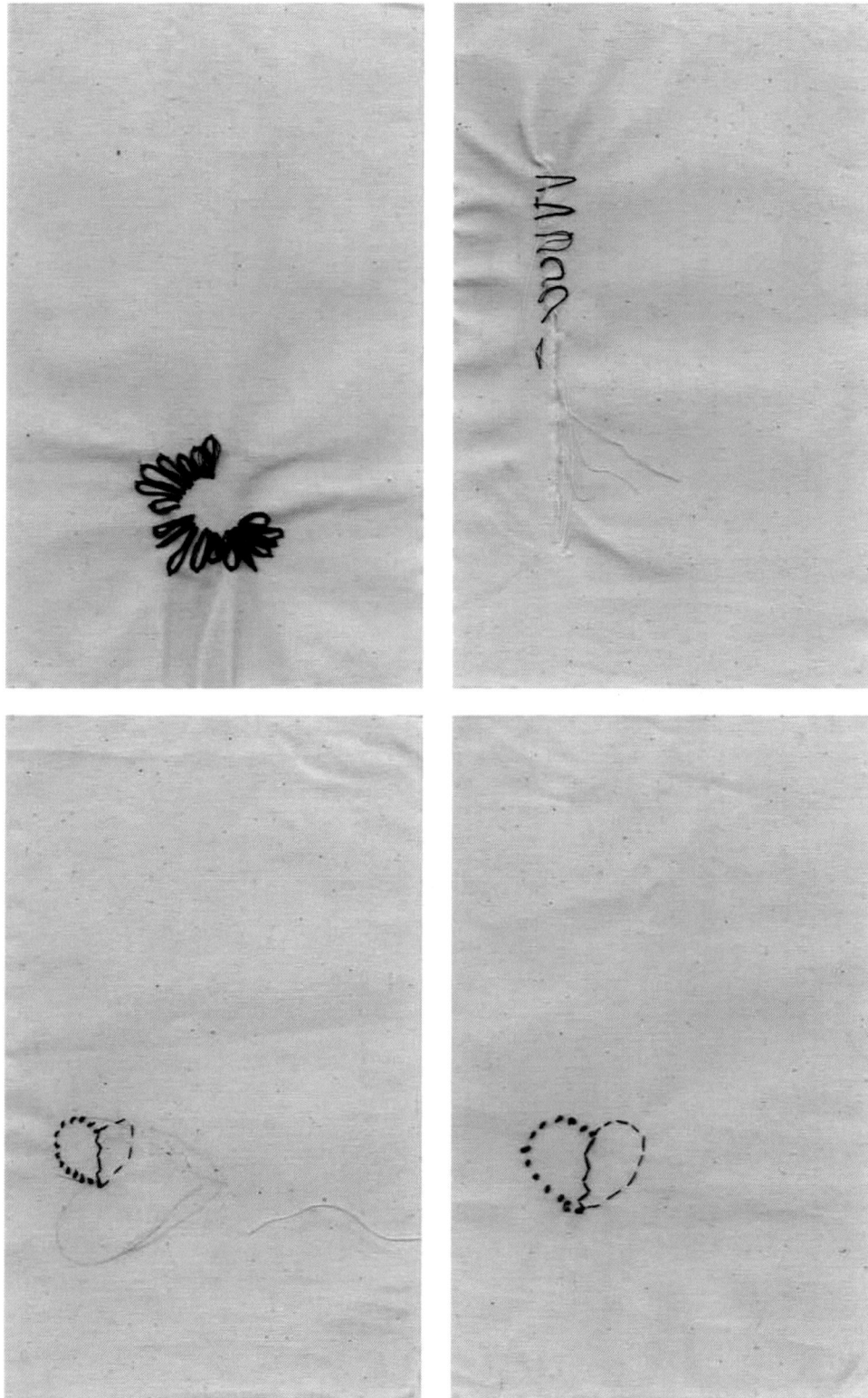

Plate 18 Samples from the third workshop held at the Arts University Bournemouth with a small group of textiles students, all able stitchers. Samples on the left are the originals and samples on the right are the reproductions. Photograph: Emma Shercliff.

Plate 19 Digital trials of image, texture, and color overlays for the second triptych. Photograph: Chris Harper. © Sonja Andrew.

Plate 20 *Closely Held Secrets* exhibition catalog, designed by Geoff Diego Litherland et al., 2010. Photograph: Katherine Townsend. © Bonington Gallery.

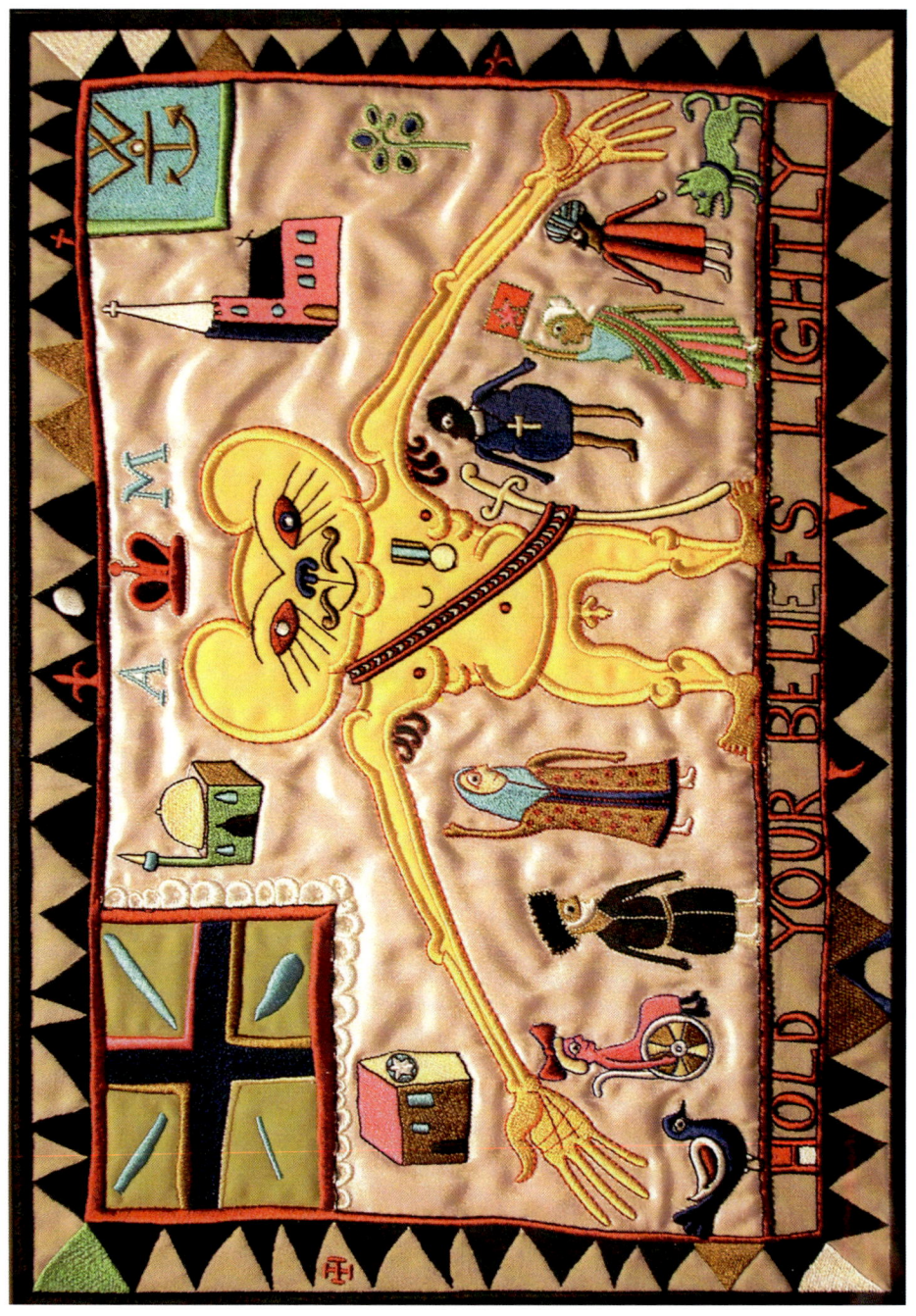

Plate 21 "Hold Your Beliefs Lightly," Grayson Perry, 2010. Photograph: Simon Beck Mather. © Grayson Perry and Tony Taylor.

Plate 22 "All the Stars," Geoff Diego Litherland, 2010. Photograph: Simon Beck Mather. © Geoff Diego Litherland.

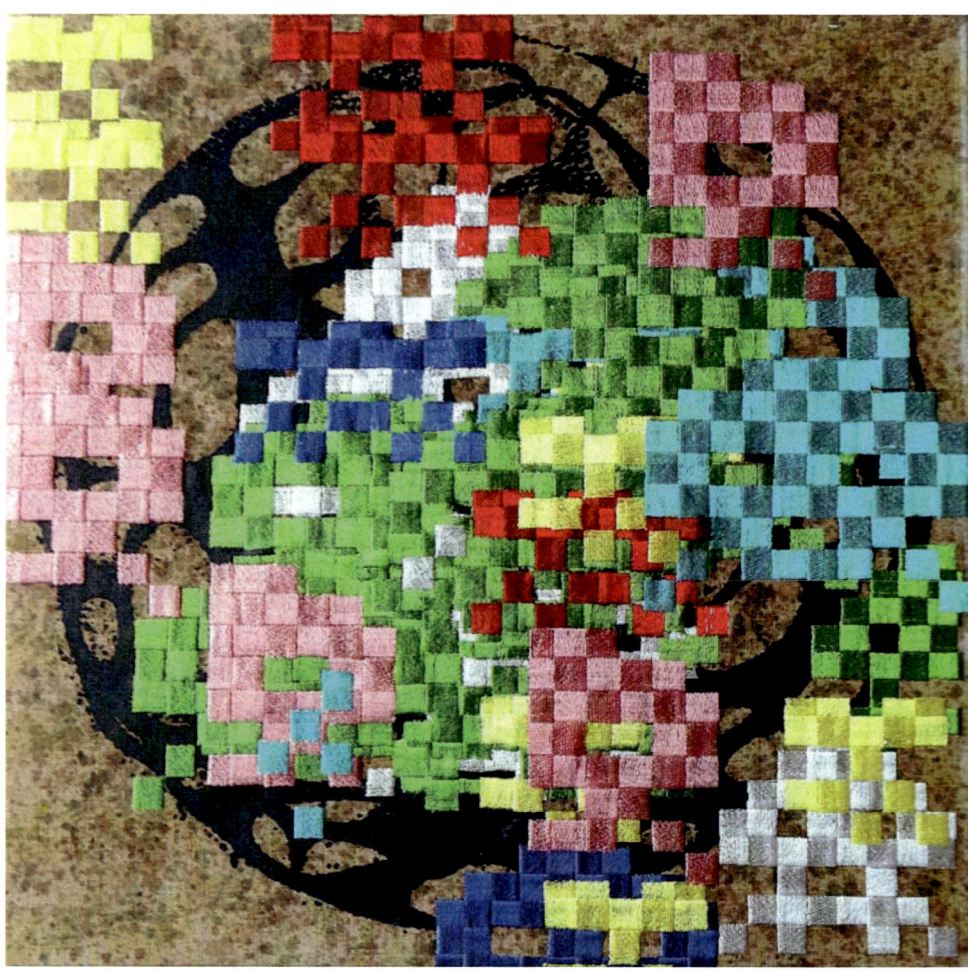

Plate 23 "Invaders," comprised of multiple layers of embroidered threads to suggest different colored pixels, Geoff Diego Litherland, 2010. Photograph: Katherine Townsend. © Geoff Diego Litherland.

technology, in which a hand-finished approach can be adopted after the first pass of the textile through an automated decorative process. Hands-on laser treatment is intended to add value through unique mark-making. In providing a digital guidance system, textile substrates offer similar advantages to creative craft processes and thus new potentials for exploring aesthetics. Inevitably, however, there is still a significant speculative element to this emerging technology; as Narendra et al. state, "manufacturing using lasers may offer extraordinary benefits in some cases or may be a total failure in others."[8]

The move from passive to active material properties will be characterized initially by a period of high-risk experimentation before technological challenges are overcome and workable design opportunities become clear.

The Schlaepfer model

Key to continuous innovation for Schlaepfer is flexible design and production, as illustrated in Figure 7.2. The methods utilized within this model are founded on various mixed-media techniques developed by the company since the 1970s. Through design and engineering skills, they enable different forms of interaction between manual, semi-automated, and automated technologies, as well as between production and the company's own fabric archives. The archives consist of fabrics produced by the company since the 1960s. They can be analyzed and reinterpreted by Schlaepfer's designers and contribute to the reinvention of techniques that would otherwise be consigned to St. Gallen's industrial past. Alternatively, they can stimulate the creation of completely new visual effects.

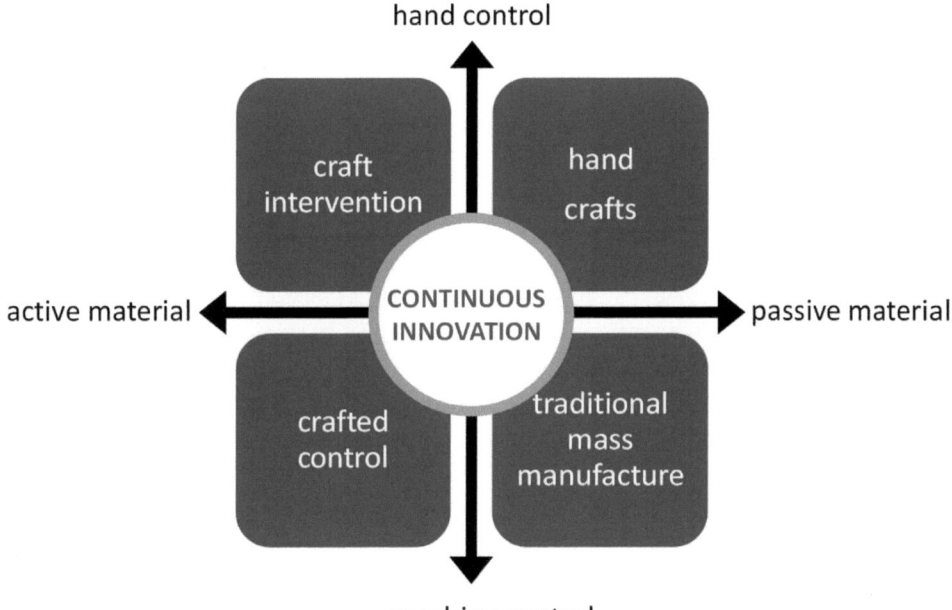

Figure 7.2 The position of craft/manufacturer at Schlaepfer. © Martin Wooley.

Schlaepfer's mixed-media methods are similarly integral to the continuous innovation model. For example, the company's development of automated laser cutting might be seen as merely a method of reducing dependency on time-consuming manual cutting. However, for Schlaepfer, rather than moving away from manual techniques completely, creative opportunities such as laser cutting make way for the invention of new craft techniques. The prospect of a technology such as a substrate guided laser system demonstrates the potential for an expanded range of techniques within the Schlaepfer model and offers a compelling pointer toward a future of crafted control within manufacturing.

Thus, the Schlaepfer archives are a dynamic resource, with new designs continuously emerging from the collection. However, one distinction between the company's use of its archives and mixed-media processes is the increased capacity of the latter to be a catalyst for automation, through laser cutting for example. Automation then progresses with the invention of new manual mixed-media processes. One can envisage a "smart grain" based on archived patterns that would have a direct physical influence on making, either through manual and/or automated processes.

The contribution of a substrate guidance system to the creative process

Looking at this potential more closely, it is possible to identify several advantages that a substrate guidance system could contribute to creative processes using smart grain. First, smart grain opens up a spectrum of manual, semi-, and fully automated interactions and applications. Second, cycles of manual, semi-, and fully automated analog and digital processes can be integrated into a range of production technologies. Third, it offers the opportunity to absorb techniques from a wide range of making processes, such as the loosely washed application of a ceramic glaze drawn into pre-inscribed or incised lines, and drawn through a layer of applied slip to a clay body, known traditionally as Sgraffito. Fourth, laser precision can be translated through a smart grain material into crafted control, whereby qualities of risk and certainty are available as flexible options. An example of risk in this context would be the inability to exercise sufficient manual control to create successful designs. Conversely, certainty could relate to the ability to arrive at pre-planned designs, while still combining manual and automated processes. Finally, the new work process promotes a shift of attention from tool work to substrate. Thus, specific Schlaepfer craft and industrial knowledge contributes increasingly to wider laser and substrate technology, reconnecting long-standing traditional skills with new bespoke textile technologies.

Traditional craft knowledge influence on new creative technological processes

The term craft here embraces a range of industrial disciplines:

1 Craft/industrial knowledge based on a rich textile history influences the creative and production capacities of an emerging technology such as the laser and substrate guidance system.
2 The capacity of such a guidance system offers manual, semi-, and fully automated options and has potential for the development of integrated hand and automated operations within a single flow of work.
3 Rather than acting as a veneer of added-on craft finishes or craft resemblances, craft practice is central to determining creative production methods.
4 The direct experience of physical manipulation—craft practice—brings a deeper knowledge of materials and processes, enabling craft inputs to transcend surface effects or mere replication.
5 Supported through crafted control, and facilitated by the adaptation of technologies such as the smart grain, craft values are integral to the creative process, regardless of the use of actual manual techniques or direct physical manipulation.

The model illustrates methods of exploring craft influence beyond traditional notions of craft as a subsidiary activity within a serial or mass production setting. The model also proposes that creative processes and technological adaptations, such as a smart grain, increase the potential for crafted control at a fundamental level, for example allowing for the production of new materials that radically reinvent rather than mimic their historic sources. Alternatively, engaging with materials without historical precedent could be proposed within the same model. While the conventional process deploys tacit knowledge and traditional techniques, when interfacing with a new technology, the more experimental approach would explore the unpredictable.

New production technologies often provide such opportunities to transcend familiar design boundaries and question what can be achieved, which disciplines might best support development, and the role of craft practice. The properties of advanced materials deployed in relation to laser and textile technology offer similar possibilities and challenges.

The machine as prototype and the craftsperson as prototype developer

Throughout the long history of the crafts, practitioners have been responsible for making artifacts, processing materials, and the design and fabrication of tools. In the pre-industrial age when hand tools predominated, this was straightforward, with tools developed, refined over generations, and handed down with craft knowledge and skills. With mechanization, this direct tool creation was replaced by commercial tools and machines, such as the move from hand-constructed to mass-produced kilns. Through this transition, practitioners became consumers of equipment, deriving considerable benefits: cheaper, higher performance, a greater range of functions, and increased efficiency. Inevitably, this transition meant that the craftsperson had less input to the form and range of tools and equipment, and therefore had to adapt their capabilities. Although adaptation can release new and original potential, withdrawal from direct development or refinement of tools removed an important strategic activity from the craft profession, including the ability to influence the operational characteristics and application of relevant production technologies. In the case of advanced complex technologies, craft intervention is unlikely to succeed alone and would depend on support from other disciplines, namely optics, production, and textile engineering. Higher education institutions are a suitable environment to facilitate this multidisciplinary support.

The application of laser technology to intelligent textile substrates is a nascent technology only partially evolved, but a craft influence could and should be brought to bear. The benefits for a craft intervention in the design and development of this technology are assumed to include the abilities to: (1) transpose the results of hands-on experimentation with laser devices and textile substrates to the mechanized equivalent; (2) refine the production technology options to engage with full as well as partial automation—in the way digital semi-professional cameras facilitate both automated and manual control; (3) optimize the potential aesthetic and functional qualities of the machine outputs for particular markets, e.g. luxury commodities, low-volume products, customized products; and (4) deliver a process of continuous innovation to relevant markets such as haute couture. Taking account of the benefits, the generic properties that equipment might possess include: (1) a variable level of physical control—from manual to full automation and points between; (2) a capacity for updating, e.g. incorporating the latest software development; (3) optimized flexibility, e.g. choice of materials and finishes; and (4) development of methodologies refined by craft influences and interventions, optimized to produce maximum production potential and choice.

Figure 7.3 summarizes the above in terms of the interplay between substrate pattern, archive influence, and hand and automated control.

Textile innovation is evolving as a means of commercial survival through adaptation, using and developing new technology, especially in niche markets. Such approaches and the technological spin-off might be adapted to incorporate craft skills and sensibilities for strategic purposes. As part of this, it is essential to apply an appropriate creative interface between the designer and the means of production, which optimizes crafted control and benefits from a "pervasive craft ethos."[9] This development may lead to the emergence of surrogate craft methods which are fully integrated into digital production processes. It may even result in a direct craft responsibility for determining the format of the production process through the design of prototype machines.

> Numerous debates have centred on technologies' potential to negate craft and potentially the craft-based traditions, but the desire to integrate technologies into craft

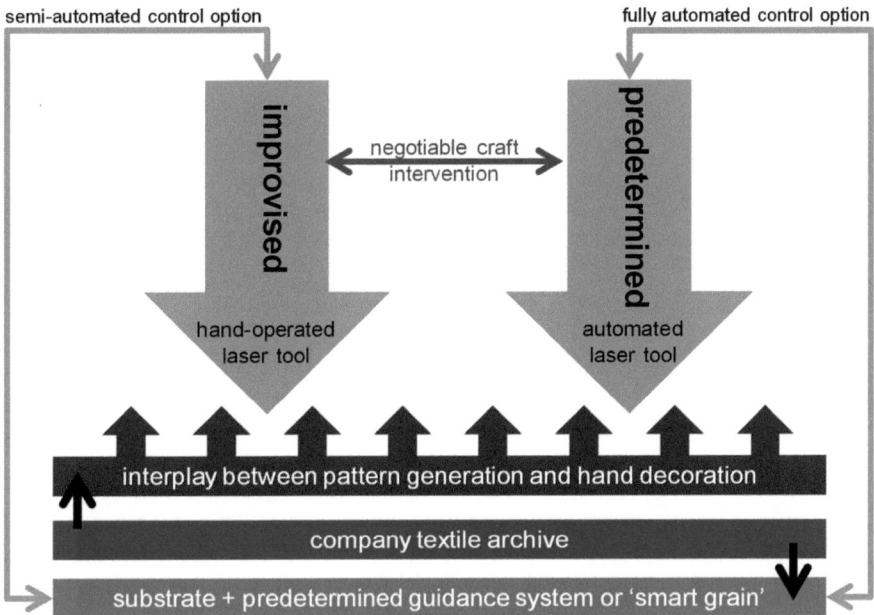

Figure 7.3 Improvised and predetermined treatments. © Martin Wooley.

practices is real. The trend is not simply based in a desire to experiment with the new, but is growing from a recognition that the digital tools provide enhanced means to communicate craft goals.[10]

Such an approach may be a vital component of craft continuity in the twenty-first century, a step which builds on the age-old tradition of adapting tools to produce original work.

Digital production technologies often possess the capacity to render manual skills redundant, without the true nature and value of the craft contribution being fully recognized. In some successful industries, however, craft processes have been retained with much success, notably in the luxury fashion, fashion accessory, and automotive industries. The potential for embedding crafted control capabilities into production technologies that link laser tools with smart textiles provides a similar but uniquely flexible means of adding value through unique design processes and outcomes.

Notes

1   Malcolm McCullough, *Abstracting Craft: The Practiced Digital Hand* (Cambridge, MA: MIT Press, 1998), 203.
2   Martin Woolley, "A Pervasive Craft Ethos," *Studio—Craft and Design in Canada* (Fall/Winter 2009–10). http://www.craftontario.com/magazine/past-issues.html [accessed November 11, 2014].
3   McCullough, *Abstracting Craft,* 193.

4   Ibid., 194.
5   Peter Dormer, *The Culture of Craft: Status and Future* (Manchester: Manchester University Press, 1997), 168.
6   Robert Huddleston and Paul Whittaker, "Jakob Schlaepfer: A Case Study in Laser Innovation and the Unexpected," *Craft Research* 1 (1) (2010): 127.
7   Robert Huddleston and Paul Whittaker, "Jakob Schlaepfer: A Vision for Innovation Enabled by Laser Technologies," (Loughborough University, UK, 2009). http://www.cuttingedgesymposium.com/20-minute-papers/huddleston-whittaker.html [accessed November 11, 2014].
8   Narendra B. Dahotre and Sandip Harimkar, *Laser Fabrication and Machining of Materials* (New York: Springer, 2008), 69.
9   Woolley, "A Pervasive Craft Ethos"; Martin Woolley, "Crafting the Mainstream—Sustaining Research and Practice Through Wider Production Engagement", *Making Futures* 2 (2011). http://mfarchive.plymouthart.ac.uk/journalvol2/pdf/Woolley_Martin.pdf [accessed April 20, 2015].
10 J. R. Campbell, "Digital Craft Aesthetic: Craft-Minded Application of Electronic Tools," in *Proceedings of New Craft Future Voices*, ed. Georgina Follett (Dundee: Duncan of Jordanstone College of Art & Design, 2007), 169.

Bibliography

Campbell, J. R., "Digital Craft Aesthetic: Craft-Minded Application of Electronic Tools," in *Proceedings of New Craft Future Voices*, ed. Georgina Follett (Dundee: Duncan of Jordanstone College of Art & Design, 2007).
Dahotre, Narendra B., and Sandip Harimkar, *Laser Fabrication and Machining of Materials* (New York: Springer, 2008).
Dormer, Peter, *The Culture of Craft: Status and Future* (Manchester: Manchester University Press, 1997).
Huddleston, Robert, and Paul Whittaker, "Jakob Schlaepfer: A Case Study in Laser Innovation and the Unexpected," *Craft Research* 1 (1) (2010): 125–32.
McCullough, Malcolm, *Abstracting Craft: The Practiced Digital Hand* (Cambridge, MA: MIT Press, 1998).
Woolley, Martin, "A Pervasive Craft Ethos," *Studio—Craft and Design in Canada* (Fall/Winter 2009–10). http://www.craftontario.com/magazine/past-issues.html [accessed November 11, 2014].
Woolley, Martin, "Crafting the Mainstream—Sustaining Research and Practice Through Wider Production Engagement," *Making Futures*, 2 (2011). http://mfarchive.plymouthart.ac.uk/journalvol2/pdf/Woolley_Martin.pdf [accessed April 20, 2015].

8
GARMENT ID: TEXTILE PATTERNING TECHNIQUES FOR HYBRID FUNCTIONAL CLOTHING

Kerri Akiwowo

Traditional and technological techniques in contemporary textile design

Today, in a time when modern technologies enable new options for creative thought, expression, and production, designers often embrace traditional craft processes and techniques in the development of contemporary textile design. As such, this approach can in some way lead "to the creation of fabrics that are evocative of the past and yet totally modern,"[1] demonstrating the relevance and impact of history, culture, and convention towards achieving innovation. In her discussion, "Respect for Tradition, Curiosity for Technology,"[2] Braddock further describes this synergy between old and new:

> Traditional processes can be given new meaning and value by modern technology, which will expand the role of textiles. Textile artists and designers world-wide are looking to the latest technology and recent developments to bring new life and fresh meaning to their craft. Some use traditional materials combined with new manufacturing technologies, others work with sophisticated textile materials and ancient techniques. In both cases it is the union of tradition and technology that will yield innovative results and provide a new aesthetic.[3]

In line with these ideas, the work discussed in this chapter attempts to utilize both traditional and technological "craft" approaches in order to consider novel textile concepts relevant to contemporary garment design. A practice-led approach together with artistic outputs suggests ways in which it is possible to integrate characteristics, processes, and techniques from the past with current developments and modern or unconventional materials. This being the case, opportunities to redefine familiar "objects" exist in a way that seamlessly encompasses established systems, alternative fabrics, and new tools, led by creative input from a textile design perspective.

In recent years, new fibers, fabrics, processes, and technologies have advanced material capability, encouraging high-performance products and inspiring cutting-edge design. Performance apparel, such as sports and active wear in particular, represents one of the fastest-growing sectors across clothing and textile industries. Designer and researcher Sabine Seymour refers to advances in science and technology that have influenced this growth in her book, *Fashionable Technology: The Intersection of Design, Science and Technology*.[4] In doing so, she identifies the ability to enhance and modify garment functionality such as heat regulation, impact protection, communication, and antimicrobials, for example.

Innovations in industrial and creative textile technologies, in the design of both machines and processes, have been integrated into the production of mainstream sportswear and other apparel items. Embedded characteristics for active clothing have redefined "performance" in sport. For example, modern versions of knitted garments demonstrate advancements in industrial technologies and equipment that have revolutionized garment construction techniques in sportswear, such as ultrasound used to seamlessly weld rather than stitch garment pieces together, for example.

New fibers, fabrics, construction techniques, and novel applications steer ongoing developments in textile sectors. Fashion designers and high street brands have also explored functional materials and approaches in ready-to-wear garments, and as a result, functional clothing has become increasingly accessible for the average consumer. The marketplace for performance clothes has expanded to reflect an increase in demand and usage of these goods. In terms of aesthetics, a shift from active and sport-specific performance garments to fashionable "sporty" items has evolved. This progression demonstrates interactions between design, science, and technology to create innovative, stylish, and wearable products. Subsequently, the "wearability" of a garment may not only be defined by its use, appearance, and comfort characteristics. Instead, a more holistic understanding can be perceived due to an increasing general awareness of materials, properties, and life cycle considerations, such as fibers and their acquisition, manufacturing methods, distribution information, product use/functionality, disposal, recyclability, and other environmental aspects. Parallel to this notion, in *Future Fashion: Innovative Materials and Technology*, Macarena San Martin comments: "Clothing does not merely serve to cover ourselves up or to keep us warm, it says a lot more. It is common sense that nowadays we take advantage of technological advances … to create garments with an added value."[5]

Interdisciplinary approaches in design continue to shape an inherent relationship between fashion and textiles. This in turn facilitates the generation of novel, ambitious, and forward-thinking creative outcomes within this community. Collaboration may involve researchers, designers, scientists, and manufacturers to promote innovation. As such, this approach to creativity aids the contribution of diverse knowledge and expertise from different disciplines. Creative vision essentially steers such collective experiences, skills, technologies, and commercial opportunities that are fundamental to advancement. Developments stimulate new approaches in textile and apparel arenas and therefore impact contemporary design.

In *The Supermodern Wardrobe*,[6] Andrew Bolton, fashion and costume curator at the Metropolitan Museum of Art (New York, USA), examines how men and women dress for the urban environment. He suggests that "supermodern" clothing is determined by high style, which incorporates ideas and materials better known for their role in high-performance sportswear and protective gear combined with twenty-first-century technology. In this account, Bolton responds to the problems created by the growth in urban populations in recent years and the resulting altered perceptions of public and social space through practical, functional clothing. Similarly, Quinn discusses designer and researcher Eunjeong Jeon's engineered wearable fabrics capable of responding to the body and space around them.[7] These designs are built upon movement-based interactions that involve the body and transitional spaces such as airports and roads. Factors such as pollution, noise, temperature change, stress, and crime inspire the design of fabrics with performance features to induce comfort for the wearer in certain environments. Both Bolton's and Quinn's studies suggest clothing not only as a wearable interface that fulfils implicit standard requirements but also as functional garments which may engage with the wearer and surroundings through design and technology. Apparel items are therefore imbued with hybrid characteristics which take on unconventional uniqueness.[8]

In terms of modern materials, man-made cellulosic (MMC) fibers—which characterize Modal® fabrics, for example—challenge traditional cotton fibers and claim superiority in quality and softness as described by producers, Lenzing Group.[9] From this material perspective, garments such as a standard cotton T-shirt become updated as a new modernized wardrobe of cotton-like clothing emerges. Other MMC fibers such as TENCEL®, also produced by Lenzing, demonstrate advanced tenacity, in particular reshaping workwear apparel markets by promoting high moisture absorption, reduced bacterial growth, and skin sensory characteristics. TENCEL® clothing has entered medical, uniform, school wear, and fashion sectors. Not only do these alternative fibers challenge conventional durability and performance capabilities, they also respond to environmental issues associated with industrial fiber and textile production—MMC textiles such as TENCEL® are made from raw renewable materials and therefore promote sustainability.[10] Other examples of modern fibers entering mainstream textile and clothing sectors include those agriculturally produced from natural sources such as corn, bamboo, and nettle, for example. These materials are also known as "bio-fibers" due to their ecological origin.

In terms of design, aesthetics, and consumer appeal, a garment's attractiveness can be determined by both its surface quality and shape in relation to the textile(s) utilized. Such characteristics are typically understood as form, color, pattern/image, texture, handle, drape, and fit, as described by Jenny Udale:

> It is important to consider the function of the textile you are designing before you start. Is it required for its aesthetic qualities, how it drapes, the handle of the cloth, its texture, for its colour, pattern, surface interest, or is it required for its function, how

it will stretch around the body or maybe how it can be tailored? Will it be used for protective qualities, perhaps against rain or the cold?[11]

From a textile design perspective, surface methods add interest, value, and appeal, generating visual and tactile qualities. For example, textile dyeing and coloration, printing, patterning, and fabric manipulation techniques facilitate experimental development and encourage innovation achieved by hand, digitally, or both. New interpretations as a result of emerging technologies and processes enable combined low-tech analog practices with more advanced methods. In particular, advances in textile inkjet printing have significantly impacted apparel industries in terms of creative expression for textile surfaces and manufacture. From an environmental perspective, digital textile printing has a reduced impact compared to conventional printing and dyeing methods. Textile designers Bowles and Isaac affirm this advantage of digital textile printing: "A more sustainable future will be possible if [digital textile printing] is adopted over others."[12] In digital printing, specified designs are engineered via a controllable contained approach, minimizing waste resources such as dyes and materials. Automation enables increased production capacity at faster speeds and lower costs. Digital printing is therefore considered a more efficient approach to achieve patterned fabric compared to traditional screen printing, dye-based techniques, and other applied methods.

In a design context, the look of a garment is fundamental to both perception and adoption by the consumer. For mainstream acceptance, hybrid concepts need to follow or even exceed traditional aesthetic ideals.[13] Factors including form, handle, quality, comfort, fit, color, and pattern require sufficient consideration and appropriate execution in modern clothing examples.

In this chapter, textile patterning methods explored were inspired by a selected group of iconic and historical familiar garments organized into a capsule wardrobe, titled *Garment ID*. This work exists within a wider body of apparel research approached from a textile design perspective. A focus on surface patterns steered the project towards design innovation through new concepts for fabrics, functional materials, and clothing. This investigation proposes a new type of aesthetic for contemporary textiles and garments by application of novel surface design methods and finishing techniques. The aim of this approach was to give individual garments a new identity by establishing a platform for the design and development of hybrid performance clothing as "everyday" wear.

More broadly, new textile and apparel concepts may be influenced by science or crafted by advancements in technology, ultimately underpinned by creative adeptness— vision, experiential involvement, and tacit design knowledge. *Garment ID,* to some extent, symbolizes this.

Garment ID: Textile design research

The *Garment ID* study was carried out using a qualitative practice-led research approach.[14] Data gathering involved exploring different patterning methods to generate experimental fabric samples that embodied individual thought and expression: creative vision and hands-on involvement leading to a range of surface finishes potentially for new hybrid clothing. According to Creswell, "The qualitative researcher is the primary instrument for data collection and analysis."[15] In this manner, data is mediated through this "human" instrument—in this case the textile designer.

As a practitioner, my experiential first-hand involvement with processes and textile materials was fundamental to the investigation. This approach facilitated experimentation through "knowing by doing," which is defined by an ability to reflect upon processes and ongoing results while actively doing the investigation. It is described by Schön as "reflection-in-action,"[16] a model that encompasses intuitive thinking as a function for knowing. Therefore, knowledge acquired was generated by an empirical approach through direct interaction with practices.[17]

Regarding the creation of a fabric sample or product that involves working with materials, textile designer Anni Albers comments: "Free experimentation here can result in the fulfillment of an inner urge to give form and to give permanence to ideas."[18] Andrew Harrison also highlights the relationship between thinking and making: "[T]o make something may be to do something that is informed by thought, reflection, knowledge and speculation may have its outcome in doing."[19] Practical engagement by the researcher-practitioner involves creative intuition, implicit behavior, and tacit knowledge through experimental sampling, designing, and documenting research processes.[20] The making process of textile patterning in this study followed the same line of the above thoughts.

Textile patterning for apparel

A preoccupation with surface pattern as a textile designer specializing in printed textiles for apparel underpinned this study. The aim of the project to investigate textile patterning techniques for hybrid functional clothing therefore facilitated existing specialist knowledge and skills within this discipline.

The starting point for design practice within the scope of this study (Figure 8.1) introduces an "Iconic Capsule Wardrobe" (ICW) (Figure 8.2). The wardrobe contains a selected group of garments to aid design development based on identifiable inspiration from the past, encompassing aesthetic, social, cultural, and historical connotations. In doing so, a systematic approach undertaken provided the basis for new methods of creating patterns regarding textile imaging and print design linked to pre-existing garments and specific clothing types.[21] Collectively, these garments were defined by the following characteristics: (1) *iconic*—symbolic or representative of a particular period of time, event, uniform, fashion trend, generic term, textile development, or process; (2) *capsule*—a term commonly used in fashion and apparel sectors to describe a notably small collection of garments; and (3) *wardrobe*—a particular group of clothing items that exist together as a complete style, trend, or look. The wardrobe comprised five key garments: (1) a handmade and un-dyed cable-knitted 100% wool jumper; (2) a pair of denim "blue jeans"; (3) a white cotton T-shirt; (4) nylon tights; and (5) a black leather bomber jacket.

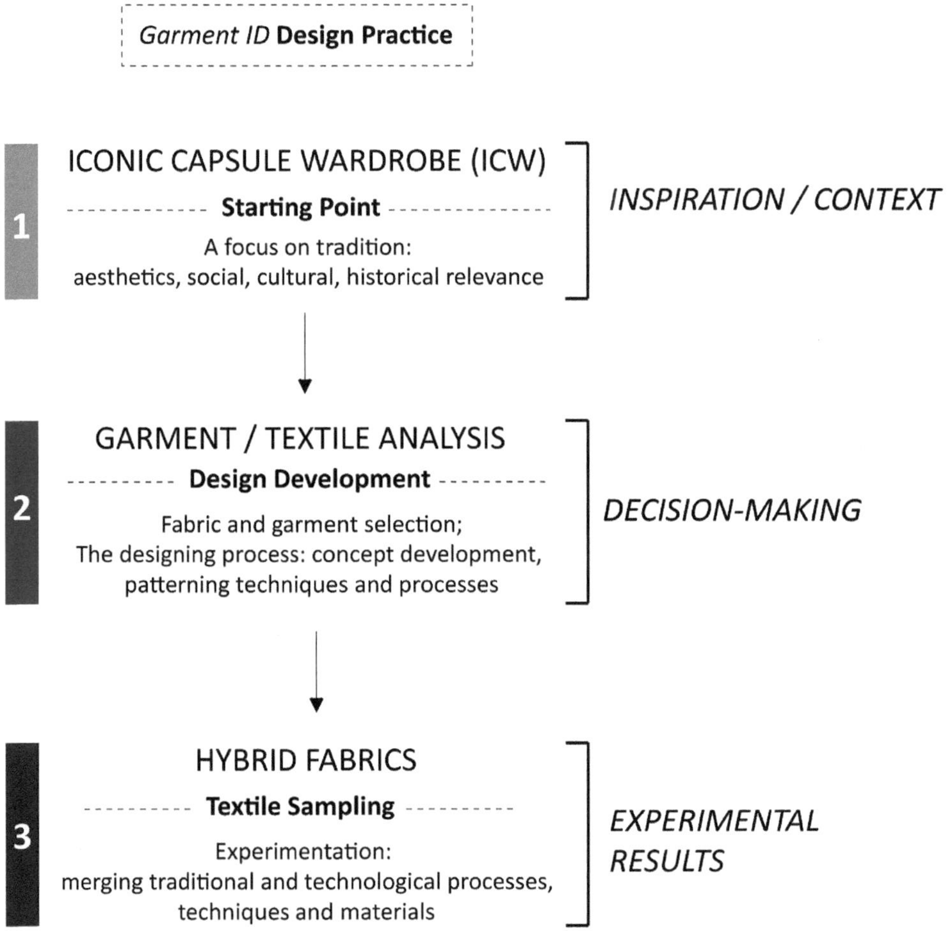

Garment ID **Design Practice**

1 — ICONIC CAPSULE WARDROBE (ICW)
Starting Point
A focus on tradition: aesthetics, social, cultural, historical relevance
— *INSPIRATION / CONTEXT*

2 — GARMENT / TEXTILE ANALYSIS
Design Development
Fabric and garment selection; The designing process: concept development, patterning techniques and processes
— *DECISION-MAKING*

3 — HYBRID FABRICS
Textile Sampling
Experimentation: merging traditional and technological processes, techniques and materials
— *EXPERIMENTAL RESULTS*

Figure 8.1 Design practice. Diagram: Kerri Akiwowo.

Figure 8.2 Iconic Capsule Wardrobe, 2008. Photograph: Kerri Akiwowo.

Each garment represented the basis for an innovative textile collection using functional fabrics, inspired by an original iconic garment. Individually, the garments provided a foundation for themed exploration of generating patterns onto textile surfaces. To aid design development and the decision-making process in terms of garment or textile selection, comparisons were made between an ICW garment and a performance garment or functional fiber, relevant to the "hybrid" ideas of the work. An examination of characteristics such as appearance, structure, and performance properties attempted to identify any common features that in some way united the two entities. At the same time, uniqueness was exploited in the consideration and proposal of new textile or garment concepts and identities.

Having established a context to initiate experimentation by proposing a relationship between old and new appearance and materials, the design process began by examining a traditional handmade cable-knitted 100% wool jumper alongside a typical fleece garment. The construction and overall aesthetics of each garment were compared and further challenged, aesthetically and structurally, through experimentation with a variety of fabrics and patterning techniques. This approach attempted to exploit both parallels and differences in a way that could inform the patterning process for textile designing and conceptual garment development.

Hand-knitted garments represent a traditional craft skill and tend to bear a distinct aesthetic, which is often decorative and constructed by different knitting patterns and stitches achievable. In this study, visual and physical characteristics of a traditional hand-knitted wool garment were first examined in order to consider the creative attributes of the item. Factors included: (1) style, such as garment shape, color, and weight; and (2) artistic qualities, such as pattern or decoration, form, texture, and composition. This inquiry stimulated the development of new patterns whereby conventional and technological methods were employed. Experimental fabric samples echoed physical qualities of the original garment and owed to designs that emulated knitted structures taking on a distinctive *trompe-l'oeil* (optical illusion) appearance.

Knitted wool garments are typically known for comfort and ease due to their inter-looping yarn construction—wool fibers are bulky and so provide good insulation and warmth. They allow stretch recovery as the body moves and are hygroscopic, readily absorbing and releasing moisture, unlike synthetic fibers. Alternatively, fleece or polar fleece is a soft, lightweight, warm, comfortable, synthetic "woolly" material made from recycled and recyclable PET (polyethylene terephthalate) or other synthetic fibers.

The first forms of polar fleece were created in 1979 by Malden Mills, who produced Polarfleece® and Polartec® technical fabrics. The emergence of polar fleece presented a new strong and light pile fabric created to mimic and exceed wool in performance—e.g. comfort, tenacity, and easy care. As synthetic fleece is highly breathable and fast wicking, typical fleece garments including jackets, jumpers, or sweaters are suitable for physical activity and used as outdoor, cool weather clothing. Often, the desired effect of fleece is that, unlike wool, it does not absorb moisture and dries quickly when wet, with the ability to insulate and remain warm under wet conditions due to its hydrophobic properties. Like wool, fleece can be damaged or affected if washed at high temperatures. But in general, fleece is easier to care for and can be machine washed at 30–40°C without shrinkage.

Fleece garments can be line dried, unlike wool clothing prone to stretch out of shape, and need little or no ironing to maintain a rich textural or smooth appearance.

This study also explored neoprene performance fabrics. Also known as polychloroprene, neoprene was developed by DuPont in 1930 as a man-made material alternative to rubber.[22] Although physically dissimilar to wool or knitwear due to a lack of bulk characteristics, neoprene is highly insulating like wool and resistant to weather elements such as rain water, and solvents, oils, and greases. Superior to wool, neoprene boasts good toughness and dimensional stability, unlikely to change its structure under thermal or physical pressure. In this study, high functionality combined with high-level creative input from a textile design perspective has been investigated. As such, this work proposes neoprene as a novel material applicable for modern "everyday" garment design explorations. Experimental surface design concepts for hybrid functional clothing are linked to historical textile crafts by application of hand and digital patterning approaches.

Among types traded, foam-backed neoprene is common for wearable products such as wetsuits, gloves, jackets, and protective gear associated with active and recreational sports such as surfing, cycling, and climbing. In terms of contemporary fashion, a trend-driven "pullover" style neoprene garment is more recognizable within this context, demonstrating enhanced creativity in the design outcomes. However, artistic input encompassing both structure (garment design) and surface (textile design) is often not expressed in neoprene sportswear and gear. Therefore, the potential to develop a smoother interchange between the two—neoprene fashion and neoprene sportswear—can be considered via the textile patterning approach and was therefore explored in this research.

Additionally, a reclaimed knitted fabric was used during experimental sampling, but due to the method of sourcing the exact fiber content was not specified. However, results of a burns test revealed both burn and melt characteristics, and it was therefore assumed that the fabric was a mixed fiber textile containing both natural (or regenerated) and synthetic fibers such as polyester/cotton, nylon/cotton, or polyester/viscose. A larger synthetic content was presumed due to increased hardening of the fibers during the burn test.

Practical investigation into textile patterning techniques for functional hybrid clothing involved hands-on experimentation with fabrics, screen printing pastes and binders as well as manually operated equipment, digital machines, and computer-aided design (CAD) software. The study was carried out with PET fleece, neoprene, and the reclaimed knitted mixed fiber fabric relevant to the traditional wool jumper identified within the ICW. Parallels between fabric and the garment were achieved through the experimental exploration of knit-like screen and digital print designs and laser etching techniques. Designs were developed by observing and recording existing knitted jumpers using hand drawing, photography, and CAD methods. The purpose of this approach was to engineer new "knitted" surface patterns onto functional fabrics essentially inspired by the iconic cable-knitted jumper. The aim was for designs to in some way mimic recognizable knitted structures but with a novel identity via varied types of pattern, rather than an actual knitted fabric formed from yarns.

Experimental parameters and methods

Experimental parameters and methods (summarized in Table 8.1) used to carry out this investigation were decided upon and employed based on three main factors: (1) a foreknowledge of and experience with the patterning processes explored—i.e. screen and digital printing methods; (2) the design potential of unfamiliar surface and imaging tools—i.e. laser technology; and (3) creative opportunities suggested by combining the selected fabrics with specific patterning techniques. As such, this experimental framework aided the qualitative aspects of the research.

Fundamentally, the aim of the research was to investigate alternative textile patterning techniques and design concepts for everyday clothing using performance or functional

Table 8.1. Experimental Parameters and Methods

Parameters	Methods
(1) Fabric*	**(1) Patterning process**
- 100% PET Polartec®[24] fleece: different varieties - Commercially available neoprene: two varieties - Reclaimed knitted fabric: mixed fiber content * All samples: 150 mm x 100 mm (approx.) unless stated otherwise	**Traditional screen printing (wet method)** Hand application of print pastes and binders onto fabric via screen **CAD: Dye sublimation printing (dry method)** Disperse dye/digital image transfer via heat/pressure **CAD: Laser etching (dry method)** CO_2 laser technology as an image-making tool to inscribe textile surfaces with patterns via beam output energy
(2) Equipment - Nylon mesh print screens - UV exposure unit (artwork/screen preparation) - Heat press machine - Digital sublimation printer - Computer (PC); CAD: Adobe Photoshop and Illustrator - CO_2 laser bed system	**(2) Themed experimentation** **Theme 1: Conventional** Screen printing **Theme 2: Technological** Dye sublimation printing; Laser etching
(3) Printing pastes, binders, dyes, laser beam - Discharge paste (screen printing) - 3D "puff" binder (screen printing) - Disperse dyes (sublimation printing) - Laser beam energy (surface etching)	**(3) Pairing: fabric-to-theme/process** **Theme 1: Conventional—screen printing** Neoprene; Reclaimed knitted mixed fiber fabric **Theme 2: Technological—dye sublimation printing and laser etching** Polartec® fleece; Neoprene

fabrics rather than conventional or traditional materials and methods. In an attempt to do so, it was anticipated that new "garment identities" could be considered through textile design interventions that encompassed distinctive craft qualities via creative contemporary outcomes. Specified processes and parameters facilitated subtle, simplistic decorative effects inspired by the original hand-knitted woollen jumper. This was achieved through the use of color, tone, image, and texture in order to mimic and reinterpret traditional aesthetic qualities in a modern way.

Experimentation was carried in two themes: (1) conventional—screen printing; and (2) technological—sublimation printing and laser etching. The thematic experimentation was adopted to celebrate, distinguish, update, and exploit both hand and digital patterning techniques. A focused approach facilitated unique tailored surface effects generated by pairing selected fabrics with particular processes. At this point, garment and textile analysis (outlined in Stage 2 of Table 8.1) aided decision making during design development towards final outcomes. Experimental results merged traditional and technological features in order to propose novel textile patterning techniques for hybrid functional clothing.

Experimental results and discussion: Creative outcomes and textile design opportunities for hybrid garment identities

This section presents the experimental fabric samples generated in the study. The creative results have been organized according to two main themes, conventional and technological, as introduced in the previous section. Selected functional fabrics and patterning processes explored have been discussed within this framework regarding decisions made during the design development phase.

Theme 1: Conventional—screen printing

This theme focuses on a conventional screen printing method. Two fabric types were investigated: neoprene and reclaimed knitted mixed-fiber fabric. A discharge printing process was investigated for the neoprene and a 3D "puff" process for the mixed-fiber fabric.

Neoprene

Commercially sourced off-white and cream-colored neoprene textile samples were screen printed with designs manipulated from hand drawings and further engineered via CAD methods to depict knitted textile structures (Plate 12). A clear (or white) "bleaching out" discharge paste was used to apply the design to the fabric surface. The digital design file was reproduced in different scales, i.e. small, medium, and large, in order to observe any differences in visual outcomes in terms of aesthetics.

Through the pairing of fabric to process (identified in Table 8.1), it was anticipated that tonal subtleties between the textile material and the pattern or print would be achieved through knit-inspired designs. This visual outcome was confirmed by the results and a "two-toned effect" was produced. In relation to the cable-knitted jumper, this gentle color shift mimicked areas of light and shade created by the decorative three-dimensional wool structure. In contrast, the fluidity and regularity of the printed knit structure displayed a visual simplicity bearing resemblance to traditional craft, updated by modern tools, traditional techniques, and unconventional materials.

Scale variation altered the resolution of the pattern; as a small-scale design, sharpness was reduced, creating a softer, more natural appearance due to a blurring effect. This outcome was influenced by the thread count of the woven screen mesh and viscosity associated with the discharge paste. In comparison, larger patterns enhanced structural detail and therefore exhibited greater intricacy. These differences aided variation regarding the textile design possibilities of this approach. Conceptually, such nuances may in some way symbolize the hairy woollen yarns of jumpers. For example, an inherent fuzziness on the surface of an actual knitted textile tends to obscure structural detail in places, especially in areas of wear on a garment. As such, this creates textural variation, often adding to the overall aesthetic. The design development potential in exploiting this innate characteristic through print design draws attention to the potential for the creation of further patterns that embody such subtleties.

Reclaimed knitted mixed-fiber fabric

Figure 8.3 shows a reclaimed knitted beige-colored textile sample that was screen printed with a design mimicking knit structure using miner foam "puff" binder. Characteristically, puff creates three-dimensional qualities on the cloth upon contact with heat such as an

Figure 8.3 Puff print onto reclaimed knitted fabric, 2008. Photograph: Kerri Akiwowo.

iron or hair dryer, making it possible to manually control the final raised effect. It was anticipated that this process altered both the original performance properties and the visual features of the fabric such as lustre and elasticity. Compared to the discharge printing method previously discussed, this process enabled tactile qualities rather than a smooth finish due to an elevated surface. This effect generated a distinct difference between the fabric and the print, adding uniqueness to the design.

Conceptually, printing a knitted pattern onto a knitted fabric playfully entwines both knitted and printed textile processes. In doing so, both fabric construction and surface design methods are combined in a way that challenges scale, tone, handle, and textile performance. This can be achieved through "fresh" exploration of a familiar technique and a new way of generating patterns as a textile practitioner. The aim of this approach is to challenge the identity and perception of what a "knitted" garment is, or could be, in the realm of apparel.

Theme 2: Technological—digital sublimation printing and laser etching

This theme focuses on two technological patterning processes: digital dye sublimation printing, suitable for synthetic materials; and laser etching. Experimentation with these patterning processes was carried out with two fabric types: Polartec® fleece and neoprene.

Polartec® fleece: dye sublimation and digital CAD method

The Polartec® fleece sample in Figure 8.4 was digitally printed using a disperse dye sublimation method outlined in Table 8.1. Pre-colored Polartec® fleece varieties were used for all sampling, as un-dyed fleece fabrics are not commonly manufactured. Print designs were photographically generated from actual knitted fabrics and garments and engineered to form repeat prints that directly referenced knitted patterns in order to display *trompe-l'oeil* qualities that imitate realistic visual characteristics. Conceptually, this approach further challenged the notion of garment identity from a textile design perspective through mimicry inspired surface impressions. The softness of the fleece combined with expectations of comfort and luxury associated with the knitted wool jumper are to some extent emulated in the sublimation printed designs.

The challenge presented by working with pre-colored fabrics allowed a degree of serendipity in the printing process due to a lack of control over the color of fabrics at the start. Consequently, this resulted in somewhat unplanned aesthetic outcomes, as it was difficult to predict the final exact shade of printed samples. The "true" overall color and appearance of the print designs as represented on the computer screen altered. This change was caused by the imposing original base color of the textile along with the transparency characteristics associated with the sublimation process, which determined the extent of this effect.

It is thought that in order to control the color parameter of this fabric, it may be necessary to carry out further extended experimentation involving the adjustment of

TEXTILE PATTERNING TECHNIQUES FOR HYBRID FUNCTIONAL CLOTHING

Figure 8.4 Dye sublimation printed pre-colored Polartec® fleece fabric with photo-generated knitted pattern, 2008. Photograph: Kerri Akiwowo.

digital patterns via CAD color functions. In doing so, the serendipitous effect could be reversed or compensated for through an in-depth exploration of digital color in relation to Polartec® fabric in a specific color. It is therefore anticipated that such investigation would produce truer color likeness using a bespoke approach that facilitates tweaking and complete alteration. Therefore, the potential to specify and control processing parameters suggests customization design development opportunities regarding this work. In relation to traditional textile craft approaches, this would modernize and reinterpret yarn-dyeing and hand-knitting methods by considering novel concepts and implementing technological techniques relevant to today.

Neoprene: dye sublimation and digital CAD method

Dye sublimation printed neoprene samples can be seen in Figure 8.5. Off-white and cream-colored fabrics led to results that closely matched computer-generated designs in terms of both color likeness and image quality. However, the fine ribbed surface of the neoprene produced a subtle, out-of-focus, blurred effect that altered the intended sharpness of patterns. Upon reflection on the outcomes, it was decided that the results did not hinder the aesthetic appeal of the design. Instead, a visual softness was created

Figure 8.5 Dye sublimation printed neoprene: photo-generated knitted patterns, 2008. Photograph: Kerri Akiwowo.

due to the reduced resolution of the print design. This anomaly benefitted the overall appearance and enhanced the design concept regarding digital patterns inspired by traditional hand-knitted woollen textiles and clothing. For example, in terms of textile design input, a usually stark synthetic rubber was transformed into a more tactile and dynamic textile material. Creative explorations involved reworking traditional features to produce engineered patterns, combined with high-performance fabric functionality and a technological textile printing approach underpinned by hybrid garment design concepts.

Polartec® fleece: laser etching and digital CAD method

Computer-generated patterns were laser etched onto Polartec® fleece samples using a raster (or filling in) image-based CAD approach enabled by the technology and design software. Laser-treated areas melted during processing due to the chemical and physical properties of the synthetic material formed from PET fibers. As such, this result produced a solid plastic-like surface caused by exposure to heat via laser irradiation. Therefore, laser-etched and untreated areas were easily distinguishable, especially when handled due to a change in tactile qualities.

Three-dimensional qualities were achieved through intricate fragmented digital patterns. CAD designs were generated from initial hand drawings of organic microstructures. Using digital manipulation techniques during the designing stage, drawn impressions were transformed into simple small-scale repeating structural compositions inspired by decorative knits or knitting patterns, commonly seen in both traditional and contemporary textiles. This approach attempted to redefine a conventional understanding and perception of a "textile structure" by using a laser-etching surface approach rather than a construction technique. As such, experimental results challenged the notion of a textile structure by focusing on a surface imaging approach in order to convey form instead of the actual formation of the fabric by knitting.

Further experimentation in terms of pattern would expand opportunities for mimicking knitted structures for fleece fabric or garments through textile design development. An in-depth technical study of processing parameters together with scientific analysis of treated fibers would address the wearable practicalities of laser-treated fleece garments based on the melting effect caused by PET and laser beam interaction.

Neoprene: laser etching and digital CAD method

Digital "knit" patterns were laser etched onto off-white and cream-colored neoprene fabrics using a vector CAD, rather than a raster method discussed in the previous section (Figure 8.6). This fabric and process pairing aimed to integrate craft elements inspired by the iconic jumper with high-performance characteristics provided by the neoprene in order to initiate new garment concepts through a textile design input. In terms of style, designs were distinctly graphic and precise, creating a notably different aesthetic compared to the aforementioned outcomes discussed in this chapter. Linear digital laser imaging enabled fine detailed repeat patterns that were developed from hand drawings and delicately emulated decorative features of knitted garments.

Experimental parameters relating to fabric, process, and design aspects attempted to merge traditional characteristics attributed to the knitted jumper with modern design considerations relating to style, function, and creativity. In doing so, alternative "knitted textile" identities have been proposed from a textile design perspective and a focus on a surface pattern approach. Creative outcomes suggest new hybrid garment forms that

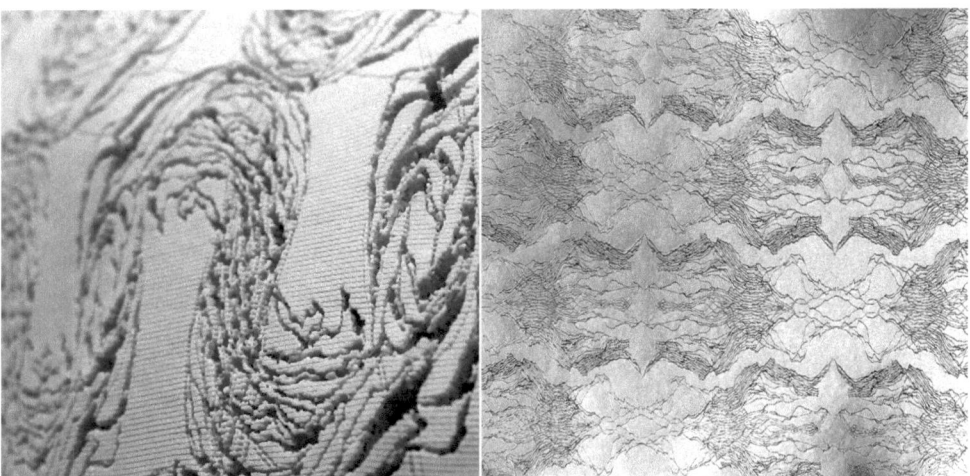

Figure 8.6 Laser-etched neoprene: vector "knit" design, 2008. Photograph: Kerri Akiwowo.

make reference to a traditional textile knit process in a contemporary manner, relevant to today.

Conclusion

This chapter presents the reinterpretation of a traditional knitting craft process through conventional and technological textile patterning interventions using functional fabrics. The aim of such interventions was to propose new "hybrid" garment identities inspired by craft techniques, linked to specific clothing types and informed by textile performance properties.

The reinterpretation of existing methods along with the adoption of technological systems for design and craft processes produced experimental results that redefined traditional techniques for modern textiles and garments. In this manner, knowledge of traditional hand skills and applied methods informed design opportunities relevant to contemporary clothing. This was due to a textile practitioner's know-how of specific techniques while exploring modern tools and methods and in turn acquiring new skills. In doing so, this investigation has identified:

1. textile design practice as a method for articulating combined traditional and contemporary craft processes, techniques, and concepts;
2. a novel textile patterning design approach informed by garment or textile construction; and
3. possibilities to integrate visual characteristics and textile techniques from the past with modern technologies and materials.

An artistic mix of craft and technology was achieved by exploring both traditional practices and digital methods: (1) screen printing reflected conventions in printed textile design via a hand approach and through the manual preparation and application of imagery; (2) dye sublimation digital printing enabled realistic photographic qualities made possible with CAD techniques; and (3) laser etching provided further digital design opportunities. Overall, textile patterns were created by modernizing hand approaches with digital methods and by focused experimentation using digital imaging technologies.

Patterning processes in relation to functional materials explored in this project acknowledge a platform for hybrid clothing. Traditional and technologically advanced pattern creation tools offered some insight into how a textile design approach might contribute to developments in "performance clothing." An attempt was made to understand how functional fabrics might be visually identified and further integrated into wider apparel sectors such as fashion markets, where "style" and "attractiveness" are paramount.

Further work aims to validate the processes involved in terms of wearability, by studying technical and creative parameters together with design development towards innovation, relevant to both textiles and garment sectors. Effective application of the ideas discussed in this chapter will ultimately contribute to defining the platform for hybrid clothing within contemporary textile or apparel environments.

Notes

1. Sarah Braddock, "Respect for Tradition, Curiosity for Technology," in *Textiles and New Technology 2010*, ed. Marie O'Mahony and Sarah Braddock (London: Artemis London Limited, 1994), 18.
2. Braddock, "Respect for Tradition, Curiosity for Technology," 18.
3. Ibid.
4. Sabine Seymour, *Fashionable Technology: The Intersection of Design, Science, and Technology* (Vienna: SpringerWienNewYork, 2008), 11.
5. Macarena San Martin, *Future Fashion: Innovative Materials and Technology* (Barcelona: Promopress, 2010), 164.
6. Andrew Bolton, *The Supermodern Wardrobe* (London: V&A, 2002), 7.
7. Bradley Quinn, *Textile Visionaries: Innovation and Sustainability in Textile Design* (London: Laurence King, 2013), 222–31.
8. Bolton, *The Supermodern Wardrobe*, 7; Quinn, *Textile Visionaries*, 222–31.
9. Lenzing Group is a leading fiber production company which specializes in innovation. The company supplies textiles and nonwovens globally. A sustainability focus within the business is attributed to their man-made cellulose manufacture derived from wood—a renewable raw material. See http://www.lenzing.com [accessed June 7, 2015].
10. Lenzing Group, "Focus Sustainability Report: Sustainability in the Lenzing Group" (2012). http://www.lenzing.com/fileadmin/template/pdf/konzern/nachhaltigkeit/Sustainability_Report_2012_EN.pdf [accessed September 20, 2013].
11. Jenny Udale, *Textiles and Fashion* (London: AVA Publishing, 2008), 10.
12. Melanie Bowles and Ceri Isaac, *Digital Textile Design* (2nd edn) (London: Laurence King, 2012), 178.
13. Suzanne Lee, *Fashioning the Future: Tomorrows Wardrobe* (London: Thames and Hudson, 2005), 124.
14. The study started as an independent project in 2008 at Central Saint Martins College of Art and Design (CSM), University of the Arts London (UAL). As a dye technician working in the School of Fashion and Textiles at CSM at the time, this position facilitated practice-led explorations in terms of being in a creative environment and access to facilities and equipment.
15. John W. Creswell, *Research Design: Qualitative & Quantitative Approaches* (London: Sage, 1994), 145.
16. Donald Schön, *The Reflective Practitioner: How Professionals Think in Action* (2nd edn) (New York: Basic Books, 1991).
17. Pat Drake and Linda Heath, *Practitioner Research at Doctoral Level: Developing Coherent Research Methodologies* (London: Routledge, 2011), 63.
18. Anni Albers, *Anni Albers: On Designing* (2nd edn) (Middletown, CT: Wesleyan University Press, 1962), 51.
19. Andrew Harrison, *Making and Thinking: A Study of Intelligent Activities* (Sussex: The Harvester Press, 1978), 13.
20. Schön, *The Reflective Practitioner*.
21. Quinn, *Textile Visionaries*, 267.
22. DuPont is an industrial chemical company founded in 1802. During the twentieth century, the

company produced a number of polymers including neoprene, which was invented in 1931. See http://www.dupont.com/products-and-services/plastics-polymers-resins/elastomers/brands/neoprene-polychloroprene.html [accessed September 19, 2014].

Bibliography

Albers, Anni, *Anni Albers: On Designing* (2nd edn) (Middletown, CT: Wesleyan University Press, 1962).

Bolton, Andrew, *The Supermodern Wardrobe* (London: V&A, 2002).

Bowles, Melanie, and Ceri Isaac, *Digital Textile Design* (2nd edn) (London: Laurence King, 2012).

Braddock, Sarah, "Respect for Tradition, Curiosity for Technology," in *Textiles and New Technology 2010*, ed. Marie O'Mahony and Sarah Braddock (London: Artemis London Limited, 1994), 18–23.

Creswell, John W., *Research Design: Qualitative & Quantitative Approaches* (London: Sage, 1994).

Drake, Pat, and Linda Heath, *Practitioner Research at Doctoral Level: Developing Coherent Research Methodologies* (London: Routledge, 2011).

Harrison, Andrew, *Making and Thinking: A Study of Intelligent Activities* (Sussex: The Harvester Press, 1978).

Lee, Suzanne, *Fashioning the Future: Tomorrow's Wardrobe* (London: Thames and Hudson, 2005).

Lenzing Group, "Focus Sustainability Report: Sustainability in the Lenzing Group" (2012). http://www.lenzing.com/fileadmin/template/pdf/konzern/nachhaltigkeit/Sustainability_Report_2012_EN.pdf [accessed September 20, 2013].

Quinn, Bradley, *Textile Visionaries: Innovation and Sustainability in Textile Design* (London: Laurence King, 2013).

San Martin, Macarena, *Future Fashion: Innovative Materials and Technology* (Barcelona, Spain: Promopress, 2010).

Schön, Donald, *The Reflective Practitioner: How Professionals Think in Action* (2nd edn) (New York: Basic Books, 1991).

Seymour, Sabine, *Fashionable Technology: The Intersection of Design, Science, and Technology* (Vienna: SpringerWienNewYork, 2008).

Udale, Jenny, *Textiles and Fashion* (London: AVA Publishing, 2008).

9
PROCESSES WITHIN DIGITALLY PRINTED TEXTILE DESIGN

Susan Carden

Introduction

This chapter explains the discovery of a novel process for producing textiles with cooling properties developed during a doctoral research project titled *Innovative Synthesis of Craft and Digital Processes: Theory Building Through Textile Design Practice* in the Centre for Advanced Textiles (CAT) at the Glasgow School of Art. One of the objectives of the study was to explore the potential for hand-crafting techniques to be used as interventions in the digital printing of textiles. The project was approached from the perspective of a practitioner-researcher in order to better understand the value and future potential of hand making during the creation and production of digitally printed textiles. However, during the early stages of the study an unexpected phenomenon was identified: the surface temperature of a set of textile samples was observed to drop in excess of five degrees Celsius below the ambient room temperature. As this discovery was further investigated, it became important to focus on the process of practice, rather than to lead the research along a more science-based path. By selecting a methodology that combined the grounded theory method with textile design practice, the invention was discovered during the study and led to a patent application afterwards. This chapter describes how a discovery that was found during a practice-led project could be later used outside the project and be developed into a full patent application.

Technology, such as a large-format inkjet printer, is developed to fulfil very specific functions, and therefore produces predetermined outcomes.[1] This is what Pye calls the "workmanship of certainty."[2] The more complex technology becomes, the greater our desire to control it.[3] Likewise, Eco asserts that our non-human relationship with technology is so unpalatable that we instinctively attempt to merge aesthetically attractive features with the functional aspects of the machines so as to forget that they control us.[4] A concern for textile designers is that they must be able to react quickly to evolving changes in advanced technology, while simultaneously bearing in mind the requirements of the society for whom they are working.[5] Using technology allows us to take what is out there in the environment and manufacture with it. In this way, we increasingly exchange the inherited knowledge associated with working by hand for the acquired knowledge that is embodied in the technology and the successive tools used to create it.[6] The designer using evolving advanced technology thus becomes increasingly less natural in the way they work, and what they create is subsequently more artificial.[7]

Designing with advanced technology places practitioners in a dichotomy between rules linked to empirical measurements and creative skill involving connoisseurship.[8] Being able to measure something gives a level of objectivity and consistency, meaning that anyone can obtain similar results. By incorporating hand-crafting in digital textile printing, the author provides a balance between the objectivity of the advanced technology and the subjective element of her own practice. The author's design knowledge adds a valuable connoisseurship to the outputs while the large-format inkjet printer supplies a degree of objectivity to the work in practice. As Flusser explains, a designer is the constant when using hand tools, while it is the tool that is replaced when it wears out or breaks; however, with advanced technology the machine becomes the constant, while the human operators come and go.[9] We are closer to nature when we design and make by hand, less so when we use tools, and still further away when we work with advanced technology.[10] McCullough maintains that we are able to create more interesting outcomes when partnerships are forged between the human input and the technology itself.[11] A practicing designer undertakes a subjective role when they create using their hands in the studio, but this activity becomes objective when the practitioner stands back and passes over the final stages of the printing to be undertaken by advanced technology. Also, for digital printing, what is a natural role for hand making—the human viewpoint—is not natural for advanced technology. As a result, this project attempts to position the practitioner in many different roles and perspectives. To date, few theories have been developed to better inform practitioners of how artists and designers are combining advanced technology with traditional craft skills in their work. From the perspective of advanced technology, the focus of this chapter is to explore how hand making can be introduced into the process of digital textile printing involving the large-format inkjet printer plus the fullest range of hardware and software that supports it.

While Dewey proposes that every medium has its own language,[12] Hughes claims that there are inbuilt restrictions to working with different materials, and part of our task as designers is to find out what these constraints are and utilize them to our own advantage.[13] This means that each of the various materials and processes involved in digital textile printing has its own distinctive characteristics and when taken as a whole, these provide a complex range of features and challenges. This was a key reason for the author deciding to explore the potential for a theory, or theories, in order to help practitioners create more effectively. One restriction for digital textile printing is that the medium used to create an initial image is not the same as the one used to print the final textile. However, similarities can be recognized between contemporary digital textile printing and the individuality of techniques used historically, for example, those used in Japanese woodblock printing of the Edo period.[14] During the Edo period, an artist would start by having a clear idea of the final print firmly in mind, just as digital print designers are required to do. First, the Japanese artist created the image on paper. Second, a highly skilled cutter who was not an artist would translate that image onto wood. Finally, the printer inked up the woodblock and transferred the image onto a substrate. Thus three different people, each with their own personal skills and visual styles, carry out distinct actions. The final artifact would therefore combine to reflect aspects of all three. For digital textile printing, the designer creates an image, but instead of going to a woodcutter to have it interpreted, the image is converted into a digital file for printing by a large-format inkjet printer. So, instead of three different craftspeople with their own unique skills, a digital textile print is created by three different entities: one human, one virtual, and one machine.

This helps to explain why no one designer is completely responsible for any single digital print. Just as the artists of the Edo period worked most efficiently when the artist was familiar with the material (e.g. wood), its strengths and weaknesses,[15] the cutter worked best when the artist's image was suitable for cutting from that specific type of wood, and the printer was kept in mind throughout the creation and production of the first two stages. As there is only one human involved at the frontline of digital printing, the designer must act alone from all three perspectives. The designer must be able to appreciate all three constituent entities in order to create effectively. It is also important that the designer does not feel enslaved by advanced technology but is aware that many different outcomes could result from a small number of constants. The decisions that may impact on the final outcome include the type of dye, the choice of large-format inkjet printer, the selection of base cloth, the selected color management system, the humidity of the print environment, the handling of the fixing and pre-coating solution, and other variables encountered at every stage of the digital textile printing process. However, as Campbell explains, designers are trained to work within the anomalies of natural materials and textile processes, and are well placed to accommodate and work around them.[16] The empirical measurements used in science to grade measurements, as mentioned by Polanyi,[17] are few and far between in textile design, although the possibility to send files digitally to be printed in geographically diverse locations provides one constant—the design represented as code—that can be measured and predicted.

Methodology

The choice of research methods and methodology in this project helped to create an environment in which play and error encouraged new discoveries to take place. The author decided to use her own design practice, as this would enable her to make use of, and reflect upon, her previously mastered skills in constructed textiles and craft alongside the process of creating digitally printed textiles. The author's intention was to intertwine hand-crafting with digital technology in order to develop innovative techniques. While admitting that she was not an impartial spectator of her own practice, the author found that by reflecting on the various documented outcomes of the study, her role as a designer led her to gain a unique perspective into her own particular way of making. This allowed for a personal understanding of how digital textile prints are created. Although the author was taking a multifaceted approach to her practice during the research, she acknowledged that it was not feasible to see the complete picture from every possible angle. She was mindful that this would result in different outcomes from other researchers viewing the same material. This was important in research terms in which the ability to reproduce a situation is key. However, the author was in a perfect position to observe and experience the situation from the viewpoint of an insider who is immersed in the process of making, rather than solely witnessing, recording, or surveying how such practice is conducted.

Scrivener claims that Schön's definition of the reflective practitioner enables us to access the way creativity works from the inside, including influences from previous experiences, by providing multiple perspectives on the act of making that is to be revealed.[18] Scrivener and Chapman also propose that reflective practice is grounded in any current creative work and can be further realized in future projects.[19] Adopting this approach meant that an interactive cycle carried the practice forward from an initial phase to consecutive stages in which the various aspects of the research problematic were repeatedly revisited. The methodology that involved textile practice-led research with the application of the grounded theory approach allowed the author to build a theory by richly documenting the studio activity at the same time as the creative work was being carried out. In this way procedural knowledge was made explicit, while the contextualization and development of new techniques synthesized emerging ideas into theories.

Grounded theory is a qualitative research method developed by Barney Glaser and Anselm Strauss in 1967 to generate theory from within the discipline for which it is to be used.[20] As a textile practitioner, this method enabled data to be gathered during the creation of work in the studio. By stopping and reflecting on the work in progress, a hypothesis was proposed, and in order to test the robustness of this hypothesis, a counter-theory was put forward. This process was then repeated six times until a final theory was reached for which no further alternative hypotheses were found. Grounded theory, explains Creswell, provides a framework for identifying categories and guidelines on how to join these categories.[21] Therefore, as a research method, this framework allowed the author to understand how the digital reproduction of images takes place and—key to theory building—enabled her to forge connections between ideas and concepts while making her work in the studio. She used the full version of grounded theory,[22] rather than an abbreviated form, as this allowed her to regularly revisit the ongoing practice with each successive emerging substantive theory. The author therefore looked for negative cases to challenge the emerging hypotheses, and used the outcomes to inform and amend each successive new theory.[23]

The first hypothesis was: *The digitally printed image seems to skim or float on the surface of the fabric, resulting in outcomes that are perceived as fake*, and the properties of their substantive theory were: *False outcomes due to digitally printed image not integrating with substrate*. So, in an attempt to find a negative scenario, or an exception in order to challenge the hypothesis,[24] ways of better integrating the digital image with the base cloth were explored. To do this, the role of each core ingredient of the digital printing process was analyzed within the digital image; the large-format inkjet printer; the reactive dyes; the pre-coating solution; and the post-fixing techniques.

Processes

Alginate is a key material or component in digital textile printing; it is required in the application of the reactive dye and is also used in a solution to fix the dye to the base cloth. The author's visit to the dentist provided an idea for a possible avenue to explore. In dental

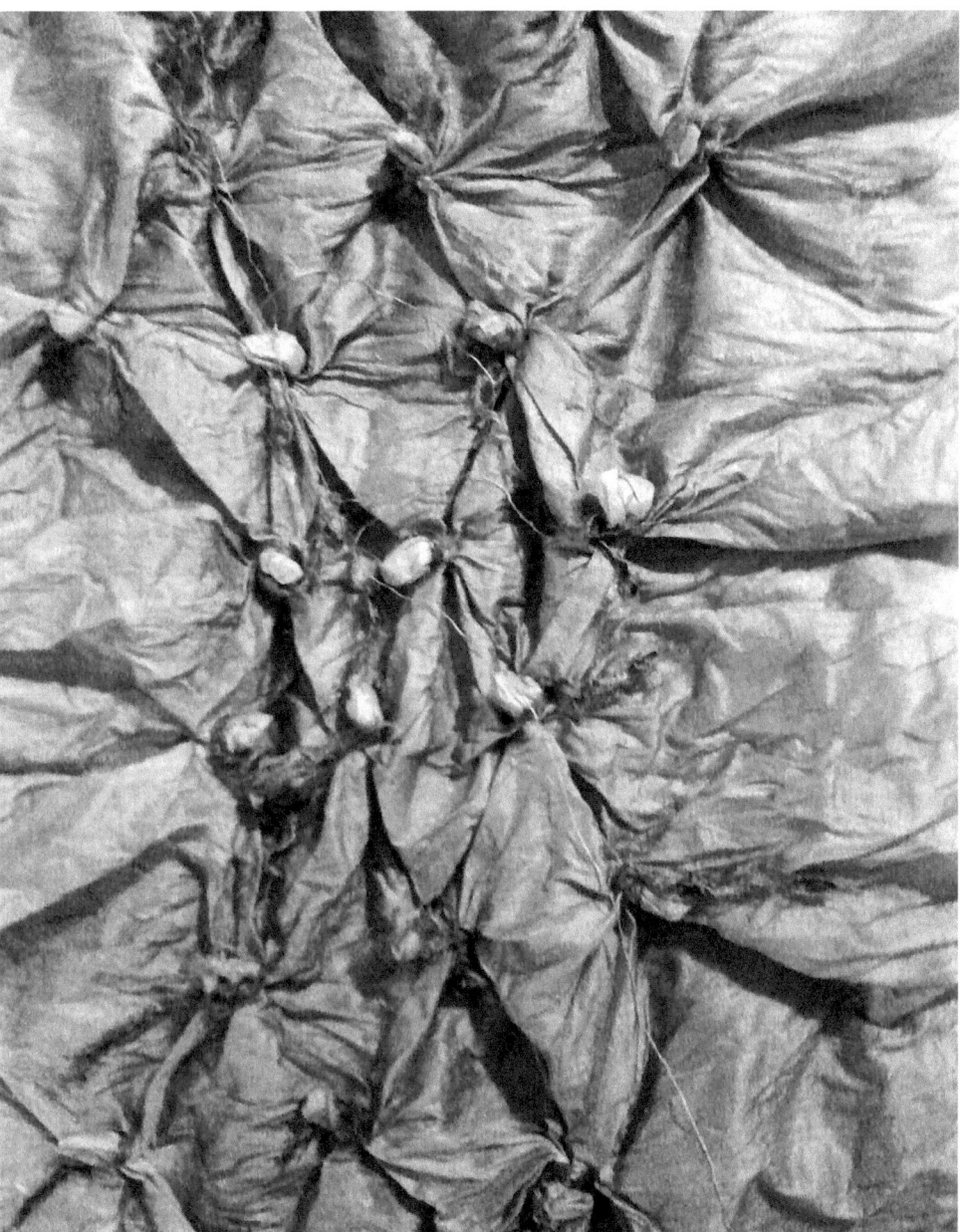

Figure 9.1 Hand-crafted silk sample, tied and saturated with water prior to applying the alginate solution, 2010. Photograph: Susan Carden.

treatment, a mixture containing alginate is used to make an impression of teeth and this can set quickly and firmly, depending on the alginate reacting with a source of calcium. In the studio the author experimented with alginate combined with water and a range of calcium-rich materials that she knew from a priori knowledge as sources of calcium.

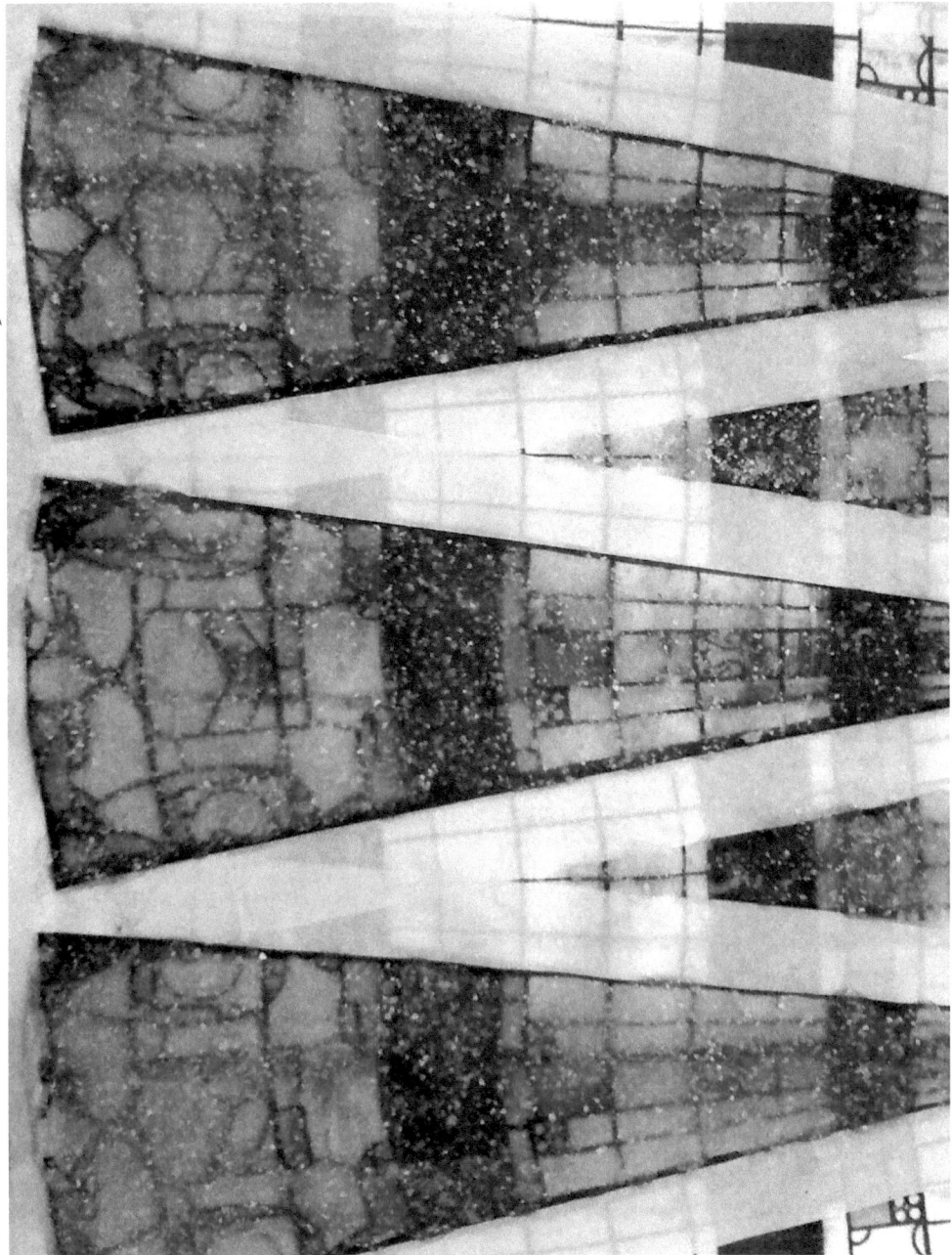

Figure 9.2 Digitally printed constructed silk sample, masked and coated with the alginate solution, 2010. Photograph: Susan Carden.

Once the author had produced a gel that thickened as anticipated, she continued to mix different quantities of these ingredients and undertook a number of experiments to test the saturation levels of various digital textile prints (Figure 9.1). The author then prepared a range of alginate mixtures at different temperatures and proportions to familiarize herself with the texture, consistency, handle, and odour of the resultant gel. After this, another approach was tried. Instead of using the prepared gel, the dry powdered alginate was combined with a wider range of calcium-rich sources and sprinkled over the surface of the following substrates: (1) digital textile prints on silk dupion, satin, and chiffon; (2) digital prints on paper of 80gsm; and (3) digital prints on glossy photographic paper of 256gsm. Water was also added to these samples. When printed silk dupion, satin, and chiffon dried out after two days, a coating of clear polythene film was added and the edges were sealed by heating (Figure 9.2). When the sample cooled, the sides of the composite had joined and the gel remained firm, providing an additional vibrancy when the light was reflected off the surface at different angles. This gave the printed textiles a new visual depth and texture (Plates 14 and 15). Surprisingly, the temperature of the samples was significantly cooler than that of the surrounding area, and this was an unexpected outcome. The samples' temperature remained far lower than the ambient room temperature for the next three weeks.

The next stage was to produce a series of samples varying the materials for the base cloth and the proportions of the ingredients. The author discovered that the temperature

Figure 9.3 Testing temperatures of silk samples in laboratory, using thermocouples, 2010. Photograph: Susan Carden.

drop across the different surfaces could be controlled to 5.5 degrees below the ambient room temperature. Technical staff at Glasgow University's Electrical Engineering Department undertook a series of laboratory tests, involving highly sensitive thermocouples in order to accurately measure the temperature drop of each textile sample (Figure 9.3). The cooling effect inadvertently created on the surface of the textiles was the result of an endothermic reaction, meaning that the textile absorbs heat from the surrounding area. In the laboratory, at 25 degrees Celsius, the temperature of the samples was as low as 19.5 degrees. The implications of this endothermic reaction, although not appropriate for the author's doctoral project, were discussed with colleagues, and a number of suggestions were made for further research. The possibilities included: (1) medical situations in which rapid temperature reduction is required; (2) circumstances where no electricity supply is present and a cool surface is necessary; (3) cooling properties that might help prevent pressure sores; and (4) the potential to create novel garments or fashion accessories due to the unusual, cool, tactile quality of the textiles. However, the aim of the study was to develop processes for theory building, so a patent application was drawn up with the assistance of a patent attorney and submitted to safeguard the discovery for a later investigation.

Invention

Chance discovery is most likely when we indulge in play and error.[25] The act of engaging with materials or systems without a deliberate outcome in mind enables us to reveal unexpected outcomes. It also allows someone to get things wrong and, in doing so, discover useful facts about how those materials and processes behave. According to Pye, there is essentially little difference between discovery and invention, as each reveals facts about the nature of something or groups of materials and systems.[26] Polanyi points out that when someone applies for a patent to safeguard an invention, they must first attempt to explain how their idea is unique, out of the ordinary.[27] They will seek to obtain a patent that covers the widest possible terms, so that the concept may be formed from as wide a variety of materials, shapes, and sizes as possible, thereby maximizing the coverage of the patent application.[28] It makes sense that when seeking to discover new processes, including those appropriate for a patent application, there should be a significant period of play and error combined with reflection and documentation in order to evaluate whether a new process is an invention or solely creative practice undertaken along logical steps and traceable stages.

Inventions require unexpected outcomes and situations that are not the commonplace in studio practice. For example, bringing together a traditional handcraft such as embroidery with digital printing, either at the pre- or post-printing stages, may alter the base cloth and produce novel outcomes. But this will not qualify as an invention, because each stage has a traceability that excludes such categorization. According to Polanyi, a true invention is not reached by a series of logical steps, as this would be an improvement; for an invention there needs to be an unpredictable element, something unexpected that makes the idea unique.[29] If, however, a combination of materials not normally associated with textile design is included in the digital printing process and this leads to unexpected results that are neither anticipated nor explained, then the process may be suitable for a patent application. In this situation, it is not the individual chemical or physical composition of the fabrics nor the dye that is being disclosed, but the manner in which these are brought together and applied. It is the operational principle that is patentable: how each part functions in relation to the others, and altogether as a whole.[30] In this way, it is the language of the combined crafts, digital technology, materials, and processes that is being used as a collective tool once sufficient skills and mastery have been assimilated to enable the practitioner to fully understand and effectively play with the grouped materials and processes. As the use of the materials, techniques, and advanced technology are mastered, it is then possible to jointly create with them, thus designing in a new way.

Materials

While materials themselves suggest patterns, structure, composition, and forms,[31] each material has its own language.[32] Thus, it is understandable that hand-crafting with individual fabrics and dyes will result in outcomes that are informed as much by the practitioner as by their materials. When a practitioner extends the range of tools, materials, and techniques or processes at their disposal to include hand-crafting and advanced technology, it is not surprising that the conversation between a maker, tools, fabrics, and dyes reaches out in a multitude of ways, and increasingly the synergy of the outcomes often exceeds initial expectations. For example, the novel process for creating textiles with cooling surfaces is long-lasting; it employs only food-grade materials and can be recycled at the end of its useful lifespan in the same manner as current domestic textiles.

Frayling tells us that designers should think of their workshops as a form of laboratory and in this way they can link crafts with sustainability.[33] Similarly, Polanyi suggests that for an inventor, a sketchbook acts as their personal laboratory.[34] In this study the author also utilized her sketchbook to manipulate ideas and pieces of information in a manner similar to conducting experiments in a science laboratory (Figure 9.4). From a workshop and sketchbook scenario, what this newly discovered process achieves is a reflective use of crafting by hand in response to playing with materials and advanced technology. This encourages a crossover of craft skills into evolving advanced technological systems.

When combining craft with advanced technology, designers should also reassess the authenticity and integrity of the context in which they are creating.[35] The question that needs to be addressed concerns the methods and processes of production as well as the nature of the final crafted artifact itself. The relationship that is forged between the designer-maker and the materials, processes, final aesthetic, function, and concept defines its integrity.[36] This honesty also relies on a sufficiently high level of skill,[37] as it permits the maker to fully understand the manual and intellectual knowledge involved in realizing integrity.[38]

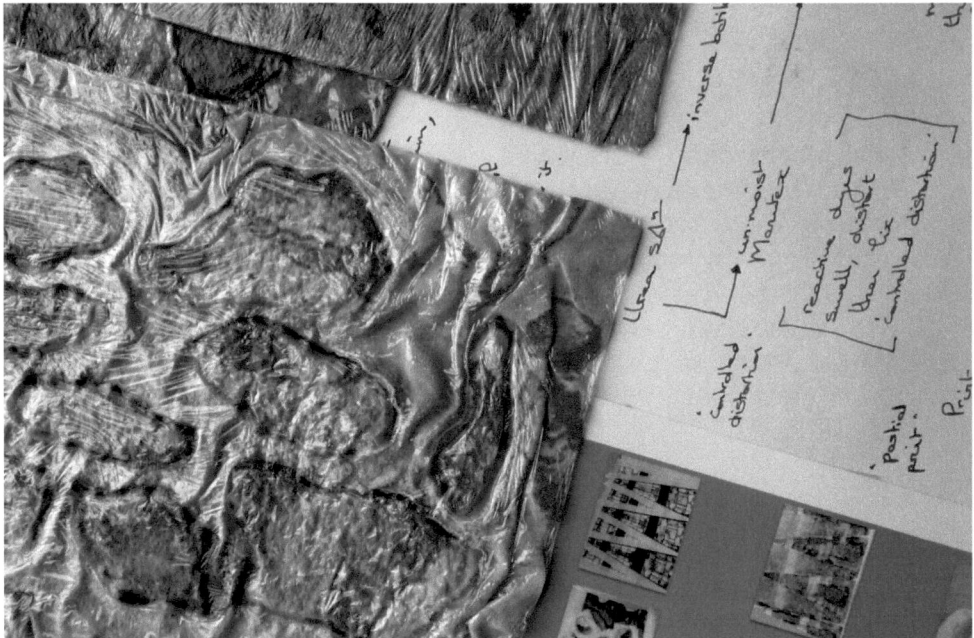

Figure 9.4 Coated silk samples and cooling process being explored in the sketchbook, 2011. Photograph: Susan Carden.

With every new technology, there is a readjustment by default of the dialogue between each aspect of this creativity. New fabrics or dyes necessitate a re-evaluation of their application within the manufacturing process. For example, advances in pigment ink technology offer alternative methods for digital printing that do not require pre-coating or post-fixing, thereby reducing chemical waste and water consumption. This in turn influences the aesthetics of the final outputs. Whether material, process, or technology, each component is so intertwined within the digital textile printing process that a change in one element impacts on the others. This is why the integrity of the design process should be reflectively analyzed to safeguard the context, implications, and the effect of emerging production methods from both the designer's and the client's point of view.

Evolving digital printing technologies, plus diverse materials and functions, feed into neighboring disciplines and systems, helping to create "super-black-boxes," in Latour's term, that comprise many individual black boxes.[39] Latour uses a black box to describe a situation in which the input and output are known, but the complex workings of the internal mechanisms are not.[40] However, the human input into the black boxes has increasingly become less aware. For example, there is no requirement for a designer to understand the minutiae of all the components of a large-format inkjet printer that act as one when we set it to work. Stakeholders involved in creating this digital tool may include dye manufacturers, their chemists and marketing teams, the technology and interfaces expert who installed the machine, substrate producers, pre-coating solution manufacturers, the software specialist who connected the computer to the printer, the programmer who enabled the image to be created and shared, and the institution that educated the individual who is currently developing tomorrow's hardware and software.[41] Every small step impacts in many ways; it is essential, yet not always visible.

Hand-crafting values

When the British Crafts Council produced the Craft Blueprint for developing craft within the UK workforce, they helped to recognize the value that "vernacular technologies, materials and form" can add to artifacts, and also the added value in economic terms through increased profit.[42] In addition, growing awareness of sustainability issues assists in the promotion of the benefits of making by hand, such as in slow design.[43] Such recognition comes with an acknowledgement of the many hours spent mastering the materials and processes involved.[44] The craftsperson's pride in their practice[45] is reflected when they take ownership of the skills and processes that are demonstrated and embodied in their work, although mastering such expertise takes a great deal of time, estimated at between ten thousand hours[46] and ten years.[47] For those who have neither the time, the inclination, nor perhaps the talent for such skill perfecting, an appreciation can still be brought about through an acquisition of fine craft pieces which can be seen as a transference of mastery in materials and processes, produced by one individual for another. In Japan, for example, the aesthetic essence associated with materials and craft is revered and inherent in their traditions and culture.[48] In the West the desire to seek or obtain an awareness of worth is similarly responded to by contemporary craftspeople when they demonstrate an economic method for producing a balance between their time, the environment, and financial security that is necessary to enable them to fully develop their ideas.[49]

Studio practice is central to textile design research, and from within it, this new process for producing textiles with cool surfaces was developed. In trying to make sense of the context, it was necessary to look both backwards and forwards—not only to the various methods of production and the impact of the materials, processes, and technologies deployed, but also to the perspective of the client who will eventually use the craft piece.[50] In this sense the author placed herself in the position of the artifact and attempted to better understand the object by making a version of it with her own hands and advanced technology. As Dormer maintains that a machine represents a system that is the culmination of many previous hand tools, it is important for us to understand this model, so that we can more fully comprehend how and where ideas and suggestions come from in the development of any new process.[51]

Conclusion

This chapter has explained how the author approached her research objective of introducing hand-crafting into digital textile printing within a doctoral research project. By reflecting on key points that emerged during the study, she has shown how a novel cooling process was discovered, while explaining how this revelation generated data that were used to support the project's primary aim of theory building through studio practice. The patent application enabled her to safeguard the details of this discovery for later consideration and development.

Using craft practices across disciplines can be seen as a valuable way of making connections with other fields,[52] as this concept allows practitioners to absorb ideas and aspects of expertise from one area of knowledge and extend them to include the domain of another. Practice, by its nature, is an investigative, hands-on activity and is therefore well placed to encourage play scenarios, reflection, and risk taking. The author found that the development and value of procedural knowledge within crafts, as opposed to the worth of the artifact when viewed as an object alone, allowed her to extend from practice-centric contexts into evolving new areas of process and theory. These emerging opportunities complement and expand the traditional domains of the contemporary craft maker's practice and provide hand-crafted artifacts with a new audience and relevance. The author's final outputs were thus enriched through association with a wider range of perspectives. "Craft makers are experts in two things: the workmanship of risk, and how to apply their tacit knowledge to the tools, systems and opportunities created by distributed knowledge."[53]

In the context of this research, it has been demonstrated that craft has the capacity to forge new relationships for creating by hand. This means that the act of forming artifacts can be analyzed from multiple perspectives, including material, function, process, final aesthetics, and concept, all of which inform the integrity of the crafted object. The number of technologies currently being introduced into digital textile printing increases, and so does the breadth of outcomes. Therefore, it is necessary to outline the parameters of existing authenticity and integrity in order that contextual considerations are not permitted to distract the practitioner-researcher. The discovery of the new process outlined in this chapter required abductive reasoning, something that instinctively comes out of nowhere,[54] but as a researcher, the author needed to generate data from the act of creating in order to produce new knowledge from within the studio enquiry. By remaining faithful to the original research problematic and adhering to the grounded theory approach with digital textile design practice as a methodology, it was possible to utilize the data generated through observation, reflection, and documentation during the discovery to enable the primary aim of the project, theory building, to be achieved successfully.

Notes

1 Michael Polanyi, *Personal Knowledge: Towards a Post-Critical Philosophy* (Chicago, IL: Chicago University Press, 1974), 176; Martin Heidegger, *The Question Concerning Technology and Other Essays*, trans. William Lovitt (New York: Harper Perennial, 1977), 23; David Pye, *The Nature and Art of Workmanship* (London: Fox Chapel Publishing, 1968), 6.

2 David Pye, *The Nature and Aesthetics of Design* (London: Cambium Press, 1978), 24.

3   Heidegger, *The Question Concerning Technology and Other Essays*, 5; Soetsu Yanagi, *The Unknown Craftsman* (Tokyo: Kodashana, 1977), 108.
4   Umberto Eco, *The Open Work* (Cambridge, MA: Harvard University Press, 1989), 128.
5   Harvey Brooks, "The Dilemmas of Engineering Education," *IEEE* Spectrum 4 (2) (1967): 89–91.
6   Vilém Flusser, *The Shape of Things: A Philosophy of Design*, trans. Anthony Matthews (London: Reaktion Books, 1999), 44.
7   Flusser, *The Shape of Things*, 44.
8   Polanyi, *Personal Knowledge*, 88.
9   Flusser, *The Shape of Things*, 45.
10 Ibid.
11 Malcolm McCullough, *Abstracting Craft: The Practiced Digital Hand* (Cambridge, MA: MIT Press, 1996), 193.
12 John Dewey, *Art as Experience* (New York: Perigee Books, 1934), 110.
13 Bob Hughes, *Dust or Magic: Secrets of Successful Multimedia* (London: Addison-Wesley, 1999), 14.
14 Hiroshi Yoshida, *Japanese Woodblock Printing* (Tokyo: Sanseido, 1939), 11.
15 Ibid.
16 J. R. Campbell, "Digital Printing of Textiles for Improved Apparel Production," in *Advances in Apparel Production*, ed. Catherine Fairhurst (Cambridge: Woodhead, 2008), 222–49.
17 Polanyi, *Personal Knowledge*, 55.
18 Stephen Scrivener, "Characterising Creative-Production Doctoral Projects in Art and Design," *International Journal of Design Sciences and Technology* 10 (2) (2002): 25–44; Donald Schön, *The Reflective Practitioner: How Professionals Think in Action* (New York: Basic Books, 1983).
19 Stephen Scrivener and Peter Chapman, "The Practical Implications of Applying a Theory of Practice Based Research: A Case Study," *Working Papers in Art and Design* 3 (2004). https://www.herts.ac.uk/__data/assets/pdf_file/0019/12367/WPIAAD_vol3_scrivener_chapman.pdf [accessed February 29, 2016].
20 Barney Glaser and Anselm L. Strauss, *The Discovery of Grounded Theory: Strategies for Qualitative Research* (New York: Aldine, 1967).
21 John W. Creswell, *Qualitative Inquiry and Research Design: Choosing Among Five Approaches* (Washington, DC: Sage, 2012), 12.
22 Anselm L. Strauss and Juliet M. Corbin, *Basics of Qualitative Research: Techniques and Procedures for Developing Grounded Theory* (Thousand Oaks, CA: Sage, 1998), viii.
23 Karl Popper, *Conjectures and Refutations: The Growth of Scientific Knowledge* (London: Routledge, 1991), 48.
24 Glaser and Strauss, *The Discovery of Grounded Theory*, 230.
25 Pye, *The Nature and Aesthetics of Design*, 63.
26 Ibid., 21.
27 Polanyi, *Personal Knowledge*, 177.
28 Ibid., 328.
29 Ibid.
30 Ibid., 123.

31 Yanagi, *The Unknown Craftsman*, 118.

32 Dewey, *Art as Experience*, 110.

33 Christopher Frayling, *On Craftsmanship: Towards a New Bauhaus* (London: Oberon Masters, 2011), 142.

34 Polanyi, *Personal Knowledge*, 85.

35 Kristina Niedderer, "Sustainability of Craft as a Discipline?", *Making Futures* 1 (2009): 165–74. http://mfarchive.plymouthart.ac.uk/journalvol1/papers/kristina-niedderer.pdf [accessed May 8, 2015].

36 Kristina Niedderer, "Relating the Production of Artefacts and the Production of Knowledge in Research," in *Reflections and Connections: On the Relationship Between Creative Production and Academic Research*, ed. Nithikul Nimkulrat and Tim O'Riley (Helsinki: University of Art and Design Helsinki, 2009), 59–67.

37 Howard Gardner, *Multiple Intelligences: New Horizons* (New York: Basic Books, 2006), 67; Richard Sennett, *The Craftsman* (New Haven, CT: Yale University Press, 2008), 52.

38 Glenn Adamson, *Thinking Through Craft* (Oxford: Berg, 2007), 5.

39 Flusser, *The Shape of Things*, 48.

40 Bruno Latour, *Science in Action* (Cambridge, MA: Harvard University Press, 1987), 140.

41 Latour, *Science in Action*, 3.

42 Crafts Council, *The Craft Blueprint: Developing the Craft Workforce in the UK* (2009), 22. http://ccskills.org.uk/downloads/1319724056-11_20_Craft-blueprint.pdf [accessed May 1, 2015].

43 Alastair Faud-Luke, *The Eco-Design Handbook* (London: Thames and Hudson, 2002), 110.

44 Gardner, *Multiple Intelligences*, 49; Sennett, *The Craftsman*, 38.

45 Mike Press, "Handmade Futures: The Emerging Role of Craft Knowledge in Our Digital Culture," in *NeoCraft: Modernity and the Crafts*, ed. Sandra Alfoldy (Nova Scotia: Nova Scotia College of Art and Design, 2007), 251–68.

46 Sennett, *The Craftsman*, 172.

47 Gardner, *Multiple Intelligences*, 41.

48 Sarah E. Braddock Clarke and Marie O'Mahoney, *Techno Textiles 2: Revolutionary Fabrics for Fashion and Design* (London: Thames and Hudson, 2007), 13.

49 Helen Rees, "Patterns of Making: Thinking and Making in Industrial Design," in *The Culture of Craft: Status and Future Studies in Design & Material Culture*, ed. Peter Dormer (Manchester: Manchester University Press, 1997), 116–36.

50 Martin Heidegger, *Being and Time*, trans. John Macquarrie and Edward Robinson (Malden, MA: Blackwell, 1962), 200.

51 Peter Dormer, "The Salon de Refuse?", in *The Culture of Craft: Status and Future Studies in Design & Material Culture*, ed. Peter Dormer (Manchester: Manchester University Press, 1997), 7.

52 Press, "Handmade Futures," 249.

53 Ibid., 264.

54 Polanyi, *Personal Knowledge*, 328.

Bibliography

Adamson, Glenn, *Thinking Through Craft* (Oxford: Berg, 2007).
Braddock Clarke, Sarah E. and O'Mahoney, Marie, *Techno Textiles 2: Revolutionary Fabrics for Fashion and Design* (London: Thames and Hudson, 2007).
Brooks, Harvey, "The Dilemmas of Engineering Education," *IEEE* Spectrum 4 (2) (1967): 89–91.
Campbell, J. R. "Digital Printing of Textiles for Improved Apparel Production," in *Advances in Apparel Production*, ed. Catherine Fairhurst (Cambridge: Woodhead, 2008), 222–49.
Crafts Council, *The Craft Blueprint: Developing the Craft Workforce in the UK* (2009). http://ccskills.org.uk/downloads/1319724056-11_20_Craft-blueprint.pdf [accessed May 1, 2015].
Creswell, John W., *Qualitative Inquiry and Research Design: Choosing Among Five Approaches* (Washington, DC: Sage, 2012).
Dewey, John, *How We Think* (Lexington, MA: D. C. Heath, 1910).
Dewey, John, *Art as Experience* (New York: Perigee Books, 1934).
Dormer, Peter, "The Salon de Refuse?" in *The Culture of Craft: Status and Future Studies in Design & Material Culture*, ed. Peter Dormer (Manchester: Manchester University Press, 1997), 2–16.
Eco, Umberto, *The Open Work* (Cambridge, MA: Harvard University Press, 1989).
Flusser, Vilém, *The Shape of Things: A Philosophy of Design*, trans. Anthony Matthews (London: Reaktion Books, 1999).
Frayling, Christopher, *On Craftsmanship: Towards a New Bauhaus* (London: Oberon Masters, 2011).
Fuad-Luke, Alistair, *The Eco-Design Handbook* (London: Thames and Hudson, 2002).
Gardner, Howard, *Multiple Intelligences: New Horizons* (New York: Basic Books, 2006).
Glaser, Barney, and Anselm L. Strauss, *The Discovery of Grounded Theory: Strategies for Qualitative Research* (New York: Aldine, 1967).
Heidegger, Martin, *Being and Time*, trans. John Macquarrie and Edward Robinson (Malden, MA: Blackwell, 1962).
Heidegger, Martin, *The Question Concerning Technology and Other Essays*, trans. William Lovitt (New York: Harper Perennial, 1977).
Hughes, Bob, *Dust or Magic: Secrets of Successful Multimedia* (London: Addison-Wesley, 1999).
Latour, Bruno, *Science in Action* (Cambridge. MA: Harvard University Press, 1987).
McCullough, Malcolm, *Abstracting Craft: The Practiced Digital Hand* (Cambridge, MA: MIT Press, 1996).
Niedderer, Kristina, "Sustainability of Craft as a Discipline?", *Making Futures* 1 (2009): 165–74. http://mfarchive.plymouthart.ac.uk/journalvol1/papers/kristina-niedderer.pdf [accessed May 8, 2015].
Niedderer, Kristina, "Relating the Production of Artefacts and the Production of Knowledge in Research," In *Reflections and Connections: On the Relationship Between Creative Production and Academic Research*, ed. Nithikul Nimkulrat and Tim O'Riley (Helsinki: University of Art and Design Helsinki, 2009), 59–67.
Polanyi, Michael, *Personal Knowledge: Towards a Post-Critical Philosophy* (Chicago: Chicago University Press, 1974).
Popper, Karl, *Conjectures and Refutations: The Growth of Scientific Knowledge* (London: Routledge, 1991).
Press, Mike, "Handmade Futures: The Emerging Role of Craft Knowledge in Our Digital Culture," in *NeoCraft: Modernity and the Crafts*, ed. Sandra Alfoldy (Nova Scotia: Nova Scotia College of Art and Design, 2007), 251–68.
Pye, David, *The Nature and Art of Workmanship* (London: Fox Chapel Publishing, 1968).
Pye, David, *The Nature and Aesthetics of Design* (London: Cambium Press, 1978).
Rees, Helen, "Patterns of Making: Thinking and Making in Industrial Design," in *The Culture of*

Craft: Status and Future Studies in Design & Material Culture, ed. Peter Dormer (Manchester: Manchester University Press, 1999), 116–36.

Schön, Donald, *The Reflective Practitioner: How Professionals Think in Action*. (New York: Basic Books, 1983).

Scrivener, Stephen, "Characterising Creative-Production Doctoral Projects in Art and Design," *International Journal of Design Sciences and Technology* 10 (2) (2002): 25–44.

Scrivener, Stephen and Peter Chapman, "The Practical Implications of Applying a Theory of Practice Based Research: A Case Study," *Working Papers in Art and Design* 3 (2004). https://www.herts.ac.uk/__data/assets/pdf_file/0019/12367/WPIAAD_vol3_scrivener_chapman.pdf [accessed February 29, 2016].

Sennett, Richard, *The Craftsman* (New Haven, CT: Yale University Press, 2008).

Strauss, Anselm L. and Juliet M. Corbin, *Basics of Qualitative Research: Techniques and Procedures for Developing Grounded Theory* (Thousand Oaks, CA: Sage, 1998).

Yanagi, Soetsu, *The Unknown Craftsman* (Tokyo: Kodashana, 1974).

Yoshida, Hiroshi, *Japanese Woodblock Printing* (Tokyo: Sanseido, 1939).

PART THREE
CRAFT THINKING IN A DIGITAL AGE

10
HAND KNITTING IN A DIGITAL ERA

Josephine Steed

Introduction

This chapter seeks to develop an argument for a more nuanced language in our critical understanding of the cultural and contextual significance of hand knitting within contemporary craft practice. It aims at developing a clearer articulation of the intrinsic complexities within this craft practice set against emergent digital contexts, technologies, and new modes of collaborative socially engaged practices.

The physical activity of hand knitting is a relatively simple repetitive action that has often been described as requiring limited skill or ability. Knitting at its most basic can be described as the transformation of a linear thread into an interwoven layered construct, whether as a hand-knitted flat-paneled jumper knitted on two pins or a complex multi-paneled whole garment produced on a high-end computer-controlled seamless 3D knitting machine. However, with these basic actions and processes, the transformation of yarn into artifacts is not the whole story or the starting point of this chapter. Instead, the author suggests deeper levels of complexity that are embedded within the hand knitting language informed by haptic, temporal, and cultural indices. There are greater levels of embodied tacit and experiential knowledge together with complex associations across cultures and customs that call for the development of a far more precise and appropriate language in contextualizing knitting against preconceptions of craft.

Through exploring a range of knitting practice together with new emergent designers working across conventional boundaries within knitting, this chapter challenges past perceptions by re-evaluating knitting as a unique skill and offers some thoughts on the process and knowledge embedded within knitting. The chapter attempts to develop a more meaningful language that clearly reflects and contextualizes the actual nature of knitting both practically and philosophically, seen against a digital technological and social backdrop.

Knitting as a "living" craft

In Sabrina Gschwandtner's article "Knitting is ...,"[1] the artist seeks to articulate the different characteristics of knitting when manifested within cultures as a language for participatory practice and community engagement. The article attempts to reposition knitting as a physical knowledge of culture where the knitted artifact is a living embodiment of human activity. This re-evaluation recognizes the innate complexities of knitting as a craft that is embedded in and reflective of broader cultural and social developments.[2]

We might look back to the lineage of knitting itself in order to start unpacking these predeterminations. As an ancient craft with its origins dating back to 1000 BC, knitting originated from hand knotting or twisting of yarns using fingers.[3] The word "knit" developed from the old English term *cnyttan*, and the German *knütten* developed to knot. Hand knitting rapidly advanced from fingers to hand tools known as pins into a skilled and complex craft where, by the fifth century AD, knitted objects such as socks are recorded, combining fashioning, seaming, and circular knitting together with patterning techniques simultaneously.[4] The deep associations and connections we have with knitting may also be tracked in many common phrases having their origin or meaning, where "knit" is often predicated in pronouncing this sense of connectedness—for example, "a close-knit family," "a tightly knit community," "knitted brows," "bones knitted together." This common linguistic adoption and the associations we have with "knit" as a verb reveal deep-rooted societal connections with the craft as an expression of broader cultural associations.

For a wider renewal of hand knitting, we must perhaps look to the pre- and post-war periods of the 1930s and 1940s where knitting was promoted as a patriotic and positive activity for those on the "home front" as part of their contribution to the war effort. Post-war hand knitting became part of the "make-do-and-mend" austerity campaign both in Britain and the United States, where novel knitted artifacts were created as tangible expressions of very personalized creativity and innovation. The campaign involved both deconstructing, "decoding," and redesigning old knitted goods, patterns, and yarns to produce unique knitted objects which quite often suggested or explicitly embedded personal narratives into the very "fabric" of the artifacts. Post-war industrialization and the commodification of knitted artifacts shifted knitting out of the home and onto the high street, subverting or undermining the status of hand knitting as a parochial craft merely concerned with preserving the past. Innovation in knitting was now firmly associated with mechanized manufacture, where the language or individual maker's vocabulary became simplified and ultimately alienated through the commodification and industrialization process itself.[5]

As hand knitting inclined to the margins as a viable manufacturing process, it was its long history of connecting people with their environment that came to the fore—from material source to the makers' largely unwritten generational knowledge of patterns and techniques—in clearly locating the craft of knitting against distinct communities and indigenous practices. The results of these knitted artifacts embodied more complex layers of narrative with hidden biographies and histories together with the "taciturn" knowledge of the maker. This phenomenon is clearly evidenced within indigenous craft. For example, in Iceland's sub-Arctic climate, the natural characteristics of Icelandic wool (both insulating and water-repellent), together with cultural pattern and garment construction work, visually and aesthetically differentiate the iconic Icelandic jumper. Likewise, in Shetland hand knitting still plays an important cultural and societal role whereby, due to the Islands' geographical remoteness and links with European traders, the traditions and customs of knitting have adapted and been preserved and continue to make an important contribution to the Islands' heritage, where the living skills of knitting are still retained.[6] The cultural identity of this remote archipelago is firmly bound up with hand knitting production, where it has been a prime creative and economic activity for around 5,000 years.[7] Knitting practitioners in Shetland today, such as Andrea Williamson, seamlessly combine traditional materials and patterns and demonstrate a renewal of interest in indigenous knitting. Williamson explains:

> Traditional Shetland knitting which has absorbed influences from centuries of trade links with Europe and Scandinavia is a constant source of inspiration. Old notebooks of patterns collected by family members, and garments that have survived over generations but are still vibrant and innovative, are a great reference.[8]

Inspired by national events such as the Royal Wedding and the Tall Ships arrival in Shetland, Williamson reappropriates traditional anchor and crown Fair Isle and lace patterns widely used in traditional Shetland knitting, giving new contemporary meaning to indigenous knitting (Plate 16). Further, this notion of these craft skills being alive and connected can be seen in the designer-researcher Hazel White's work "Hamefarers' Kist" inspired by Shetland life. She uses knitting as an interactive tool for generating collective memories across generations by sharing online photo albums with people who do not routinely use computers. The small box containing knitted pincushions, each one with a different pattern, is associated with people, places, or events (Figure 10.1). Using a "knitted remote," the Kist is an intuitive way of accessing online content and speculates how objects like these might be usefully integrated into our lives. Knitting within this context is intended to engage users with technology in an accessible and unobtrusive way.

Hand knitting is experiencing a revival of interest that challenges many previous assumptions that it is more concerned with the preservation of the past rather than as a medium that can be forward-thinking and progressive. New modes of practice, such as seen in Amy Twigger Holroyd's work, are emerging, which find new meaning for knitting—in Holroyd's case, re-knitting as a "craft of use" tool for exploring the potential of knitting as a strategy for sustainability.[9] Otto von Busch alludes to this wider contextual premise as the "Zen of knitting," being not merely a method of production but "a process of investigation and intervention" not unlike the game of chess.[10] Von Busch emphasizes that the whole entity of the human experience of knitting needs to be examined for future innovation rather than singular aspects such as process, tools, and finished artifact. "Crafts like knitting are not usually connected to the idea of progress, yet innovation is an inherent but often overlooked part of the practice," says von Busch.[11]

Figure 10.1 "Hamefarers' Kist," Hazel White, 2009. Photograph: Hazel White.

The evolution of knitting as a "living craft," then, clearly does embrace new iterations as an integrated and embedded craft within contemporary design, technology, and fashion innovation and recognizes a need for more critical analysis of the aesthetic and contemporary cultural narrative elements associated with the products of this medium. This renewal of interest, in particular of knitting as social intervention or collaborative movement, has been played out particularly within Europe and North America with socially proactive knitting groups, for instance Stitch 'n' Bitch,[12] or the politically motivated performance pieces of Liz Collins's Knitting Nation,[13] challenging our frames of reference. New generations of knitters across different demographics, generations, and types of practice, both amateur and professional, have emerged, who are "blogging," "twittering," "bombing," and "guerrilla-ing" their knitting.[14] In *The Culture of Knitting*, Turney recognizes the need for greater understanding and more critical approaches in re-examining the value and impact of knitting on contemporary culture and society.[15] Set against our physical communities' increased fragmentation into new cyberspace global villages, knitting has the potential to restore a sense of self and locality by better connecting people to places and history through both the haptic and temporal processes of making something by hand from start to finish.

Extending the language of knitting

The physical process of knitting is "easy." It is essentially created using two sticks or pins based on two stitches. It is highly accessible, portable, and simple, which may suggest that little skill or mental application is required.[16] However this assumption fails to recognize that the actual practice of knitting can also be complex, highly skilled, and difficult. In many respects, knitting is full of contradictions, cleverly disguising its true attributes and thus appearing harmless, non-threatening, and familiar. It is the "softer" skills of knitting that enable the medium to address "hard" issues in witty and creative ways. For example, Freddie Robins uses knitting to question issues related to domesticity, gender, and the human condition.[17] Due to the strong cultural preconceptions associated with knitting, her work disrupts the notion of craft being passive and benevolent.

In "Knitted Homes of Crime" (Figure 10.2), Robins uses knitting as a medium to address crimes by women in a soft yet provocative manner.[18] Through knitting she disrupts our assumptions of the home as a place of safety and domesticity. Another piece by Robins,

Figure 10.2 "Knitted Homes of Crime," Freddie Robins, 2002. Photograph: Douglas Atfield. © Freddie Robins.

"How to make a piece of work when you are too tired to make decisions," focuses on the process of making rather than the product as the main driver for her work. This relationship between the process and the product is central to understanding some of the key attributes of knitting. Each piece of knitting tells a story where the making process is an integral part of an experience, which often results in unfinished pieces. Referred to as "ephemeral joy,"[19] this phenomenon is well known in knitting circles, where the pleasure experienced by the knitter during making outweighs the need to produce a finished garment. Rachael Matthews, co-founder of a socially engaged network of knitters, refers to these as uFOs (un-Finished Objects), where uncompleted knitting projects lie dormant in homes, representing hours of invested time and memories.[20] Matthews's "uFO Project Administration Service" rehomes these abandoned knitted enterprises by inviting participants to engage with their history and embedding them with new knitted narratives.

In another sphere literally, Daina Taimina, a mathematician at Cornell University and the author of *Crocheting Adventures with Hyperbolic Plane*, uses crochet to visually understand complex three-dimensional forms.[21] Taimina invents and utilizes "hyperbolic crochet" to describe a space with a negative curvature that increases exponentially (Plate 17). With no formula available for this complex form, mathematicians were unable to physically visualize a hyberbolic curve and it was not until 1997, when Taimina made the first usable model of the curve using crochet, that mathematicians were for the first time able to visualize this form. She further explains:

> I have crocheted a number of these models and what I find so interesting is that when you make them you get a very concrete sense of the space expanding exponentially. The first rows take no time but the later rows can take literally hours, they have so many stitches. You get a visceral sense of what "hyperbolic" really means.[22]

The three examples here point to the diversity of the craft that explores and communicates a range of complex issues and contexts. In the case of Robins, the assumptions of knitting as "soft" and non-threatening are maneuvered away from the familiar safe territory of female domesticity towards a darker and more sinister perspective. Matthews explores the underlying process of knitting, reflecting on why we knit by inviting discussion based upon unfinished objects. In both cases, their knitting practices are focused on articulating human behavior and exposing personal lives through knitting. In contrast to this, Taimina's "hyberbolic crochet" uses soft craft skills to illustrate complex mathematical problems. Through using crocheted models in her teaching of complex geometry, she makes mathematics accessible and enables the boundaries of scientific and creative disciplines to converge.

Further to this and perhaps more importantly, knitting has become a powerful tool for politically and socially engaged practitioners, where it is at the forefront of forging new meaning for craft practice. In her collaborative performance work *Knitting Nation: Knitting During Wartime*, American artist and designer Liz Collins facilitates large groups of knitters to produce knitted banners and garments that contend with issues of nationalism, globalism, and community.[23] In addition, politically active knitting groups such as Knitta, a Houston-based group of amateur knitters who began the "knit graffitti" movement in 2005, posits knitting as an illegal activity.[24] Ranging in age from 23 to 71, these "guerrilla" knitters anonymously "tag" street lamps, public and private property, and bring new meaning by juxtaposing craft, graffiti, and vandalism. Thus, they reappropriate activity normally associated with male-dominated media. As the artist statement for the group explains further: "We prove that disobedience can be beautiful and that knitting can be outlaw."[25]

However, philosopher Michel Foucault challenges this perspective of knowledge, by advocating an "insurrection of subjugated knowledges" that revalues indigenous and naive knowledge in order to develop a better and more meaningful language appropriate for the real world.[26] Foucault's comments are focused upon here to illustrate that knowledge is primarily driven by our own human activity and social organization. Therefore the knowledge of knitting as an indigenous craft is by its nature inherently complex and multilayered, mirroring the desires and needs of society at any given time. In *Abstracting Craft: The Practiced Digital Hand,* Malcolm McCullough argues for the acceptance of digital technology into the craftsman's toolbox and questions why these new manifestations should be excluded from the presence of the craftsman's "hand" in these digital artifacts.[27] Linguistically, the term "craft" has been applied to any number of activities that are personal and require some mastery. Whereas the advancement of 3D printing and other rapid prototyping technologies are now able to separate digital craft practices from industrial design by producing "individually prepared" objects, digital craft may need to become more "haptic," or manipulated by the different aspects of touch, in order to be considered craft.

A social medium through new technology

The Web 2.0 and social networking have produced completely new modes of engagement and levels of collaboration. The egalitarian nature of the web has created platforms which are no longer limited by geographic or culturally fixed practices. This has transformed our understanding of networked interactions, insofar as online sites and services are no longer about passive audiences but building proactive communities of collaborators whereby DIY (do-it-yourself) online communities drive a new form of creative practice through sharing experiences via websites and blogs. Online knitting communities are driven by amateurs and consist of hobbyists and enthusiasts who evaluate and learn from one another to bring new methods of interaction across different areas of society, where free access to information and resources are blurring previous boundaries. This new wave of practitioners, the "amateur expert,"[28] brings new meaning to knitting, which is not motivated by commercial practice, and suggests alternative aims based on personal satisfaction, community values, and the intrinsic gratification experienced in the act of "making." The widespread use of the internet has introduced new tools for knitting where practitioners simultaneously use mouse and needle, knitting and blogging to develop new knitting communities that operate both locally and globally. This phenomenon is manifested in a project instigated through Ravelry, a social network for knitters that demonstrates the power of internet craft communities to foster new types of collaborative practice.[29] Called "The Queen Susan Shawl project," members recently recreated a "lost" knitting pattern. Through distributing the only existing record of the Queen Susan Shawl, a photograph available on the Shetland Museum Photographic Archive, knitters from across the world worked continuously in their different time zones to create a chart of the original design and produce a pattern that could be downloaded free of charge from Ravelry. A member's blog posting clearly summarizes the project thus:

> Think of it—a piece knitted before the turn of the last century, designed by a close group of family/friends living in an isolated area, preserved in a photograph, being recreated by a far-flung band brought together by technology and a love of this craft.[30]

In his book *Making is Connecting*, David Gauntlett discusses the power of the internet to drive a new direction for craft.[31] Seemingly contrary to values of hand making, knitters across the globe have embraced the web as a medium to inspire, encourage, and collaborate with an intensity and pace not previously possible.

We tend to view the final artifact as the only true expression of knitting, where innovation lies within the final object. However, as Otto von Busch points out, there is another layer of mathematical innovation, which he refers to as "micro-interventions," which can provide another perspective on our understanding of knitting.[32] At this micro level where a continuous thread or yarn is repeatedly looped and reconnected to itself, the craft has analogies to software protocols where a multitude of iterations are made possible. This mathematical coding of knitting, similar to weaving, is inextricably linked to technology, where the coding embedded within knitting patterns can be easily translated into the 0 and 1 binary code within computer circuitry.[33] Technology has for a long time been a major driver within knitting innovation, where the development of three-dimensional knitting machines in the mid-1990s in particular signified a paradigm shift in seamless knitwear manufacture.[34] Referred to as "New Craft,"[35] emergent digital interfaces for knitting provide an alternative craft practice which challenges established skills of hand making. New technological capabilities require a different set of design skills that go beyond merely production to "machine-thinking,"[36] making possible new types of design practice. New modes of knitting innovation are taking place—for example, the ideas and techniques employed by designer Rudiger Schlömer, whereby he attempts to reappropriate knitting technologies as well as their production methods to use them as tools with which to "hack." As Schlömer explains:

> The parallel to pixel graphics is probably one of the first things you notice when you look at knitting patterns, yes. And using patterns you're really counting the whole time. Knitting is a really repetitive movement—it's a loop out of a loop out of a loop; over, under, out of, into. It's very algorithmic, like analog programming.[37]

New flexible manufacturing technologies, for instance 3D scanning and printing, are set to further revolutionize traditional methods of production, and have major implications for knitting in the future.[38] Initially developed for the car and medical industries, users of the technology have started to research into softer products such as textiles. The

Dutch company Freedom of Creation[39] investigates the making of "immediate products" to create rapid prototyped stretch products that mimic the inherent characteristics of knitting. The company have high ambitions, stating: "Our goal is to replace traditional knitting."[40]

Technology also drives other types of innovation, namely a shift in focus from product towards experience. Japanese fashion designer Issey Miyake provides an example of innovation in this area through his A-POC (A Piece of Cloth) collection. A-POC utilizes knitting technology to produce knitted tubular fabric with integrated garment shapes that can be modified by the wearer to create customized body pieces. Developed in the late 1990s, this collection transformed the retail experience for Miyake's customers. Through creating a retail laboratory environment, Miyake engaged the wearer as co-designer, whereby their input became part of the design process. Similarly, the Considerate Design research project "Knit to Fit," a collaboration between London College of Fashion, the Open University, and Cambridge University's Engineering Design Centre, explored the personalized fashion experience within the context of seamless garment knitting.[41] This project addressed the use of three-dimensional body scan data for the extraction of precise body measurements and translation into two-dimensional computer-aided design systems integrated with industrial knitting machines. Its final aim was the direct three-dimensional production of seam-free knitwear with enhanced fit and customization for user requirements.

When using rapid technological innovations such as three-dimensional knitting and printing, a new approach to design practice is required to facilitate a sustainable future for knitting relevant to the demands of increasingly complex twenty-first-century technology and customer experience. As Suzanne Lee surmises in her book *Fashioning the Future: Tomorrow's Wardrobe*: "Technology is nothing without craft."[42]

This acknowledgement of the importance of craft is further expressed through the Emotional Wardrobe research project at the Central Saint Martins College of Art and Design.[43] The project focused on how fashion as an emotional and expressive medium can impact on the development of digital systems for clothing. The research discussed a number of issues concerning the future of design where, in the face of so much technological complexity, an understanding of a designer's core skills is paramount when working within transdisciplinary environments.

Conclusion

The perception of knitting as a mere "pastime" fails to recognize that it is unique in its simultaneous creation of surface, structure, and form. Unlike two-dimensional problem-solving, knitting explores the whole design problem and results in completed products from raw materials. This method of making uses code reading, together with additive and deductive techniques, and demonstrates that knitting is a holistic design approach. As a hybrid craft, the skills of knitting occupy the space between disciplines that embrace both craft and industry and that have over time developed through hand skills, then mechanical operation, and more recently through electronic and digital technologies.

In addition to this, knitting is a craft which is firmly rooted within society, where it has always been a method for expressing oral history, facilitating community engagement, and expressing deep personal attachments.

A new role for knitting has emerged in recent years across an increasingly diverse range of creative practices, demonstrating the intrinsic value of knitting within new contexts that challenges definitions and the language of this craft practice. Hand knitting can offer another type of perspective on problem-solving that, due to its inherent qualities as an accessible medium, enables complex themes to be explored by both experts and amateurs alike. It is in fact these qualities of inclusivity and accessibility, together with inherent participatory and collaborative values, which suggest that knitting skills and knowledge have more to offer than previously thought. Further, the ability of knitting to transform from raw material to three-dimensional forms suggests much closer synergies between knitting and complex emergent technologies, such as 3D printing, than perhaps previously considered.

The design and technology relationship is becoming ever more complex. Different approaches to design are therefore necessary with particular emphasis placed on interactions involving process, experience, and meaning embodied within the knitted artifact. As contemporary practice becomes progressively more sophisticated, new models are required, and experts from across the sciences and design disciplines need to be brought together to explore new territories. Further research is now required to examine the broader knowledge base of knitting to reveal the potential benefits of knitting methodologies, which can be applied within different scenarios. In short, we need to find out if knitting can be developed into a more nuanced language that can add new value to complex design problems.

Notes

1. Sabrina Gschwandtner, "Knitting is …", *The Journal of Modern Craft* 1 (2) (2008): 271–8. Sabrina Gschwandtner is a New York-based artist who works with a range of photographic and textile media. Her artwork has been exhibited at various international museums and galleries, including the Museum of Arts and Design, New York and the Fleming Museum. See http://sabrinag.com [accessed May 25, 2015].
2. Sandy Black, *Knitwear in Fashion* (London: Thames and Hudson, 2002), 6; Joanne Turney, *The Culture of Knitting* (Oxford: Berg, 2009), 4.
3. James Norbury, *The Penguin Knitting Book* (London: Penguin Books, 1957), 15.
4. David J. Spencer, *Knitting Technology: A Comprehensive Handbook and Practical Guide to Modern Day Principles and Practices* (Oxford: Pergamon Press, 1989), 6.
5. Claudia Eckert, Martin Stacey, and Christopher Earl, "References to Past Designs," in *Studying Designers '05*, ed. John S. Gero and Nathalie Bonnardel (Sydney, Australia: Key Centre of Design Computing and Cognition, 2005), 3–21. http://oro.open.ac.uk/7412/1/past_designs_from_SD05_PROCEEDINGS-2.pdf [accessed May 25, 2015].
6. Shetland Government, "On the Cusp … Shetland's Cultural Strategy, A Vision for Cultural Life in Shetland 2009–2013" (n.d.). http://www.shetland.gov.uk/community_planning_dev/documents/CulturalStrategyDigital.pdf [accessed May 25, 2015].

7   Linda G. Fryer, *Knitting By the Fireside and On the Hillside: A History of the Shetland Hand Knitting Industry c.1600–1950* (Lerwick: The Shetland Times, 1995).
8   Andrea Williamson. See http://www.andreawilliamson.co.uk/images/gallery/about.swf [accessed June 4, 2015].
9   Amy Twigger Holroyd is a designer, maker, and researcher. Her knitwear label *Keep & Share* explores the relationship between fashion, making, design, and sustainability. http://www.keepandshare.co.uk [accessed May 25, 2015].
10 Otto von Busch, "Zen and the Abstract Machine of Knitting," *Textile: The Journal of Cloth and Culture* 11 (1) (2013): 6–19. Otto von Busch is a researcher at Business and Design Lab, School of Design and Craft, University of Gothenburg and at Parsons The New School of Design, New York. His research topics include socially engaged craft and DIY culture, fashion, and social innovation.
11 Von Busch, "Zen and the Abstract Machine of Knitting," 7.
12 Stitch 'n' Bitch is an international social knitting network. Set up by Debbie Stoller in 1999 in New York, the network has been at the forefront of inspiring a new generation of knitters who are politically and socially active. http://www.stitchnbitch.org [accessed May 25, 2015].
13 American artist and designer Liz Collins has created a series of multimedia site-specific installations and performance projects called *Knitting Nation* as a response to working in the textiles and fashion industries, and has staged several exciting, large-scale events involving a small army of uniformed knitters and manually operated knitting machines. http://www.lizcollins.com/projects/knitting-nation [accessed May 25, 2015].
14 "Yarn bombing" and "guerrilla knitting" are types of graffiti that use knitting or crochet rather than paint or chalk.
15 Turney, *The Culture of Knitting*, 2–5.
16 Gschwandtner, "Knitting is …".
17 Freddie Robins. http://www.freddierobins.com [accessed May 25, 2015].
18 Turney, *The Culture of Knitting*, 112.
19 TECH-knitter, "Two bits of knitting theory: the 'work-to-glory' ratio and 'product plus-process'," *TECH-knitter* (9 November 2009). http://techknitting.blogspot.com/2009/11/two-bits-of-knitting-theory-work-to.html [accessed June 4, 2015].
20 Textile artist Rachael Matthews is the co-founder of the Cast Off knitting club—a democratic and proactive knitting club. See http://prickyourfinger.blogspot.co.uk/2009/04/ufo-project-administration-service.html [accessed May 25, 2015] and http://www.castoff.info [accessed May 25, 2015].
21 Daina Taimina, *Crocheting Adventures with Hyperbolic Planes* (Wellesley, MA: A. K. Peters, 2009).
22 Margaret Wertheim, David Henderson, and Daina Taimina, "Crocheting the Hyperbolic Plane: An Interview with David Henderson and Daina Taimina," *Cabinet* 16 (Winter 2004/05). http://www.cabinetmagazine.org/issues/16/crocheting.php [accessed May 25, 2015].
23 David Revere McFadden, Jennifer Scanlan, and Jennifer Steifle Edwards, *Radical Lace & Subversive Knitting* (New York: Museum of Arts and Design, 2007), 22–5.
24 Knitta is a group of artists who began the "knit graffiti" movement in Houston, Texas, in 2005. http://knitta.com [accessed May 25, 2015].
25 Sabrina Gschwandtner, *KnitKnit: Profiles + Projects from Knitting's New Wave* (New York: Stewart, Tabori and Chang, 2007), 92.
26 Michel Foucault, *Power/Knowledge: Selected Interviews and Other Writings, 1972–1977* (New York: Pantheon Books, 1980), 81.

27 Malcolm McCullough, *Abstracting Craft: The Practiced Digital Hand* (Cambridge MA: MIT Press, 1998).

28 Stacey Kuznetsov and Eric Paulos, "Rise of the Expert Amateur: DIY Projects, Communities, and Cultures," in *Proceedings of the Sixth Nordic Conference on Human–Computer Interaction* (New York: ACM, 2010), 295–304. http://www.staceyk.org/hci/KuznetsovDIY.pdf [accessed May 25, 2015].

29 Ravelry is a free social networking website, beta-launched in May 2007. It functions as an organizational tool for a variety of fiber arts including knitting, crocheting, spinning, and weaving. As of 28 February 2014, Ravelry had four million members worldwide. See http://www.ravelry.com [accessed May 25, 2015].

30 http://www.ravelry.com/patterns/library/the-queen-susan-shawl. For pattern created and blogger's quote. http://fleeglesblog.blogspot.com/2009/11/queen-susan-shawl.html [accessed May 25, 2015].

31 David Gauntlett, *Making is Connecting: The Social Meaning of Creativity, from DIY and Knitting to Youtube and Web 2.0* (Cambridge: Polity Press, 2011).

32 Von Busch, "Zen and the Abstract Machine of Knitting," 8.

33 Sabine Seymour, *Fashionable Technology: The Intersection of Design, Fashion, Science, and Technology* (Vienna: SpringerWienNewYork, 2008), 15.

34 Kate Sayer, Jacquie Wilson, and Simon Challis, "Seamless Knitwear—The Design Skills Gap," *The Design Journal* 9 (2) (2006), 39–51.

35 Robyn Healy, *The Endless Garment: The New Craft of Machine Knitting* (Melbourne: RMIT Gallery, 2010), 5.

36 Ibid.

37 Nick Currie, "From Words of Wool: An Interview with Rudiger Schlömer" (13 May 2008). http://www.aiga.org/words-of-wool-an-interview-with-rudiger-schlomer [accessed May 25, 2015].

38 Jan Brand, *Beyond Green: Sustainability & Fashion* (Arnhem: Artez Press, 2008).

39 Freedom of Creation. http://www.freedomofcreation.com [accessed May 25, 2015].

40 Brand, *Beyond Green*, 86.

41 The Considerate Design Project is a research collaboration between London College of Fashion, the Open University, and the Engineering Design Centre at Cambridge University funded by the research councils AHRC and EPSRC. http://www.consideratedesign.com/projects/knit-for-fit [accessed May 25, 2015].

42 Suzanne Lee, *Fashioning the Future: Tomorrow's Wardrobe* (London: Thames and Hudson, 2007), 18.

43 The Emotional Wardrobe (EW) was Phase 1 of Designing for the 21st Century Research Cluster supported by the UK's Engineering and Physical Sciences Research Council (EPSRC) and Arts and Humanities Research Council (AHRC). http://www.design21.dundee.ac.uk/Phase1/21Clusters/Emotional_Wardrobe.htm [accessed May 25, 2015].

Bibliography

Black, Sandy, *Knitwear in Fashion* (London: Thames and Hudson, 2002).
Brand, Jan, *Beyond Green: Sustainability & Fashion* (Arnhem: Artez Press, 2008).
Currie, Nick, "From Words of Wool: An Interview with Rudiger Schlömer" (May 13, 2008). http://www.aiga.org/words-of-wool-an-interview-with-rudiger-schlomer [accessed May 25, 2015].

Eckert, Claudia, Martin Stacey, and Christopher Earl, "References to Past Designs," in *Proceedings of Studying Designers '05, Aix-en-Provence* (Sydney: Key Centre for Design Computing and Cognition, 2005). http://oro.open.ac.uk/7412/1/past_designs_from_SD05_PROCEEDINGS-2.pdf [accessed May 25, 2015].

Foucault, Michel, *Power/Knowledge: Selected Interviews and Other Writings, 1972–1977* (New York: Pantheon Books, 1980).

Fryer, Linda G., *Knitting By the Fireside and On the Hillside, A History of the Shetland Hand Knitting Industry c.1600–1950* (Lerwick: The Shetland Times, 1995).

Gauntlett, David, *Making is Connecting: The Social Meaning of Creativity, from DIY and Knitting to Youtube and Web 2.0* (Cambridge: Polity Press, 2011).

Gschwandtner, Sabrina, *KnitKnit: Profiles + Projects from Knitting's New Wave* (New York: Stewart, Tabori and Chang, 2007).

Gschwandtner, Sabrina, "Knitting is …", *The Journal of Modern Craft* 1 (2) (2008): 271–8.

Healy, Robyn, *The Endless Garment: The New Craft of Machine Knitting* (Melbourne: RMIT Gallery, 2010).

Kuznetsov, Stacey, and Eric Paulos, "Rise of the Expert Amateur: DIY Projects, Communities, and Cultures," in *Proceedings of the Sixth Nordic Conference on Human–Computer Interaction* (New York: ACM, 2010), 295–304. http://www.staceyk.org/hci/KuznetsovDIY.pdf [accessed May 25, 2015].

Lee, Suzanne, *Fashioning the Future: Tomorrow's Wardrobe* (London: Thames and Hudson, 2007).

McCullough, Malcolm, *Abstracting Craft: The Practiced Digital Hand* (Cambridge, MA: MIT Press, 1998).

McFadden, David Revere, Jennifer Scanlan, and Jennifer Steifle, *Radical Lace & Subversive Knitting* (New York: Museum of Arts and Design, 2007).

Norbury, James, *The Penguin Knitting Book* (London: Penguin Books, 1957).

Sayer, Kate, Jacquie Wilson, and Simon Challis, "Seamless Knitwear—The Design Skills Gap," *The Design Journal* 9 (2) (2006): 39–51.

Seymour, Sabine, *Fashionable Technology: The Intersection of Design, Fashion, Science, and Technology* (Vienna: SpringerWienNewYork, 2008).

Shetland Government, "On the Cusp: Shetland's Cultural Strategy, A Vision for Cultural Life in Shetland 2009–2013" (n.d.). http://www.shetland.gov.uk/community_planning_dev/documents/CulturalStrategyDigital.pdf [accessed May 25, 2015].

Spencer, David J., *Knitting Technology: A Comprehensive Handbook and Practical Guide to Modern Day Principles and Practices*, 2nd edn (Oxford: Pergamon Press, 1989).

Taimina, Daina, *Crocheting Adventures with Hyperbolic Planes* (Wellesley, MA: A. K. Peters, 2009).

TECH-knitter. "Two bits of knitting theory: the 'work-to-glory' ratio and 'product-plus-process'," *TECH-knitter* (9 November 2009). http://techknitting.blogspot.com/2009/11/two-bits-of-knitting-theory-work-to.html [accessed May 25, 2015].

Turney, Joanne, *The Culture of Knitting* (Oxford: Berg, 2009).

Von Busch, Otto, "Zen and the Abstract Machine of Knitting," *Textile: The Journal of Cloth and Culture* 11 (1) (2013): 6–19.

Wertheim, Margaret, David Henderson, and Daina Taimina, "Crocheting the Hyperbolic Plane: An Interview with David Henderson and Daina Taimina," *Cabinet* 16 (Winter 2004/05). http://www.cabinetmagazine.org/issues/16/crocheting.php [accessed May 25, 2015].

11
HIDDEN VALUES AND HUMAN INCONSISTENCIES IN HAND STITCHING PROCESSES

Emma Shercliff

A new craft revival

The proliferation of interest in textile crafts in contemporary Western cultures is indisputable. Since craft in the UK was conceived as distinct from both fine art and artisanal labor in the mid-nineteenth century,[1] there have been a number of craft revivals. Each resurgence of a cultural or popular recognition of craft seems to coincide with periods when craft skills are perceived to be almost in danger of being lost, or in transition to become something else through the introduction of new technologies, economics, or politics.[2] When considered thus, as a culture that appears to be disappearing, craft is retrieved and reclaimed enthusiastically, idealized as especially meaningful or valuable.[3] Reflecting this, hand stitching tends to have an ambiguous status; it is both revered by some and ridiculed by others. This labor-intensive and precise craft currently attracts both popular and avant-garde interest as part of this wider craft revival and is visible in a variety of contexts.[4]

The phenomenon itself invites research, as each new craft revival has different historical contexts and slightly different values. With the growth of screen-mediated virtual cultures in a postmodern and post-industrial UK, the specific qualities of hand making take on new meanings and suggest new possibilities.[5] Architect Juhani Pallasmaa claims that "our embodied existence is rarely identified as the very basis of our interaction and integration with the world, or of our consciousness and self-understanding."[6] Because there are computer-aided machines to execute tedious, repetitive tasks like stitching at speed and with accuracy, the particular instances of voluntarily using our hands in time-consuming craft activities merit re-examination. I argue that hand stitching cultivates a distinctive form of attention to the self that has renewed significance in the context of the commonplace anti-haptic experiences of keyboard and screen interactions that now infiltrate daily routines in the home and the workplace. In this world overwhelmed by the convenient speed and spontaneity of visual information, where image and concept hold supremacy over sensory experience,[7] the processes involved in making things by hand remind us that we are physically grounded by our bodies in a material world. As philosopher Matthew Crawford proposes:

> Thinking about manual engagement seems to require nothing less than that we consider what a human being is. That is, we are led to consider how the specifically human manner of being is lit up, as it were, by man's interaction with his world through his hands.[8]

As a "manual" craft, to use Crawford's terms, hand stitching activates the articulation of the hand, eye, mind, memory, and material. This chapter explores some of the cognitive and emotional qualities particular to hand stitching processes in order to be able to respond to Crawford's proposition. The examples discussed suggest that the practice of hand stitching is a process that needs to be understood as a mode of interaction if it is not merely trivialized as quaint or domestic labor, or archived as ethnographic curiosity or art object.

The hegemony of digital production methods has transformed the human experience of working by hand. These new technologies currently redefine the body and the hand, as mechanization redefined manual labor in the eighteenth and nineteenth centuries.[9] Contemporary fashionable aesthetic qualities that speak seductively of the handmade might include: (1) uniquely individual products made to the customer's own specifications; (2) exclusive artifacts that demonstrate a high degree of care and attention to detail in their design and manufacture; or (3) the current trend for all things vintage, particularly the "make do and mend" revival that reflects a well-marketed, nostalgic ideal of a hand-worked past. These qualities can be and are reproduced easily by machines. However, it is the qualities a machine cannot reproduce or mimic that I am interested in. The body and the senses are not relied upon as they once were in manually skilled manufacturing processes, but the human scale of the body, its inner biological rhythms and emotional responses may be used to measure a different sort of performance.

In contrast to the reproducible perfection (or imperfection) achieved by machine-made textiles, hand making reflects the uniqueness of the individual and reminds us of our human inconsistencies. The infinite differences represented by traces of the hand no longer indicate imperfection keenly replaced by machine uniformity, but on the contrary are prized and valued representations of personal expression. The visible mark of the hand signals the physical presence of the human being. In fast-paced, digitally mediated lifestyles, much can pass us by without leaving any real impression or testament to us "being there" and "having done it." A handmade artifact is a document of close physical interaction between the maker and their world.

Making processes: "In touch" with the world

Handmade samples and artifacts demonstrate inquisitive, exploring hands knowledgeable about their world—hands that know how to handle and manipulate materials, hands that interact with the material world. This is described by Pamela Johnson as "[t]he need to make, to engage with the world in a tactile way, the need to transform materials or to respond to those transformations … an articulation of being in the world through the senses."[10] Making things can be a more complex process than might be initially thought. It involves several different kinds of processes that inform each other and overlap. As human beings we use our emotions and our senses to explore and interact with our world as an ongoing experience and evolving relationship with materials and things. On this I agree with anthropologist Tim Ingold's view. He "considers the process and practice of making, skills and intelligence as emerging from a progressive and continual adjustment of practitioners' perception and body movements in relation to their environment."[11] This view is shared by Martina Margetts, who states that "making is a revelation of the human impulse to explore and express forms of knowledge and a range of emotions; an impulse towards knowing and feeling, which shapes human action and hence the world we create."[12] She also implies that this is an ongoing process of interaction that continually transforms both the person "doing" and the world being "done to." The processes of making, like the acquisition of experience and knowledge, reveal tentative explorations towards an external world. The thing made renders these encounters and transformations visible and tangible, and contains within it a document of the processes undergone.

An encounter suggests an unfamiliar or unforeseen "coming-up-against."[13] "Coming-up-against" is critical here as it implies being "in-contact-with." There is, therefore, a physical and active dimension to an encounter. All senses are alert to the event. The sensory boundary between the self and the thing encountered is permeable and an impression is made. Through touch, smell, sound, and vision, elements of the thing encountered seep into and enmesh with the self, thereby transforming one's knowledge of the surrounding material world. Philosopher Michel Serres's writing about the sense of touch in his book *The Five Senses: A Philosophy of Mingled Bodies* proposes that the body meets the world through the skin in a mutual touching where things mingle: "I mix with the world which mixes with me. Skin intervenes between several things in the world and makes them mingle."[14]

Overlapping these processes of discovery and creation is a process of knowledge acquisition. The hands draw upon the knowledge they already hold from previous encounters and manipulations with materials; they negotiate constantly with the new idea held in the mind tacitly and new knowledge gained from the experiences had during this new encounter.[15] Artifacts are produced out of this stimulating process of encounter, exploration, and interpretation between the eye, hand, mind, materials, and method as by-products of material investigations that lead to further discoveries, acquaintances, and conversations with the world. As poet Joseph Brodsky explains, these actions are possibly more emotionally and cognitively stimulating in a maker's consciousness than the product: "the first, the second, and the last reality for him is the work itself, the very process of working. The process takes precedence over its result."[16]

Ethologist Ellen Dissanayake also considers this "behavioral tendency" to be more meaningful than the result. Her term for creative activity is "making special,"[17] which as a verb in the present continuous conveniently relocates the emphasis from the artifact to the process of making. She writes: "Making special emphasizes the idea that the arts ... have been physically, sensuously, and emotionally satisfying and pleasurable to humans."[18] Noting that a great deal of time and effort is spent on what might appear to be gratuitous pastimes that take away energy from more directly useful activities, she proposes that making might be considered as a human behavioral trait that "satisfies an intrinsic and deep human imperative."[19] She suggests that this type of pleasure derived from handling and making is "hardwired into human nature," citing the example of babies born with incipient hand movements that presage the grasping, gripping, and handling of things, leading to more sophisticated patterns of playful experimentation, and potentially to tool use and making.[20] Discovering our potential to "make" our relationship to the material world is associated with meaningful and pleasurable sensations and emotions for good reason; it fuels our curiosity and we therefore continue to make our world.

Methods used: Hand stitching workshops

I have found "hidden" a useful concept through which to study this physical quest for knowledge. The mark of the hand visible in handmade artifacts represents a store of knowledge and information that is often unwritten and non-verbalized. This "hidden" knowledge embodied in the handmade artifact implies here that such knowledge cannot be put into words and is unmeasurable and often taken for granted.

As part of my doctoral research, I conducted a series of practical workshops to explore ways of investigating and articulating elements of this "hidden" knowledge, such as the specificity of manual engagement in hand stitching processes, the sorts of embodied knowledge sought and acquired, and the nature of the interactions it makes possible. Over a period of five months, I ran three workshops with students: two at the Royal College of Art with participants of varied stitching experience, and one at the Arts University Bournemouth with experienced stitchers.[21] The workshops involved drawing and hand stitching exercises as stimuli for discussion with participants, with the expectation that the conversation prompted by the immediacy of the experience of stitching might offer different insights from those achieved by interviews or questionnaires. I discuss here observations drawn from the conversations and artifacts made during these workshops.

Paying attention

Hand stitching is precise work. The deft coordination of the hand, eye, and mind in the making of stitches demands that one pays attention. Importantly, each repeated gesture

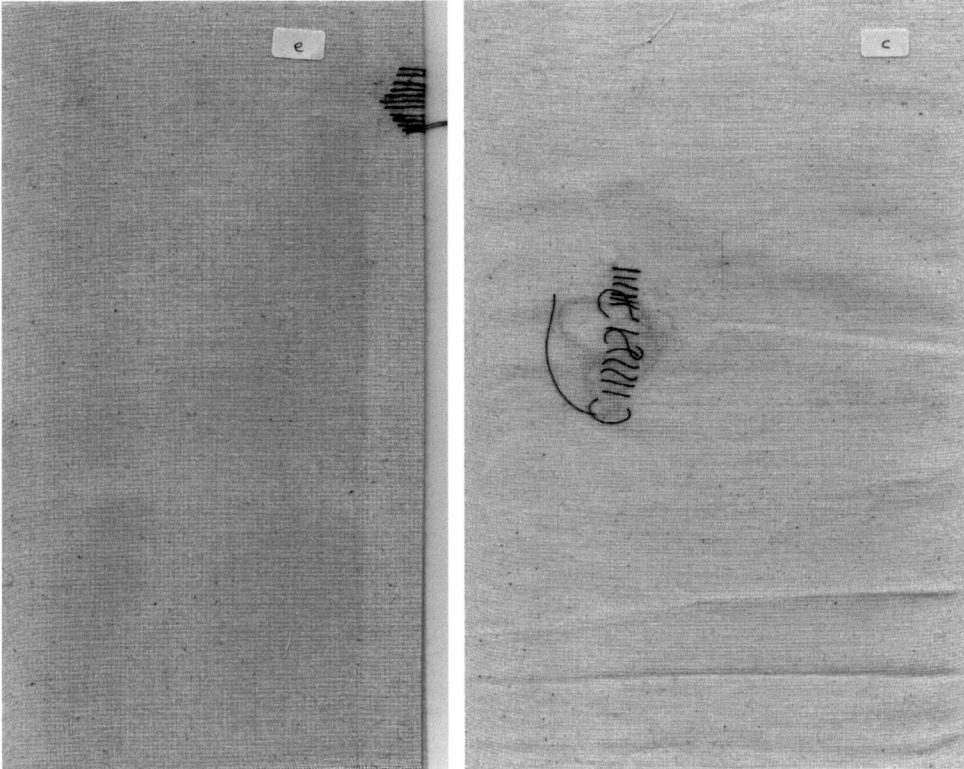

Figure 11.1 Samples from the first workshop, held at the Royal College of Art, made by participants with varied skill levels. Left: skilled in the basics, having to pay attention to the placement of the needle. Right: moderately skilled, having to pay attention not to pull the tension of the thread taut. Photograph: Emma Shercliff.

is almost the same each time—so similar that the body repeats it without having to learn a new movement, but each time a minute adjustment of placement or direction retains the mind's attention. The attention requires a combination of senses, especially touch and vision, adjusting spontaneously to constantly changing stimuli.

Depending on the task, the stage of execution, and the skill of the stitcher, the type of attention may vary. A participant with only basic skills explained her need to pay close attention: "If you come from a non-practical stitching point of view, as I do … what was difficult was to actually put the needle in the right place … I needed to concentrate more."[22] And a skilled participant unlearning a technique was acutely aware of the level of attention necessary to prevent the automatic responses of her hand: "I was automatically pulling it to make sure that the tension was right … I had to consciously pull the thread out again … I don't know how much my hand is used to it, but it kind of did it on its own." Figure 11.1 illustrates the samples from this first workshop evidencing the traces of the related hand stitching tasks made by the participants.

The slow rhythm of hand stitching sets up a particular frame of mind that absorbs the individual in the task. The rhythmic, repetitive, accumulative gestures generate conditions

Figure 11.2 With bowed head and work held close to the torso, the body manipulates itself to facilitate the close attention and focused concentration required for hand stitching. Photograph: Emma Shercliff.

that draw together mind and body and inspire a focused attention on the moment in hand. Indeed the posture adopted by the body while stitching (Figure 11.2) seems deliberately to pull the hands, eye, and mind closer together in their shared concentration. Other activities described by the participants as demanding similar types of attention include driving, drawing, and model aeroplane making. The mind and body are fully engaged in the activity, albeit while sitting still. Pallasmaa describes this "mental and material flow between the maker and the work" as "so tantalising that the work seems to be producing itself."[23]

Although David Pye was an outspoken critic of the Arts and Crafts ideals, he appears to agree with William Morris about "that mysterious bodily pleasure which goes with the deft exercise of the bodily powers."[24] Pye admits that "there can be a certain pleasure in finding that one's judgement is being exercised only half-consciously, and in letting the process continue … One can, for instance, do a great deal of sawing and chopping without quite knowing how one has arrived at the result correctly. The hands appear to do it on their own, without referring to the head."[25] The focused hand–eye coordination required for the combination of precision and repetition of these gestures engenders an almost trance-like state of mind.

The words used to describe this experience include phrases like "drawn in by," "lose myself," "disappear," which suggest the sensation of being absorbed into, merged with, or swallowed up by the work—letting oneself become part of the work without quite knowing how it happened.[26] The boundary of the self is blurred with that of the work. The self as a contained subject, normally conscious of where the body stops and the external world begins, relapses into a "lost 'oceanic' state of synaesthetic synergy, where boundaries differentiating self from other have become fluid, permeable or mutable."[27] The normally clear distinctions between the person doing and the thing being done to, between subject and object, are temporarily suspended, as is the sense of time passing, and even of location. Claire Pajaczkowska proposes the term "haptic"—the muscular action of manual dexterity and the sensory relationship between vision and touch—as a clue. Like knowledge acquired tacitly, a haptic experience is outside language, beyond the reach of words and the formal rules of syntax and grammar. It does not adhere to the rule of subject, object, verb: "'Doing' can have the meaning of 'being done to' in a way that combines active and passive both simultaneously and indivisibly."[28] Ingold writes of things leaking: "[I]t is in the opposite of capture and containment, namely discharge and leakage, that we discover the life of things."[29] Paradoxically, it is in these moments of suspending reality that we discover the life of things, that we are most in touch with the world.

Positive psychology offers another explanation. This total absorption with the task in hand, this feeling of wholeness, typically generates a heightened sense of self-awareness and a losing track of time that is described by psychologist Mihaly Csikszentmihalyi in his research into states of optimal experience as "flow."[30] Flow is understood to be a form of pleasure that arises from total absorption in an intrinsically motivating activity, as described in the words of one participant: "You really get into it and you can't stop." It is a component of an experience worth having for its own sake, independent of any other type of external reward.

On the other hand, once the pattern of the gesture is recognized and is settled into a rhythm, concentration may change its focus. This is illustrated by a participant accomplished in hand stitching who, having made her design decisions, describes the execution as "a purely enjoyable process you know, I could do anything, I could watch telly ... not something new, one of my favorite films, one I've watched a hundred times before ... I could talk on the internet with my friends."

Doing as a way of knowing

Tacit knowledge is the term used to describe the phenomenon of the body learning how to do something and to consequently store this knowledge to refer back to and use intuitively to execute tasks like cooking, driving, and making things. Craft critic Peter Dormer called it "personal" and "practical know-how."[31] It is acquired from watching others and by practicing through physically engaging the body, as opposed to reading instructions in a book. The knowledge is evidenced in the doing, and can become so habitual as to go unacknowledged. Yet these actions of the body are intentional and thereby imply an understanding of the possible consequences, explained by Christopher Frayling as "the knowledge which enables him to understand and overcome the constantly arising difficulties that grow out of variations."[32]

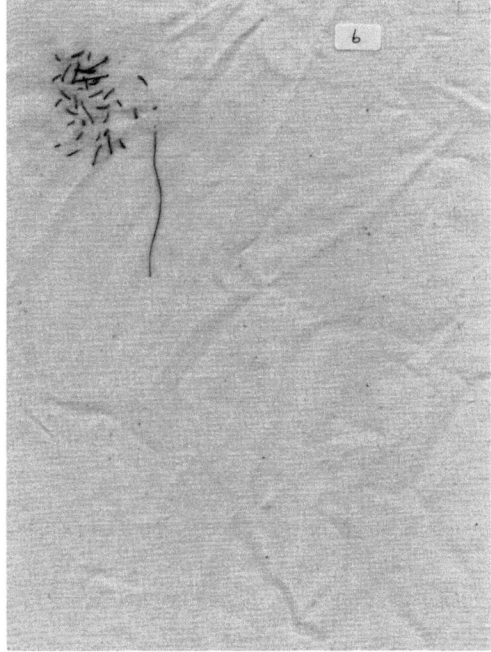

Figure 11.3 The participant initially ranked the sample on the left, executed by me prior to the workshop, as the least aesthetically pleasing. After executing the task herself, shown in the sample on the right, she then ranked it the most aesthetically pleasing. Photograph: Emma Shercliff.

Listening to participants' comments, I discovered that the knowledge gained from doing is a notably different experience from that of looking. The first workshop requested participants to make value judgements of simple stitching tasks I had executed myself prior to the workshops, first by looking and, second as a result of having done the tasks themselves. Their evaluation changed; the doing altered their perception of the stitching. Referring to the sample on the left in Figure 11.3, having made her own version (shown on the right), one participant explains: "I found that my evaluation in terms of its aesthetic qualities changed a bit after doing it according to which I enjoyed more." Other participants express similar changes of perception: "There is a change in the balance of how I appreciated the patterns and textures after I made it myself," and "[n]ow I've done it, it gives me a different insight." A process is not necessarily apparent from just looking at an artifact. Doing the tasks led to a deeper appreciation of what is perceived visually.

Embodied intelligence

The coordination of the eye, hand, and mind is therefore not limited to equipping an individual to mechanically execute practical tasks. A later exercise illuminated ways in which the careful coordination of hands that "appear to do it on their own, without referring to the head"[33] can be applied to understand and interpret hand stitching without recourse to verbal instruction.

Without prior discussion or explanation, each participant was required to reproduce a piece of stitching that had been made by another. They therefore drew on their store of tacitly acquired practical knowledge to work out which methods were used by their partner stitcher and then again to reproduce the techniques they recognized. In this workshop, all participants sought to interpret the original work with a personal response. Plate 18 illustrates two of these pairings and shows the possible extent and variation of this kind of practical understanding and interpretation.

Initially, all participants found it difficult to describe in words how they had set about the task. The activity was performed by the thinking hands without recourse to language, as described by Pallasmaa: "Artistic images expose us to images and encounters of things before they have been trapped by language. We touch things and grasp their essence before we are able to speak about them."[34] Further discussion revealed that the eye, hand, and mind were working simultaneously, intuiting how to make the work: looking closely to dissect what had been done, drawing on their own views to interpret the intentions of their partner, and on their store of practical knowledge to execute the task. Fingers holding the needle feel across the fabric and search for the exact position to reinsert the needle, in cooperation with the eyes that check resemblance and the mind that imagines the interpretive response. A sensual intelligence[35] accompanies the dexterity and precision of handling and positioning the needle as hands gauge distance and use pressure in their search, feeling when the tension of the thread is sufficient to have satisfactorily made a stitch. The tacit knowledge held by the hands means they know what the fabric and thread should feel like as they work, while their eyes consciously attend to the kind of stitch they want to be seen.[36] Richard Sennett describes this as "a constant interplay between tacit knowledge and self-conscious awareness, the tacit knowledge serving as an anchor, the explicit awareness serving as critique and corrective."[37]

Emotional responses

Such encounters as described above are perceived as emotional as well as sensory experiences. The emotions involved fall into different categories. Sometimes they are intimately entwined with the maker's sense of self, their identity, and their connections with people and places. Other categories concern the challenges encountered in solving problems, for example, the frustration felt at not finding the appropriate technique and spoiling materials by having to unpick and re-stitch, or the shyness felt when faced with

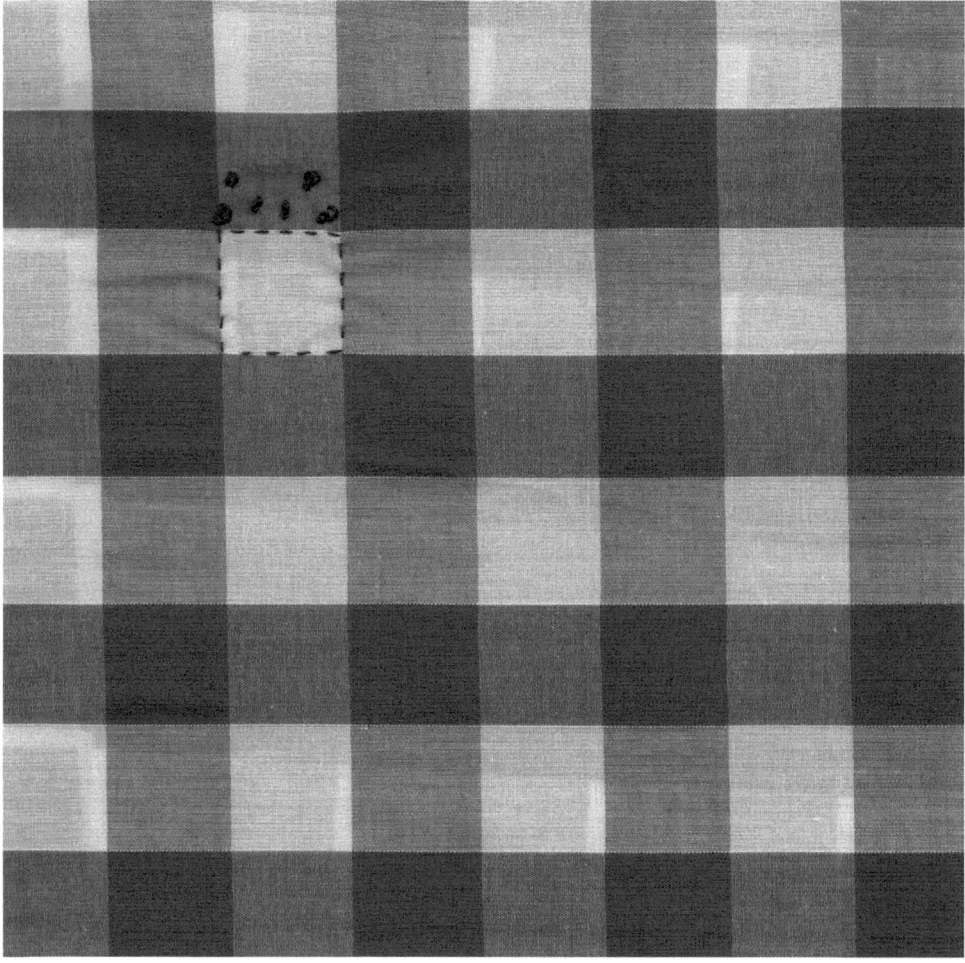

Figure 11.4 "Blending In": subtly intervening on a found fabric by neatly outlining and filling in the gingham checks. Photograph: Emma Shercliff.

a new material or method, or the nervousness when learning a new manual skill. Practical knowledge is applied and challenged, but the emotions are also called upon to drive the activity and make decisions.

On the one hand, a simple task of stitching a straight line in parallel to the edge of the cloth demonstrated how the more prescriptive the task is for an accomplished stitcher, the less the emotional involvement. One participant explains: "You didn't really have to think for that one ... not really a lot of emotion ... [I] paid attention to a certain extent, just trying to make it straight enough for it to be a line ... You could think about other things while doing it."

However, the more open to interpretation the task is, the greater the attention paid and the stronger the emotional involvement. My invitation to respond freely to found fabrics, already colored and patterned, provoked overtly emotional responses as the participants tried to find a way to intervene on the material by using hand stitching. In order to find a way of executing the task satisfactorily, the participants seemed to come up against what Pajaczkowska describes as the "paradox of destruction and creation" inherent to hand stitching.[38] They experienced this particular stitching task diversely as an empathetic integration, or aggressive possession or frustration. For instance, one participant, who had chosen a fabric she liked, followed the contours of the existing shapes with her stitching, describing that she was "using the shapes that were on the fabric already and just adding to it really ... I think I blended in a bit ... It's quite an easy fabric to add to." She felt surprised and slightly disappointed at her subtle intervention (Figure 11.4), thinking it perhaps ought to have been visibly more dramatic.

Another participant described her response as being motivated by the extreme emotions of hate, love, and anger in an attempt to overpower the material and to find a way of possessing it in order to transform it. Her intervention (Figure 11.5) is also inspired by the existing motif, but instead of blending in, her stitching almost smothers it. She explains:

> I think mine stands out. It's quite obvious that I've added to it. I didn't do it to make it blend in. For me that was like vandalism, it was like graffiti ... so I didn't want it to blend in ... I'd rather passionately hate or absolutely love something. Like if I absolutely hate something I'll try and put my stamp on it, cut into it, destroy it, make it into something I actually like. If I don't have any emotional response towards it then there's no point really ... Blank things to me are clinical, there's no life to them. I like taking something that already exists and turning it into something else.

A third explained that she found the task frustrating and felt she could not satisfactorily make her mark on top of someone else's work:

> When I started I had total lack of imagination ... I tried to break this already finished fabric ... why break this fabric? I'm not good at adding, I can't manage with scrap fabrics already completely finished. Makes me less imaginative. I usually work with completely blank fabric. So using this is not original for me. I want to create from scratch.

Figure 11.5 "Hating Flowers": stitching a strongly personal mark onto a found fabric. Photograph: Emma Shercliff.

This seems to align with the perspective of jeweler and craft writer Bruce Metcalf. He argues that the foundations of craft practice are rooted in a biological context, recounting that in his experience as a teacher, students attracted to a craft discipline discover that "the exercise of their newly discovered sensibility is both pleasurable and powerful … The motivation is felt: self-perceived as an emotion."[39]

Self-centered

The practicing of a technique embeds the practical knowledge into the body tacitly. Being unique individuals, each body that makes is different and the ability to make becomes deeply entwined with an individual's sense of self. The act of making is a non-verbal expression of "I am here and this is what I think and feel." In the above examples, responding to materials was accompanied by, and even driven by, a personally shaped emotional experience.

When probed to think beyond the stylistic intentions of their stitched work, participants began to hint at more visceral understandings of their craft that reveal the physical body to be very much at the center of their world:

It's almost like a bridge between us and the world, because textiles ... are constantly in contact with our body. For me that's why stitch is so important. Because it's almost like, a part of us ... it's almost like, at one with us. When I think of stitching, I think of mending. So I think of scars, making something better, like embellishing ... going through the body, like through the skin, from outside going in, and then coming out again.

Another imagines it to be "almost like tattoos in a way, all over us, almost like clothing ... just all over, messages and images." And "I see it as threads that go through the body but then join on to other people. So there's a link."

Conclusion

In considering some of the qualities and values of hand stitching processes, this chapter has explored ways in which textile craft skills can enrich an understanding of the material world and sustain a continually changing relationship to it, by cultivating a distinctive form of attention to the self. If screen-based work can provoke a fractured and dislocated sense of self, by contrast handwork can encourage a focused awareness of the body as a whole being literally in touch with its environment. In support of this, Serres's concept of "mingling with the world"[40] proposes "a conception of the human being not as a composite entity made up of separable but complementary parts, such as body, mind and culture, but rather as a singular locus of creative growth within a continually unfolding field of relationships."[41]

Hand skills can highlight the significance of touch, and the powerful stimulation provoked by handling materials reminds us that the body is a sensate being affording access to particular types of embodied knowledge. The illusion of experience mediated frequently today via screen technologies causes the materiality, temporality, and spatiality of real experience to stand out as novel or precious, and physical experiences of making provide "a central point of bodily reference within the fluidity of time and action."[42] The scale and pace of hand stitching match those of the body, grounding cognitive and emotional experience in a tangible process. The physical proximity of material, tools, and body enables a person to feel situated in time and space, and the relatively slow pace allows for contemplative thought and open-ended exploration as a refuge from the more habitual speedy results and instant gratification. I suggest that the focused, calm rhythm of accumulative hand stitching is one way for individuals alienated by the intangible nature of the objective world of consumption to assimilate the surrounding material world, strike up conversation with it, feel grounded by it, and articulate themselves within it—literally to make it one's own.

Notes

1. See Tanya Harrod, *The Crafts in Britain in the 20th Century* (New Haven: Yale University Press, 1999); Christopher Frayling, *On Craftsmanship: Towards a New Bauhaus* (London: Oberon Books, 2011).
2. See Harrod, *The Crafts in Britain*; Frayling, *On Craftsmanship*.
3. Raymond Williams, *The Country and the City* (London: The Hogarth Press, 1985).
4. For example, recent exhibitions include: "Quilts 1700–2010," V&A, London, 2010; "Beware of Embroidery," Pitzhanger Manor House, Ealing, 2010; Louise Bourgeois's 2010 exhibition "The Fabric Works," which opened the new Hauser and Wirth contemporary art gallery in London and was accompanied by a comprehensive catalog of her textile artworks (Celant, 2010). The following year Tracey Emin's pieced and embroidered artworks were shown at her Hayward Gallery retrospective, "Love Is What You Want." Publications include: *Contemporary Textiles: The Fabric of Fine Art* (Monem, 2008), which surveys the work of leading artists in the field from the whole spectrum of textile practices, many of whom use stitch; and *Extra/Ordinary Craft: Craft and Contemporary Art* (Buszek, 2011), with accounts of the contemporary influences of crafting, which includes textiles in large proportion, on the visual and performing arts. Popular interest is visible in the reality TV programs applied to the crafts: *Great British Sewing Bee*, in 2013, challenged candidates to a series of dressmaking projects, and in 2012 *Paul Martin's Handmade Revolution* toured the country in a contest to seek a champion "amateur maker." Lucrative business ventures capitalizing on cleverly marketed trends for nostalgic "home-made" ideals include Kirstie Allsopp's TV series *Kirstie's Handmade Britain* and its accompanying books and DVDs, and Jane Brocket's series of books *The Gentle Art of Stitching*, *The Gentle Art of Quilt-Making*, and *The Gentle Art of Knitting*. Upper Street Events, organizers of The Knitting and Stitching Show and The Festival of Quilts, attracting over 168,000 visitors per year from over 50 countries, claim: "The Knitting and Stitching Show is the largest and most highly regarded textiles and craft event in the UK and it's your opportunity to share your love of textiles with others. Whatever your craft passion it is the perfect place to find inspiration, learn new skills and shop for all your essential supplies." http://www.theknittingandstitchingshow.com/london [accessed June 18, 2015].
5. See Richard Sennett, *The Craftsman* (London: Allen Lane, 2008); Matthew Crawford, *The Case for Working With Your Hands or Why Office Work is Bad for Us and Fixing Things Feels Good* (London: Viking, 2009); Frayling, *On Craftsmanship*; Ewan Clayton, "Why heritage crafts are important," keynote speech, Heritage Crafts Association, Victoria and Albert Museum, London, March 23, 2010. http://www.heritagecrafts.org.uk/index.php/heritagecrafts/heritage-crafts/item/15-why-heritage-crafts-are-important [accessed April 10, 2015]; Claire Pajaczkowska, "Tension, Time and Tenderness: Indexical Traces of Touch in Textiles," in *Digital and Other Virtualities. New Encounters: Arts, Cultures, Concepts*, ed. Griselda Pollock (London: I.B.Tauris, 2010), 134–48.
6. Juhani Pallasmaa, *The Thinking Hand: Existential and Embodied Wisdom in Architecture* (Chichester: John Wiley & Sons, 2009), 12.
7. Jorunn Veiteberg, *Craft in Transition* (Bergen: Bergen National Academy of the Arts, 2005); Anna Konig, "The Joy of Making," *Resurgence* 263 (2010). http://www.resurgence.org/magazine/article3234-the-joy-of-making.html [accessed April 10, 2015].

8   Crawford, *The Case for Working With Your Hands*, 63.
9   Williams, *The Country and the City*.
10 Pamela Johnson, "Out of Touch: the Meaning of Making in the Digital Age," in *Obscure Objects of Desire: Reviewing the Crafts in the Twentieth Century*, ed. Tanya Harrod (London: Crafts Council, 1997), 297–8.
11 Tim Ingold quoted in Myriem Naji and Laurence Douny, "Editorial", *Journal of Material Culture* 14 (4) (2009): 413.
12 Martina Margetts, "Action Not Words," in *Power of Making: The Importance of Being Skilled*, ed. Daniel Charny (London: V&A and the Crafts Council, 2011), 39.
13 "Encounter" derives from the Latin *contra*, which means "against."
14 Michel Serres, *The Five Senses: A Philosophy of Mingled Bodies* (London: Continuum, 2008), 80.
15 Tim Dant, "The Work of Repair: Gesture, Emotion and Sensual Knowledge," *Sociological Research Online* 15 (3) (2010). http://www.socresonline.org.uk/15/3/7.html [accessed April 10, 2015].
16 Joseph Brodsky, quoted in Pallasmaa, *The Thinking Hand*, 80.
17 Ellen Dissanayake, *Homo Aestheticus: Where Art Comes From and Why* (Seattle, WA: University of Washington Press, 1995), 51.
18 Dissanayake, *Homo Aestheticus*, 59.
19 Ibid., 34.
20 Ellen Dissanayake, "The Pleasure and Meaning of Making," *American Craft* 55 (2) (1995): 41.
21 I studied for my PhD at the Royal College of Art, London, and I teach at the Arts University Bournemouth, which gave me access to the resources and participants for these workshops.
22 Quotes taken from transcripts of conversations remain verbatim. In instances where English is not the participant's first language, but the meaning of their words is clear, the quotes have not been corrected.
23 Pallasmaa, *The Thinking Hand*, 82.
24 William Morris, *Art Under Plutocracy* (1883). http://www.marxists.org/archive/morris/works/1883/pluto.htm [accessed April 10, 2015]
25 David Pye, *The Nature and Art of Workmanship* (London: The Herbert Press, 1995), 124.
26 Pye, *The Nature and Art of Workmanship*, 124.
27 Pajaczkowska, "Tension, Time and Tenderness," 145.
28 Ibid., 146.
29 Tim Ingold, "Bringing Things to Life: Creative Entanglements in a World of Materials," in *Realities: Working Paper* 15 (2010): 8. http://www.socialsciences.manchester.ac.uk/medialibrary/morgancentre/research/wps/15-2010-07-realities-bringing-things-to-life.pdf [accessed April 10, 2015].
30 Mihaly Csikszentmihalyi, *Flow: The Psychology of Optimal Experience* (New York: Harper and Row, 1990).
31 Peter Dormer, "Craft and the Turing Test for Practical Thinking," in *The Culture of Craft: Status and Future*, ed. Peter Dormer (Manchester: Manchester University Press, 1997), 147.
32 Frayling, *On Craftsmanship*, 78.
33 Pye, *The Nature and Art of Workmanship*, 124.

34 Pallasmaa, *The Thinking Hand*, 36.
35 Tim Dant, "The Work of Repair."
36 Michael Polanyi, *The Tacit Dimension* (Chicago: University of Chicago Press, 2009).
37 Sennett, *The Craftsman*, 50.
38 Pajaczkowska, "Tension, Time and Tenderness," 143.
39 Bruce Metcalf, "Craft and Art, Culture and Biology," in *The Culture of Craft: Status and Future*, ed. Peter Dormer (Manchester: Manchester University Press, 1997), 77.
40 Serres, *The Five Senses*, 80.
41 Tim Ingold, *The Perception of the Environment: Essays on Livelihood, Dwelling and Skill* (London: Routledge, 2000), 4.
42 Polly Ullrich, "Workmanship: The Hand and Body As Perceptual Tools," in *Objects and Meaning: New Perspectives on Art and Craft*, ed. M. Anna Fariello and Paula Owen (Lanham, MD: The Scarecrow Press, 2005), 211.

Bibliography

Brocket, Jane, *The Gentle Art of Stitching* (London: Collins and Brown, 2012).
Buszek, Maria Elena (ed.), *Extra/Ordinary Craft: Craft and Contemporary Art* (Durham, NC: Duke University Press, 2011).
Celant, Germano (ed.), *Louise Bourgeois: The Fabric Works* (Milan: Skira, 2010).
Clayton, Ewan, "Why Heritage Crafts Are Important," keynote speech, Heritage Crafts Association, Victoria and Albert Museum, London, March 23, 2010. http://www.heritagecrafts.org.uk/index.php/heritagecrafts/heritage-crafts/item/15-why-heritage-crafts-are-important [accessed April 10, 2015].
Crawford, Matthew, *The Case for Working With Your Hands or Why Office Work is Bad for Us and Fixing Things Feels Good* (London: Viking, 2009).
Csikszentmihalyi, Mihaly, *Flow: The Psychology of Optimal Experience* (New York: Harper and Row, 1990).
Dant, Tim, "The Work of Repair: Gesture, Emotion and Sensual Knowledge," *Sociological Research Online* 15 (3) (2010). http://www.socresonline.org.uk/15/3/7.html [accessed April 10, 2015].
Dissanayake, Ellen, *Homo Aestheticus: Where Art Comes From and Why* (Seattle, WA: University of Washington Press, 1995).
Dissanayake, Ellen, "The Pleasure and Meaning of Making," *American Craft* 55 (2) (1995): 40–5.
Dormer, Peter, "Craft and the Turing Test for Practical Thinking," in *The Culture of Craft: Status and Future*, ed. Peter Dormer (Manchester: Manchester University Press, 1997), 137–57.
Frayling, Christopher, *On Craftsmanship: Towards a New Bauhaus* (London: Oberon Books, 2011).
Harrod, Tanya, *The Crafts in Britain in the 20th Century* (New Haven: Yale University Press, 1999).
Ingold, Tim, *The Perception of the Environment: Essays on Livelihood, Dwelling and Skill* (London: Routledge, 2000).
Ingold, Tim. "Bringing Things to Life: Creative Entanglements in a World of Materials," *Realities: Working Paper* 15 (2010). http://www.socialsciences.manchester.ac.uk/medialibrary/morgancentre/research/wps/15-2010-07-realities-bringing-things-to-life.pdf [accessed April 10, 2015].
Johnson, Pamela, "Out of Touch: The Meaning of Making in the Digital Age," in *Obscure Objects of Desire: Reviewing the Crafts in the Twentieth Century,* ed. Tanya Harrod (London: Crafts Council, 1997), 292–9.

Konig, Anna, "The Joy of Making," *Resurgence* 263 (2010). http://www.resurgence.org/magazine/article3234-the-joy-of-making.html [accessed April 10, 2015].
Margetts, Martina, "Action Not Words," in *Power of Making: The Importance of Being Skilled,* ed. Daniel Charny (London: V&A and the Crafts Council, 2011), 38–43.
Metcalf, Bruce, "Craft and Art, Culture and Biology," in *The Culture of Craft: Status and Future,* ed. Peter Dormer (Manchester: Manchester University Press, 1997), 67–82.
Monem, Nadine (ed.), *Contemporary Textiles: The Fabric of Fine Art* (London: Black Dog, 2008).
Morris, William, "Art Under Plutocracy" (1883). http://www.marxists.org/archive/morris/works/1883/pluto.htm [accessed April 10, 2015].
Naji, Myriem, and Laurence Douny (eds), "Editorial," *Journal of Material Culture* 14 (4) (2009): 411–32.
Pajaczkowska, Claire, "Tension, Time and Tenderness: Indexical Traces of Touch in Textiles," in *Digital and Other Virtualities, New Encounters: Arts, Cultures, Concepts*, ed. Griselda Pollock (London: I.B.Tauris, 2010), 134–48.
Pallasmaa, Juhani, *The Thinking Hand: Existential and Embodied Wisdom in Architecture* (Chichester: John Wiley & Sons, 2009).
Polanyi, Michael, *The Tacit Dimension* (Chicago: University of Chicago Press, 2009).
Pye, David, *The Nature and Art of Workmanship* (London: The Herbert Press, 1995).
Sennett, Richard, *The Craftsman* (London: Allen Lane, 2008).
Serres, Michel, *The Five Senses: A Philosophy of Mingled Bodies*, trans. Margaret Sankey and Peter Cowley (London: Continuum, 2008).
The Knitting and Stitching Show. http://www.theknittingandstitchingshow [accessed April 10, 2015].
Ullrich, Polly, "Workmanship: The Hand and Body As Perceptual Tools," in *Objects and Meaning: New Perspectives on Art and Craft,* ed. M. Anna Fariello and Paula Owen (Lanham, MD: The Scarecrow Press, 2005), 198–213.
Veiteberg, Jorunn, *Craft in Transition* (Bergen: Bergen National Academy of the Arts, 2005).
Williams, Raymond, *The Country and the City* (London: The Hogarth Press, 1985).

12
PERSPECTIVES ON MAKING AND VIEWING: GENERATING MEANING THROUGH TEXTILES

Sonja Andrew

Introduction

As textile practitioners increasingly seek to communicate personal narratives, traditions of making, and cultural identity within their work, is shared meaning between the maker and the viewer truly generated in the way the maker intends? Can the meaning of individual images and sequential narratives extend beyond the maker to their audience? And what impact might perceptions of the "digital" and "craft" aspects of textile practice have on interpretations of the work? In *Semantic Visions in Design*, Giard writes:

> We are dealing with a visual world and a corresponding visual language. All languages are learned and the visual one is no different. To assume what we perceive is the same as our neighbour is in fact an error … not only is visual literacy a learned phenomenon, it is culturally or contextually biased … no matter how we use colour, shape, form and texture in composing our message we are sending out signals. The operative question should be "What are we communicating?"[1]

Critical discourse concerning textile practice is more usually located within cultural and theoretical paradigms such as feminism, rather than communication. Parker and Pollock discuss the high and low art distinctions drawn between fine art and craft within art history, with textiles as a gendered practice placed within the realm of "decorative crafts" and afforded lesser status. They note that this was partly achieved through distinctions made between textile production carried out in public (male) and private (female) domains, creating divisions between the professional and the domestic ascribed to place, gender, and audience for the product. Practices such as patchwork and embroidery were particularly framed through the "feminine stereotype" and defined as "domestic art."[2] As such, they were used as a means to maintain the hierarchy between fine art and craft and further establish their distinctions. The wider feminist issues discussed by Parker and Pollock continue to concern textile makers and theorists. In discussing women artists' decision to choose the textile medium on which to build their practice, Jefferies states: "It therefore becomes highly problematic, even contradictory, for women artists to acknowledge textile practices within their work without recognising the underlying hierarchical value system and hierarchical divisions outlined by Parker and Pollock."[3]

With these wider feminist issues, and others such as cultural identity embedded in textile practice and academic criticism, locating textile research within a semiotic communication paradigm is atypical. But curators and academics such as Jefferies, Atkins, and Millar encompass communication-based perspectives in their textile dialogue, examining the narrative characteristics of cloth and its relationship to cultural identity.[4] In this chapter, the dichotomy between authorial intention and viewer perception is examined via my own textile practice, discussing printed textile panels specifically developed as visual narratives on cloth for location in public spaces. Reflecting on family history, religious motivation, and social exclusion, the panels aimed to communicate the imprisonment of John Edgar Bell, a World War I Quaker and conscientious objector, and the effects of his actions on his family. The communicative potential of these textiles is explored from the perspectives of both the maker (author) and the viewer, exemplifying the influence of images and processes on the construction of meaning in, and from, the textiles.

Applying semiotic theory to encode practice

The semiotic approach adopted in the development of the textile panels focused on structural analysis and narratology,[5] examining the selection and juxtaposition of components in the construction of visual texts to create signifying systems of meaning. This approach involved considering the communicative function of individual images, textures, and colors (i.e. signifiers) incorporated into the initial stages of the textile development, the readings (i.e. signified meanings) generated when several signifiers were brought together in the second stage of the textile development, and the overall meaning created when groups of signifiers were combined within compositions for the textile panels in the final stage of the textile development. Although practitioners may carry out the initial stages of this process consciously, the later stages often involve more subconscious sets of decisions within the trial and error processes of making. As visual encoding takes place by the maker, elements within compositions are juxtaposed, removed, or reworked, and a multitude of decisions take place about relationships between elements, which, through continued practice, build tacit knowledge.

Paradigm and syntagm

Consciously or not, artists and designers make paradigmatic and syntagmatic choices when constructing their work. Referring to linguistics, Saussure suggests that meaning is generated from paradigmatic and syntagmatic differences between signifiers: the first dealing with selection and substitution, and the second with combination and arrangement.[6] Fiske notes that Saussure suggests paradigm and syntagym as the two ways in which signs can be organized into codes,[7] stating:

> A paradigm is a set of signs from which the one to be used is chosen ... A syntagm is the message into which the chosen signs are combined ... All messages involve selection (from a paradigm) and combination (into a syntagm).[8]

Semiotic structural analysis of the textile development sought to make explicit the paradigmatic and syntagmatic choices that are usually implicit within my textile practice; what actually occurred was a series of successive cycles of small deconstructions from which the communicative content of the work was built. Barthes, in his application of semiotic structural analysis to visual texts (as in *Système de la Mode*), argues the importance of dividing texts into significant small units, "then to group these units into paradigmatic classes, and finally to classify the syntagmatic relations which link these units."[9] Barthes's deconstructive process suggests an incremental semiotic method of examining the constituent elements that create meaning within a visual text, which was applied to constructing the narrative textiles to communicate the objector's story.

Visual development

A collage approach was taken to tentatively form narrative relationships between photographic images and other signifiers such as color and mark, creating "micro visual syntagms" and analyzing the potential meanings they conveyed. The communicative value of colors and textures and the age, patina, and authenticity of the source material were evaluated. Research on World War I and family photographs and anecdotes informed this process. In *The Spoken Image*, Scott notes:

> It is with the accumulation of family snaps in shoe-boxes and drawers that the viewer can take, or be compelled to take, any number of a-chronological journeys through his/her past ... surrendering to chance encounters with prints which he/she must shape into narratives—not narratives of external time but narratives of inner duration, memory, resurrected illusion; in short, narratives of the narrator.[10]

The communication intent of each image was evaluated against a framework of baseline semiotic criteria in order to consider its potential for inclusion in the final textiles. This was supplemented by sketches and notes on how the fabric might be treated. Family

Figure 12.1 Early sketchbook page, wood stain and heat transfer experiment. Photograph: Chris Harper. © Sonja Andrew.

portraits were heat-transferred over wood-stained pages (Figure 12.1) and line, collage, stitch, and type were incorporated, with test samples of flocking and screen printing produced. This experimentation with primarily hand-generated processes helped to focus the narrative direction, with definitive elements emerging that informed later digital development of the print compositions and the chronology, content, and treatment of the final textiles.

The commutation test

As the work progressed, trial compositions for the textile panels were developed by hand and digitally in Photoshop, with commutation tests taking place consciously and incrementally throughout this stage of the design process. Barthes suggests that the deconstructive function of a commutation test is to identify the characteristics and differences of individual signifiers within a paradigm or syntagym and define their significance.[11] This involves changing a signifier and examining if this leads to a change in the meaning of the elements it is grouped with.[12] The test is primarily one of substitution. A signifier is selected, one or more alternatives are considered, and the effect of the substitution is evaluated in terms of the change in meaning generated by the introduction of a different signifier. This change enables evaluation of the efficacy of the original and replacement signifier and their contribution of meaning to the paradigm or syntagm. The test can also involve rearrangement of the existing signifiers into a new configuration to determine if different meaning is created.

As with paradigmatic and syntagmatic choices, artists and designers incorporate commutation tests on a daily basis as conscious or subconscious actions within their practice. Some of the tests take place physically, examining the impact of the change of signifier or change of compositional relationship on the meaning of the work. This often takes place instinctively, as a cycle of substitution, analysis, rejection/selection, and confirmation, until the desired meaning and aesthetic placement are achieved. Commutation tests can also take the form of a mental process of substitution or rearrangement, evaluating the present–absent dichotomy of elements within the visual text. This process can happen almost instantaneously, or involve much deliberation, as the practitioner draws on prior experience to inform their decision making, with cycles of commutation occurring continuously within the practice until the work is concluded.

Reflection in action

The early stages of the textile practice encompassed a "problem finding" approach,[13] discovery orientated actions, and reframing the design problem through contextual research, development of an encoded image bank, and visual experimentation. This began the "reflection-in-action,"[14] the explicit and intuitive processes of practical and theoretical inquiry necessary to progress the practice to a communicative conclusion.

Both Schön and Dormer recognize that much of the problem solving inherent in visual practice is informed by prior experience and tacit knowledge, enabling intuitive manipulation of ideas, materials, and processes.[15] Within the textile making, discarded early ideas were revisited to inform later work as the panel compositions progressed. Visual research was interspersed throughout the process; experimental approaches converged then separated, only to converge again later as the work developed. When engaged in the actual process of making, the basic cycle extrapolated from Schön's discussion of the structure of reflective practice is much more organic and complex.[16] Schön acknowledges this, stating:

> In order to see what can be made to follow from his reframing of the situation, each practitioner tries to adapt the situation to the frame. This he does through a web of moves, discovered consequences, implications, appreciations, and further moves. Within the larger web, individual moves yield phenomena to be understood, problems to be solved, or opportunities to be exploited.[17]

Decisions and evaluations were made concerning the intended meaning of individual images (signifiers) and groups of images within compositional trials. Paradigms of signifiers were collated from which visual syntagms could be established, creating "micro narratives"; then relationships were created between the syntagms to construct the main narrative content of the work.[18] Cycles of development, review, and revision of compositional experiments emerged as the work progressed. These can be considered the action and reappreciation stages of the structure of reflection-in-action described by Schön.[19]

The two-dimensional nature of print, as opposed to the more textural presence of knitted or woven construction, was a concern when investigating perceptions of the textile medium. The print process provided clarity of visual content, but lacked the tactile qualities implicit to textiles. To enhance the surface and generate more "textile" signification, stitch, appliqué, and overprinting were applied to disrupt the single visual plane created by the digital printing process. Fabric layering experiments were also carried out to combine the reading of one image with another. When the effect was established they were trialled digitally to save time.

Applying semiotic theory to encode the textiles imposed constraints on the practice, competing with aesthetic considerations and disrupting intuitive thinking and making processes. This was frustrating, particularly as Dormer argues that the experienced maker can rely upon their tacit knowledge to solve problems as they emerge and that there is an interdependency of intention, subject matter, and process being navigated to create successful conclusions that are dependent upon the maker's expertise.[20] However, John-Steiner notes: "The shaping of a visual language of communication is a slow developmental process. In some cases, considerable time elapses between the early, impressionable period of stimulation [and the] linking of these sights and images to a more personalised form of expression."[21]

The problem finding/solving methods usually adopted in my practice had to be modified to construct narrative textiles. It was not the transition between hand and digital processes that made the practice less responsive, but the constant evaluation of the emerging communicative content. Moving between hand and digital processes is embedded in my working methodology. Positive results from commutation tests with images, textures, and colors could happen when working with layers in Photoshop or when arranging collage compositions on a table, neither having greater nor lesser value in my practice. However, the definition of craft is "an activity involving skill in making things by hand," but to craft is to "exercise skill in making (something)."[22] By the first definition, the incorporation of digital technology as part of the design and manufacturing process for the textile panels may invalidate them as craft. However, their bespoke nature, visibility of the hand-rendered textile processes, and the maker's tactile engagement with the work may assist in them being "read" as craft by the general public. The second definition leads to a question of skill. If to craft something is to exercise skill in making, what is our definition of skill in making in the digital age? Is this perceived in the same way by the maker and the viewer? Dormer notes that "every craft has a technical language" and that we "test the language against the practice," with the craft outcome assessed by peers against what is considered current good practice.[23] But the technical language of contemporary textile practice has changed to incorporate multiple streams of knowledge to inform the final artifact. As digital technical knowledge and the tacit knowledge of mastered hand processes are combined in textile making, the crafted object becomes more than the application of one specific hand-applied skill. It also becomes open to scrutiny beyond the maker's peers, as public acceptance of digital processes within textiles may shape if, and how, they are received as crafted objects.

Constructing the final textiles

Although both hand and digital processes informed the early stages of the textile development, the construction of the final textile compositions began by hand. Stained lining paper edges from old picture frames, sections of discarded fabrics, torn fragments of aged house paint and wallpapers (the detritus of past collecting) were collaged to evoke aged colors, textures, and marks for the textile background. The collage process enabled "hands-on" working with these materials, reacting to their visual qualities. Several backgrounds were formed and reworked this way, until compositions that achieved an effective balance of shape, color, and mark emerged. These were photographed, dissembled, scanned, and digitally reconstructed, the process echoing the early stages of the practice, where hand-generated experiments created components for later digital development.

 The first triptych was developed to communicate the values and social exclusion of the conscientious objector's family, the imprisonment of the objector, and the post-war stigma the family endured. An image of the objector's wife and daughter established the start of the narrative to connote family, domesticity, and home. However, my authorial intentions for the images relied heavily on their compositional juxtaposition with other elements to create meaning beyond basic significations of the maternal or familial. For example, a visual syntagm had to be created in the first panel to communicate the family as singled out for their pacifist beliefs (Figure 12.2). A medal as a redundant[24] symbol of war was positioned beneath the mother and child, then crossed out via stitching to signify rejection of war and "not heroic," communicating society's perception of the objector's actions. Crossed keys as symbols of St Peter and the gates to heaven were added via screen printing to signify a Christian family, providing an entropic signifier of faith, operating via narrowcast codes. Circling marks were added to suggest being "singled out" in their community; the marks were hand-drawn to give authenticity to the shape

Figure 12.2 The first panel of the first triptych with a visual syntagm created to communicate the family as singled out for their pacifist beliefs. Photograph: Chris Harper. © Sonja Andrew.

and screen printed in white to provide emphasis. The name/date stamp was added to suggest wartime identification. A modified crown was screen printed in white over the medal as a form of oppositional encoding. Crosses replaced traditional elements of the crown to communicate "serving God not the crown" and further symbolize the family's beliefs of faith before country, bringing together images from the paradigms of monarchy and Christianity. Stamps were added to indicate the period and, as an icon of the ruling monarch, to represent the dominant cultural code of "serving king and country" in wartime. As the panels were developed, white crosses and crossed-out medals were incorporated across the triptych to create a continuum of Christian signification and pacifism.

Key issues in constructing the communicative content for this final stage of the practice were generating intertextuality[25] between the panels to create a holistic sense of meaning from the work, and developing intratextuality between signifiers in the panels to create specific meanings to inform the narrative sequence. Some elements communicated redundantly, with an expectation of common interpretations, while others were more entropic to generate subliminal responses. Although authorial intentions for individual signifiers and panels were specific, each image and composition was open to multiple interpretations. Readings of the triptych were inevitably informed by viewers' personal and cultural experiences, their memories, histories, and wider social and historical knowledge. While some readings echoed the encoded intention of the work, others diverged from it. According to Kuhn, memories:

> do not simply spring out of the image itself, but are generated in a network, an intertext of discourses that shift between past and present, spectator and image, and between all these and cultural contexts, historical moments. In this network the image itself figures largely as a trace, a clue: necessary but not sufficient, to the activity of meaning making; always pointing somewhere else.[26]

Viewer perceptions (1)

The triptych was displayed at four different locations: (1) Walford Mill Craft Gallery in Dorset (pilot study); (2) LloydsTSB banking headquarters in Birmingham; (3) Manchester Museum of Science and Industry; and (4) Saltaire United Reformed Church in West Yorkshire. The survey was conducted with the general public via on-site questionnaires and interviews with 327 people in total. While 201 respondents (61.46%) stated their interpretation of the work would not change if it were produced in a different medium (many noting that meaning was in content, not medium), forty-one (12.53%) were unsure or did not respond to the question, and eighty-five (25.99%) stated that their interpretations would change if the work was produced in a different medium. Several did not give reasons why their interpretations were affected by the medium, but seven at Walford Mill particularly noted layering, appliqué, or collage effects within the work and five noted color as affecting their decision. One viewer particularly noted "ideas of nostalgia, a piece of fabric carries memory or layers of its lifespan." Across the remaining sites, thirteen viewers particularly felt that the textile medium made the work look older and suggested age and history, although references to these qualities were also found in other responses. One viewer stated that textiles and especially banners were strongly associated with social history and this shaped their perception of the work. Other viewers noted that textiles imply age, history, and authenticity, capturing the "essence of the images" better than other media could and making the photographic elements look more faded.

Ten viewers specifically noted the importance of tactile qualities in textiles. One viewer commented that "The medium of fabric/textiles communicates a 'naturalness,' 'wholesomeness,' 'old' technology brought to a new use. Texture so much more valuable than printed poster or computer screen. The colors are richer for being produced as textiles." Another viewer felt that texture "adds to the depth of piece," while a third noted: "The material makes it seem much more living, as if the people are here rather than simply an old photo."

Four respondents particularly felt that textiles were more emotionally expressive than other media and six viewers noted design processes, including stitching, symmetry, and integration of images with the cloth. Loss of scale and impact were also noted if the work was produced in different media. Ten viewers (five at the Manchester site and five at Saltaire) felt that the textile medium was suggestive of, or related to, the textile industry of the area, revealing the influence of local history on their perceptions of the work.

Of the 327 survey respondents, only seven (2.14%) felt that the overall meaning of the triptych related to conscientious objection. A further ten viewers (3.05%) stated that the triptych communicated an anti-war message. Responses to indivudual images showed some interpretations of aspects of the triptych that correlated with the maker's intention, particularly linking war, family, and suffering, but they did not exemplify a complete understanding of the overall communication intention. Analysis of the survey data confirmed the primary reason for this related to viewers' interpretations of individual signifiers and the communication relationships that some viewers formed between different signifiers within each composition and between signifiers in different panels of the triptych. However, contextual influences related to the function of the building and history of the area were also found to inform viewers' aberrant decoding[27] of the work.

"Back to the drawing board"

Responses to the work necessitated a re-evaluation of image and process. At the start of the investigation I had concerns about the number of redundant visual signifiers that were incorporated to communicate the narrative. I expected that there would be shared cultural consensus on the meaning of specific images, such as the white feather to signify cowardice. However, this was not the case. Even when images such as medals were clearly crossed out, the predominant readings were still heroism and bravery, and the white feather generated multiple readings, including "quill" and "for pigeon carriers at the front line." Based on viewer responses, the triptych became a paradigm from which images, colors, and surface treatments could be selected or rejected, and alternatives sought, for the development of a new set of narrative textiles to communicate the

Figure 12.3 Additions to the digitally printed textile surface via heat transfer, bonded frayed fabrics, stitch, screen printing, and flocking. Photograph: Chris Harper. © Sonja Andrew.

objector's story. At the start of this process, several images were automatically excluded due to the extent of their aberrant decoding by viewers.

Responses across the sites suggested that the color palette communicated the past, generating connotations of history. Several of the original collage elements were therefore digitally reconfigured into new compositions to form backgrounds for the second triptych, with digital color trials exploring staining effects to generate a more aged look and sombre mood (Plate 19). The narrative content of each panel was developed incorporating signifiers that provided the best match between the maker and the audience. The second triptych had the same communication objectives as the first triptych, with the values and social exclusion of the conscientious objector's family, the imprisonment of the objector, and the post-war stigma the family endured as the focus of the panels. New images were added, such as the British flag crossed out with screen printed brush marks to suggest lack of patriotism. A lock and barbed wire were also incorporated to suggest imprisonment of the objector and the virtual imprisonment of his wife (due to the social exclusion she faced), until three compositions emerged that formed a workable visual narrative for the communication test.

However, some signifiers that received substantial aberrant decoding still needed to be incorporated. The small white crosses as Christian symbols were associated with graves by a significant number of viewers due to their size and arrangement. The scale of the crosses was increased in the second triptych; more decorative examples were incorporated to evoke church altar crosses and they were flock printed to generate surface texture. As layering and collage effects were noted in some responses, digital print overlays were applied as a surface treatment on the panels, with frayed edges in areas to emphasize the additions and connote patchwork (Figure 12.3). Stitch was also incorporated to draw attention to tactile qualities implicit in the textiles medium. The stitching and patches of appliqué also aimed to generate domestic connotations in relation to the mother and child images. Screen printed and stitched tally marks were added to the center panel to signify the marking of time in prison, with small wool knots to enhance

Figure 12.4 The second textile triptych panels in situ at the Bankfield Museum and Art Gallery, West Yorkshire. Photograph: Chris Harper. © Sonja Andrew.

the digitally printed barbed wire. An image of a WW1 bomb crossed out by stitch was added to the first panel and a small appliqué cross as a Christian symbol was added over the objector's torso. The second triptych (Figure 12.4) was completed with the addition of heat-transferred *fleur de lys* to the first and final panels as an entropic signifier, a Christian symbol of purity associated with the Virgin Mary.

Viewer perceptions (2)

The second triptych was displayed at the Bankfield Museum and Art Gallery, West Yorkshire, and Manchester Museum of Science and Industry (MOSI), with 140 museum visitors surveyed in total (seventy at each site). The survey shows that sixty-five respondents stated that their interpretation of the work would change if it were produced in a different medium, thirty-five (42.85%) at the Bankfield and thirty (42.85%) at MOSI, with fifty-six providing a reason for their decision. Eight viewers particularly felt that cloth was the most appropriate medium to make the work look older and that textiles suggested authenticity, age, and history better than other media. One viewer noted: "Textiles have an added meaning to me—the history of cloth—everyday use and the fading/rotting qualities that evoke memories of their own. The images would still be strong in the other media but would lack the added layers of textile." Another wrote: "Textiles 'carry' history more intrinsically than other media— they are quite literally amplified with memory of life lived. The texture and worn nature of these pieces vividly convey the aspect of a personal memorial." A third viewer explained that they engaged more with the work due to the textile medium, stating: "Feeling of past wars through aged textiles and photographs. Lack of support from country and church subtly shown. We would not have spent as much time interpreting the works in other mediums."

References to tactile qualities, softness, and the depth/relief effects inherent to textiles occurred across several responses, but fourteen viewers particularly felt that the tactile nature of the textile medium was important, with comments such as: "Textiles are much more tactile—familiar—warm, absorbent—all metaphors for humanity—moving, soft." One viewer noted that the tactile nature of the panels gave the work more of an "old military feel," while a third wrote: "Textile enables varied surface texture and is therefore of greater visual interest: in layering, printing, stitch, fringe. Bare information would be imparted via a photo or web but additional experience of surface would be lost." The emotive qualities of textiles were also noted in several responses, particularly that textiles were more intimate than other media, with one viewer stating: "I would not have this feeling of tenderness that ragged old cloth brings to me."

Fifty-five respondents stated their interpretation of the work would not change if it were produced in a different medium, with forty-five providing a reason for their decision. Thirty-two viewers felt that the meaning was in the content not the medium, but four still exhibited preferences for the work being produced as textiles, one viewer noting:

> It wouldn't change my interpretation provided the original images were used in the various media. Textiles give a much more interesting surface and carry the weight of the symbolism of cloth, therefore resonate more for me.

Six further viewers also made comments on the design process. One said: "[I] would still interpret it in this way. However, I think it works better in textiles because of the overlapping of fabric and techniques used—example—the way the wire comes out of the fabric has more meaning than being flat on a poster or web design." Another viewer explained:

> I relate to all visual work but prefer the tactile qualities of fabrics/textiles. I love the way color can be absorbed and also can "sit" on the surface. The stitching is also a time-consuming activity that engages you with the work, the "make do and mend" connection also.

Ten viewers were unsure if their interpretation of the work would change if it were produced in a different medium. However, seven of these still demonstrated a preference for the work being produced as textiles, with two viewers particularly noting domestic associations with cloth. One stated: "Soft 'domestic' medium like textile is very powerful in depicting a harsh subject," while the other noted:

> There would be a loss of detail and texture. The fact that the work is textile makes it seem more domestic and homely, it has a texture which is comforting, in contrast with the darker elements and images. Other media would be less personal and more distancing—we wear cloth and have it all around us for most of our lives—the work being on cloth and of cloth makes me feel more closely associated with it.

From the survey, twenty-one (15%) of the 140 viewers interpreted pacifist meanings from the triptych, and thirteen of these (9.28%) specifically noted conscientious objection, with five interpretations corresponding closely to the encoded meaning for the triptych. One viewer noted:

> It's a family saga and that only impinges on me more strongly as I look and see the same people in different pieces. It's about war and imprisonment, the way the women back home are trapped behind their windows, in domestic static-ness, in a way similar to the man trapped behind the barbed wire of his POW camp. I wonder if he was imprisoned for being a conscientious objector—as there is a crucifix and a crossed-out projectile? And his hand suggests attesting—e.g. to a belief.

Another viewer stated:

> The overall impression is of an ancestor of yours who was misunderstood when he became a conscientious objector in World War I. He was shown the white feather and was "obliged" to become an active participant. He was subsequently taken prisoner of war and interned for a long time. He always was an enigma to his family who misunderstood his motivations and his change of personality when he returned home from his ordeal.

The remaining three viewers interpreted the separation of the conscientious objector from his family, and his imprisonment and release, with one viewer particularly noting that the objector bore "the scars of the whole ordeal."

Further viewers also reflected on imprisonment due to religious belief, peace, and an anti-war message. Although there were fewer survey respondents for the second triptych, the number of pacifist interpretations increased. This implied that the combination of signifiers improved the communication of pacifist meanings to the audience. The remaining responses showed some correct interpretations of aspects of the triptych, with comments linking war, family, and suffering at both sites.[28] However, these responses did not show a complete understanding of the overall communication intention of the textiles. Analysis of the survey data confirmed that again this related to viewers' interpretations of individual signifiers and the communication relationships formed between different signifiers.

Conclusion

It was determined from the research that multiple factors informed viewers' interpretations of the textiles. A lifetime of personal and cultural experiences, accumulated factual knowledge, and mythology mixed with dominant cultural codes to inform readings of the visual content. This often led viewers to make different paradigmatic choices of meaning to those of the maker, thereby constructing alternate readings of the textiles. When a substantial number of viewers drew the meaning of an image from a different paradigm to that of the maker, the main cultural paradigm to which the image belonged was revealed. This would suggest that no matter how carefully visual syntagms of meaning within textile practice are constructed, viewer consensus on meaning, and shared construction of meaning between maker and audience, may be elusive. Even if viewers are sympathetic to the processes of making and image content within the work, the differences in their interpretation of individual signifiers will impact on the overall meaning they derive from the work. However, Barthes suggests that a "plural" text open to multiple interpretations is an "ideal" text, in which a multitude of codes are mobilized to generate a mass of divergent readings:

> In this ideal text, the networks are many and interact, without any one of them being able to surpass the rest; this text is a galaxy of signifiers, not a structure of signifieds; it has no beginning, it is reversible, we gain access to it by several entrances, none of which can authoritatively be declared as the main one.[29]

In contrast to viewers' divergent readings of the imagery, inherent beliefs about, and responses to, the cloth consistently emerged in the surveys, demonstrating some shared cultural understanding of the textile medium. An expectation of permanency was expressed about textiles, that the longevity of cloth made it the most appropriate medium to communicate age and history. While visual syntagms of meaning can be developed via any media that can carry an image, viewers' responses to the textiles demonstrated readings informed by the tactile qualities of cloth. Viewers connected not only with the imagery printed on the cloth but also with the processes of making. The interaction of textural components such as stitch, flock, and fabric layering created "tactile syntagms" of meaning. These were additional signifiers to the visual image and generated meaning at a much more subliminal level. Readings were informed by viewers' reactions to the cloth in situ, and by culturally embedded assumptions concerning textiles. Cloth carried connotations of warmth, intimacy, and softness, and elicited more emotive responses, although the visual content of the work may also have influenced this. While it can be argued that tactile syntagms may be developed through other processes such as sculpture, viewer responses to the textile panels suggest that textiles have their own semantic vocabulary, not only for the maker, but also the viewer. To craft narrative textiles in the digital age, the maker should be open to combining digital technologies with traditional methods of textile production to communicate meaning and engage the viewer on both visual and tactile levels with the work.

Notes

1. Jacques Giard, "Product Semantics and Communication, Matching the Meaning to the Signal," in *Semantic Visions in Design*, ed. Susann Vihma (Helsinki: University of Industrial Arts, 1990), 7.
2. Rozsika Parker and Griselda Pollock, *Old Mistresses: Women, Art and Ideology* (London: Routledge, 1981), 58–81.
3. Janis Jefferies, "Contemporary Textiles: The Art Fabric," in *Contemporary Textiles, The Fabric of Fine Art*, ed. Nadine Monem (London: Black Dog Publishing, 2008), 44.
4. See, for example, Janis Jefferies, "site-labour-cloth-trade-value-sight-light," in *Selvedges, Janis Jefferies: Writings and Artworks since 1980*, ed. Victoria Mitchell (Norwich: Norwich School of Art and Design, 2000), 81–105; Peninna Barnett, Janis Jefferies and David Ross, "Letters from the Editors: Textile and Text," *Textile: The Journal of Cloth and Culture* 1 (4) (2003): 4–5; Jacqueline Atkins, *Wearing Propaganda: Textiles on the Home Front in Japan, Britain, and the United States, 1931–1945* (New York: Yale University Press, 2005); Lesley Millar, *Jerwood Applied Arts Prize 2002 Textiles* (London: Crafts Council, 2002); Lesley Millar, *Cloth and Culture Now* (Epsom: University College for the Creative Arts, 2007).
5. Semiotic narratology (narrative theory) examines the fundamental composition of narrative, focusing on the meaning of constituent units. Originating in linguistics, it can be applied to reveal the underlying structure of visual, verbal, or written narrative forms. See Roland Barthes, *Image, Music, Text* (London: Fontana, 1977); Gerard Genette, *Narrative Discourse: An Essay in Method*, trans. Jane E. Lewin (New York: Cornell University Press, 1983).
6. Ferdinand de Saussure, *Course in General Linguistics*, trans. and ed. Roy Harris (London: Bloomsbury Academic, 2013), 144–53.
7. A code is "a system of meaning common to the members of a culture of subculture," as described by John Fiske, *Introduction to Communication Studies* (London: Routledge, 1990), 15.
8. Fiske, *Introduction to Communication Studies*, 56–8.
9. Roland Barthes, *Elements of Semiology* (London: Jonathan Cape, 1967), 48.
10. Clive Scott, *The Spoken Image, Photography and Language* (London: Reaktion Books, 1999), 235.
11. Barthes, *Elements of Semiology*, 65–7.

12   Ibid.; Daniel Chandler, *Semiotics: The Basics* (Abingdon: Routledge, 2007), 88–90; Fiske, *Introduction to Communication Studies*, 109–10.
13   Jacob Warren Getzels and Mihaly Csikszentmihalyi, *The Creative Vision: A Longitudinal Study of Problem Finding in Art* (New York: John Wiley & Sons, 1976), 77–155.
14   Donald Schön, *The Reflective Practitioner: How Practitioners Think in Action* (Aldershot: Ashgate Publishing Limited, 1991), 49–69.
15   Schön, *The Reflective Practitioner*, 49–69; Peter Dormer, *The Art of the Maker, Skill and its Meaning in Art, Craft and Design* (London: Thames and Hudson, 1994), 13–18, 100.
16   Schön, *The Reflective Practitioner*, 128–67.
17   Ibid., 131.
18   Sonja Andrew, "The Medium Carries the Message? Perspectives on Making and Viewing Textiles," *Journal of Visual Arts Practice* 12 (2) (2013): 198.
19   Schön, *The Reflective Practitioner*, 128–67.
20   Dormer, *The Art of the Maker*, 13–18.
21   Vera John-Steiner, *Notebooks of the Mind: Explorations of Thinking* (Oxford: Oxford University Press, 1997), 91.
22   Catherine Soanes and Angus Stevenson (eds), *Oxford Dictionary of English* (2nd edn) (Oxford: Oxford University Press, 2003), 402.
23   Dormer, *The Art of the Maker*, 17–8.
24   Redundancy is that which is expected to be predictable or conventional in a verbal, written, or visual message. See Fiske, *Introduction to Communication Studies*, 10–16.
25   Intertextuality refers to links in form and content that bind a text to other texts. See Chandler, *Semiotics: The Basics*, 251.
26   Annette Kuhn, *Family Secrets, Acts of Memory and Imagination* (London: Verso, 1995), 12.
27   Aberrant decoding particularly applies to visual images and arises when a message is misunderstood due to differences in the (cultural) codes shared by the originator of the message and the reader/viewer. See Fiske, *Introduction to Communication Studies*, 77–9.
28   Sonja Andrew, "Image and Interpretation: Encoding and Decoding a Narrative Textile Installation," *Journal of Textile Design Research and Practice* 2 (2) (2014): 168–82.
29   Roland Barthes, *S/Z* (New York: Hill and Wang, 1974), 5–6.

Excerpts from this chapter were originally published in the *Journal of Visual Arts Practice* 12 (2) (2013) and the *Journal of Textile Design Research and Practice* 2 (2) (2014).

Bibliography

Andrew, Sonja, "The Medium Carries the Message? Perspectives on Making and Viewing Textiles," *Journal of Visual Arts Practice* 12 (2) (2013): 195–221.
Andrew, Sonja, "Image and Interpretation: Encoding and Decoding a Narrative Textile Installation," *Journal of Textile Design Research and Practice* 2 (2) (2014): 153–86.
Atkins, Jacqueline, *Wearing Propaganda: Textiles on the Home Front in Japan, Britain, and the United States, 1931–1945* (New York: Yale University Press, 2005).
Barnett, Peninna, Janis Jefferies, and David Ross, "Letters from the Editors: Textile and Text," *Textile, The Journal of Cloth and Culture* 1 (4) (2003): 4–5.

Barthes, Roland, *Elements of Semiology* (London: Jonathan Cape, 1967; originally published in French by Editions du Seuil, Paris, 1964).
Barthes, Roland, *S/Z (*New York: Hill and Wang, 1974; originally published in French by Editions du Seuil, Paris, 1970).
Barthes, Roland, *Image, Music, Text* (London: Fontana, 1977).
Chandler, Daniel, *Semiotics: The Basics* (Abingdon: Routledge, 2007).
De Saussure, Ferdinand, *Course in General Linguistics* (1916), trans. and ed. Roy Harris (London: Duckworth, 1983).
Dormer, Peter, *The Art of the Maker, Skill and its Meaning in Art, Craft and Design* (London: Thames and Hudson, 1994).
Fiske, John, *Introduction to Communication Studies* (London: Routledge, 1990).
Genette, Gerard, *Narrative Discourse: An Essay in Method*, trans. Jane E. Lewin (New York: Cornell University Press, 1983).
Getzel, Jacob Warren, and Mihaly Csikszentmihalyi, *The Creative Vision: A Longitudinal Study of Problem Finding in Art* (New York: John Wiley & Sons, 1976).
Giard, Jacques, "Product Semantics and Communication, Matching the Meaning to the Signal," in *Semantic Visions in Design*, ed. Susann Vihma (Helsinki: University of Industrial Arts, 1990), section b: 1–7
Jefferies, Janis, "site-labour-cloth-trade-value-sight-light," in *Selvedges, Janis Jefferies: Writings and Artworks since 1980*, ed. Victoria Mitchell (Norwich: Norwich School of Art and Design, 2000), 81–105.
Jefferies, Janis, "Contemporary Textiles: The Art Fabric," in *Contemporary Textiles: The Fabric of Fine Art,* ed. Nadine Monem (London: Black Dog Publishing, 2008), 34–61.
John-Steiner, Vera, *Notebooks of the Mind: Explorations of Thinking* (Oxford: Oxford University Press, 1997).
Kuhn, Annette, *Family Secrets, Acts of Memory and Imagination* (London: Verso, 1995).
Millar, Lesley, *Jerwood Applied Arts Prize 2002 Textiles* (London: Crafts Council, 2002).
Millar, Lesley, *Cloth and Culture Now* (Epsom: University College for the Creative Arts, 2007).
Parker, Rozsika, and Griselda Pollock, *Old Mistresses: Women, Art and Ideology* (London: Routledge, 1981).
Schön, Donald, *The Reflective Practitioner: How Practitioners Think in Action* (Aldershot: Ashgate Publishing Limited, 1991).
Scott, Clive, *The Spoken Image, Photography and Language* (London: Reaktion Books, 1999).

13
CLOSELY HELD SECRETS: EMBODIED KNOWLEDGE IN DIGITALLY CRAFTED TEXTILES

Katherine Townsend

Introduction

"Hold Your Beliefs Lightly" (Perry, 2010), "They Are Taking It to the People" (Whalley, 2010), and "What a Load of Shit" (Fisher, 2010) do not immediately conjure up the world of "embroidery." However, as titles of contemporary artworks, they do represent a significant moment in art and design where digital technology is accessible to all-comers and can be used—and, some may say, misused—accordingly.

This chapter explores the aesthetic and expressive potential of digital embroidery through reflection on a textile research project and exhibition, *Closely Held Secrets* (2008–10). This two-year project was inspired by the working relationship between the artist Grayson Perry and technical embroidery designer Tony Taylor, and was further developed by Geoff Diego Litherland (exhibitions co-ordinator/artist) and the author, Katherine Townsend (principal investigator/textile practitioner). Supported and funded by the School of Art & Design, Nottingham Trent University, the outcomes of the investigation culminated in an exhibition at the Bonington Gallery, opened by Janis Jefferies on October 29, 2010. The show featured artworks by Perry and eight other visual artists, most using digital embroidery as a creative medium for the first time.

The key aim of *Closely Held Secrets* was to examine and reveal the often hidden, yet reciprocal, relationship between technician and artist/designer—how the embodied knowledge of both parties is instrumental in the advancement of digital craft practice. The chapter includes insights into (1) the private dialogue between the originator of an idea and the agent (and mode) of interpretation, and (2) how innovative outcomes are informed by vision but are ultimately achieved through collaborative, human/machine interactions involving tacit knowledge, skills, and trust.

Analysis of selected artworks from *Closely Held Secrets* illustrates how the multi-head embroidery machine can be used in a variety of ways: meticulously to replicate full color, hand-embroidered techniques, expressively to convey abstract phenomena, and intuitively to just "see what happens." The examples and accompanying narratives both question and demonstrate (1) the flexibility of textiles as an aspect of multi-disciplinary practice, and (2) how creative collaboration and intervention with digital embroidery technology can lead to novel outcomes that address diverse contexts such as gender, ornamentation, mechanization, sexuality, and space, through stitch.

The following sections discuss four aspects of the project, beginning with the *research context*, an overview of *digital embroidery* and the practice-led *research methodology* that was applied. This is followed by explanation of the two key approaches to digital embroidery which emerged through the project as a *method of replication* and an *exploratory process*. The conclusion reflects on some of the outcomes of the project and the role of embodied knowledge in digital crafting practices. The artists' voices form a significant part of the chapter, through reflections on their individual motivations and the collaborative experience.

Research context

The idea for *Closely Held Secrets* was inspired by the professional working relationship between Grayson Perry and Tony Taylor. Their creative partnership had developed since 1996 when a Nottingham embroidery company refused to digitize the artwork of an ejaculating penis, incorporated into Perry's "Tree of Death" quilt design. They however recommended another local company, Red Tape Designs, run by Taylor, who accepted the commission with an open-minded "Don't worry, you have reached the Channel 4 of embroidery."[1]

The idea to highlight the creative exchange between an artist and a technical expert grew into a research project following initial conversations between Perry and Taylor, who approached Litherland and Townsend at the Bonington Gallery at Nottingham Trent University. In addition to working with Perry, Taylor was interested in working with a group of artists who were not necessarily embroidery specialists, but were keen to explore the potential of their different artistic practices through collaborative experimentation with digital embroidery. Following a call for participation via the Bonington Gallery in October 2008, a group of nine visual artists working in a variety of art and design practices such as fine art painting, sculpture, drawing, and textiles were selected by Taylor. The group comprised Simon Beck Mather, Craig Fisher, Charlotte Hodes, Geoff Diego Litherland, Danica Maier, Grayson Perry, Stella Whalley, Derek Sprawson, and Katherine Townsend.

Digital embroidery

The digitization of textile design and production has enabled designers to devise hybrid approaches and generate digitally crafted outcomes integrating knowledge of traditional and advanced technologies. In practice, digitization has fundamentally accelerated the textile process, resulting in fabrics that are no longer inscribed with the marks of temporality or "a linear unfolding of history."[2] While some hand-embroidered textiles can be difficult to distinguish from machine-produced pieces, the capability and accessibility of digital embroidery technology has opened up the potential for a once painfully time-consuming craft to be explored by creative practitioners who are rich in ideas but time-poor. In the past an artisan would undertake hand embroidery to order, while a traditional craft practice is now often sourced offshore by luxury brands. In the commercial textile sector, handwork has generally been replaced by computer-aided design and manufacturing (CAD/CAM) whereby intricate designs can be reproduced expediently. The technicians equipped to run this technology constitute a unique group of artisans, who possess the knowledge and skills of "human-centric, analogue and digital methods of creation."[3]

Digital, or multi-head, embroidery is a technically advanced version of machine embroidery, which was invented in the 1820s to enable "a female to embroider any designs with eighty or 140 needles as accurately and expeditiously as the former could do with one!"[4] Taylor considers multi-head embroidery and the associated digitizing process to be "essentially similar to traditional hand embroidery, made stitch by stitch; it's only the tools that are different."[5] For example, hand-stitched Petit Point designs necessitated a schematic, literally a "plot," and digitizing requires a similar encoding process, whether as a physical working drawing (on squared paper) or as a virtual "map" of the design on screen. As Taylor and Perry's creative relationship exemplifies, the automation of hand-crafting processes using CAD/CAM has extended the possibilities for conceptual artists to diversify their practice using nontraditional media. As the specialist nature of digital embroidery technology can be difficult to access, it proved easy to assemble a group of artists interested in exploring it as an "interdisciplinary/intermedial" practice, with support from experts in this area.[6]

The title of the project and exhibition was suggested by Taylor through the following citation:

> It's a traditional art, it's creation, it's mechanical, it's electronic; it's difficult and at the same time easy. It's working with your hands, your head and your heart. Knowledge is gained by working with others who learned by doing and who are willing to divulge closely held secrets.[7]

Closely Held Secrets sought to reveal the nature of the often hidden dialogue between the originator of an idea and the agent of interpretation. The project challenged the myth that it is the technology that transposes an artist's ideas, rather than a skilled technician acting as a creative conduit between the artist *and* the technology. It explored how the exchange and realization of ideas require each party to draw on embodied knowledge, to inform new methodologies and outcomes that extend the parameters of a particular medium. The exhibition catalog was designed to reflect upon how creative practice often happens through collaborative engagement over time, but can often be unacknowledged and forgotten (see Plate 20).

Research methodology

The methodology adopted for the project was based on case studies of nine artists, undertaking a reflective, practice-led "research *through* Art and Design"[8] approach, over a nine-month period. The individual artists applied a variety of materials, developmental and action research methods to investigate digital embroidery, by customizing the technology to make new artworks.[9] Emphasis was placed on experimental collaboration, informed by the existing tacit skills of the technical experts and the developing knowledge of the artists, to provide new insights into the creative process of digital textile/art production.[10]

The iterative "research as a learning process"[11] was documented by each group member using a variety of recording methods, including note and image making, photography, video and sound recording. Perry, who had used the medium before, had the clearest idea of an envisioned final outcome, but an exploratory "what if?"[12] approach based on trust, intuition, and at times leaps of faith, was embraced by most of the other members of the group. The physical translation of nine different artists' concepts proved intense during the realization stage between April and October 2010. It therefore became necessary to engage a second digital embroidery specialist, Tessa Acti, a recent postgraduate from Nottingham Trent University. Acti's MA Textile Design Innovation project explored "the beauty of thread" by challenging the use of the multi-head technology to produce stitch structures to the optimum dimensions of the machine's working area. Her abstract design style together with her knowledge of programming and operating the machinery provided a symbiotic skill set to Taylor's artisanal approach of translating a master copy of an artwork onto point paper.

The level of exchange between Taylor and Acti as the "experts" and the artists as "novices" varied according to their experiential knowledge. So although all the partnerships were cross-disciplinary in a general sense, those with established textile skills such as Maier, Fisher, and Townsend became more involved in the process, as a natural extension of their existing skill base, and therefore relied less on the technicians to make aesthetic decisions for them. Similarly, Perry had worked with Taylor on numerous occasions, so was clear in his instructions and expectations. Perhaps the most reciprocal technical and aesthetic collaborations, which underpin the notion of cross-disciplinary engagement, were those undertaken by Beck Mather and Taylor; Sprawson, Taylor, and Acti; and Litherland and Acti. Interestingly, these three artists were the least familiar with textiles, but the most open to its potential as an expressive medium.

Digital embroidery as a method of replication

This section discusses artworks created by Grayson Perry, Simon Beck Mather, and Charlotte Hodes, which were translated by Taylor into embroideries that placed strong emphasis on the original, graphic qualities of the artwork. It also considers works by Danica Maier and Craig Fisher, who worked with Taylor initially but went on to collaborate with Acti in the digitization and stitching out stages, resulting in intricate, decorative wall panels and a conceptual installation, respectively.

Grayson Perry: "Hold Your Beliefs Lightly"

Perry designed a new artwork for *Closely Held Secrets*, inspired by African Asafo flags, prompting Taylor to question the artist whether the embroidery should be suitably "rough and ready" in the general style of these textiles. Perry's response was to suggest the contrary—that the stitching should be "precise and luxurious like a pair of professional boxer's shorts."[13] The final design (Plate 21) was translated by hand from a drawing. The design depicts Perry's famous teddy bear, Alan Measles, as a tribal leader in a surreal composition featuring leaders of the world's religions and Perry's alter ego, Claire (in a wheelchair), combined in the style of African ethnic insignia.

Through discussion, Perry and Taylor agreed that a combination of three satin appliqués, together with embroidered replication of the rich, colorful imagery, would produce the desired effect. The application of satin stitches on silk in carefully selected shades is visually seductive, while demonstrating the professional finish that can be achieved with all fifteen needles of the multi-head machine. The graphic, shiny finish met Perry's brief perfectly, but is paradoxical in terms of the subject matter depicted. The subversion of the use of stitch lies in the subject matter and detail inherent in the imagery rather than the meticulous process and quality of translation "imprecise by design rather than in its execution."[14]

Having worked together for so long, an understanding has evolved whereby Taylor can grasp Perry's requirements regarding the "feel" of each piece. In contrast with his ceramics, which though controversial visually often appear sketchy, spontaneous, and naive, Perry uses embroidery in a more prescriptive, yet highly seductive manner. For example, the imagery on Claire's "Coming Out Dress" (2000), also featured in the exhibition, incorporates images from the artist's childhood, including Alan Measles as an avenging primitive god. It also shows a struggling butterfly, symbolic of the transvestite coming out of the cocoon of puberty, and a "decriminalized penis with a bow around it, made to look cute like a pair of cherries on a child's dress."[15]

Simon Beck Mather: "Yew Tree Avenue–Children's Nightgarden"

Beck Mather's series of geometric embroideries were based on his painted wooden maquettes. Embroidery was completely new territory for the artist, who was open-minded about how his work could be translated, allowing Taylor to take the lead. Though abstract in terms of their patterning, they fit within the "replication" category because of the painterly exactitude with which Taylor carefully interpreted the intricate reliefs using various stitching methods and contrasting stitch directions to create a new entity (Figure 13.1: left).

> Whilst the artist's original pieces are 3D by design, the thread patterns gave the embroideries a more subtle shifting physicality, dependent on both the position of the viewer and the light source.[16]

Figure 13.1 Left: an interpretation of "Yew Tree Avenue–Children's Nightgarden" as an embroidered artwork, Simon Beck Mather, 2010. Photograph: Simon Beck Mather. Right: section of embroidered appliqué based on the series of wave drawings and paper cuts, Charlotte Hodes, 2010. Photograph: Debbie Whitmore. © Charlotte Hodes.

For Taylor, working with Beck Mather was the ultimate exchange between the artist and the artisan in *Closely Held Secrets*, inasmuch as he had to "prise out" the artist's original intentions regarding his existing pieces, and then engineer the new artworks by means of the "secrets" of embroidery digitizing.[17] This relationship is in stark contrast to the one Taylor experienced with Perry, who originated his artwork with the embroidered outcome clearly in mind, whereas Beck Mather was working in unknown aesthetic territory.

Charlotte Hodes: "Wave"

Hodes provided Taylor with finished artwork for "Wave" (2009/10), a collection of large-scale (A0) printed/paper cuts inspired by classical Greek figures, which he synthesized to create a single, intricate piece. Hodes was fascinated by the possibilities of translating her work, recognizing that the tactile, collaged surfaces of imagery and pattern of her paper cuts shared many of the qualities that are inherent in embroidery. The major challenge was how to use the paper cuts as a starting point for digital embroidery through combining inkjet printing with multi-head embroidery to articulate the layered qualities of the drawings.

We were acutely aware of the embroidery threads being my drawing tool, equivalent to the cut lines of the scalpel blade in the paper. These threads weave a complex, intricate layer across the surface, holding together the digitally printed areas, patterns, and shapes.[18]

The resulting piece (Figure 13.1: right) featured richly colored floral elements juxtaposed with a figure and fan-shaped skirt translated as monochromatic, lace-patterned appliqués, superimposed upon a digital print. Taylor considered this synthesis of textile approaches to illustrate a "tacit conspiracy" between the artist and the artisan:

The "physicality" of embroidery is important here; the relatively muscular quality of the stitches and appliqué set against the fine precision of Charlotte's original paper cuts was particularly effective.[19]

Craig Fisher: "What a Load of Shit"

In the exhibition catalog for *Closely Held Secrets*, Fisher tells an amusing tale of how he once spent an entire two-week package holiday sewing sequins onto an artwork, and the attention and amusement it created among his fellow holidaymakers when they discovered it was not a map of Majorca, but "a big pile of vomit!"[20] Fisher's account underpins his ongoing exploration of the subversive potential of "the ornamental" through his process of making. In *Closely Held Secrets*, his aim was to work with Taylor and digital technology to make "the most beautiful pile of crap" that he could.[21]

In the event, Taylor digitized Fisher's numerous, varying-sized motifs designed to resemble cartoon-style bird droppings and Acti stitched them out to the artist's specific requirements. As Acti observed, Fisher "explored layering, placement, tonal colour and replication, slightly changing each piece so it challenged the perception of repetition."[22]

Figure 13.2 Views of the installation, "What a Load of Shit" by Craig Fisher, 2010, Bonington Gallery, Nottingham Trent University. Photographs: Simon Beck Mather. © Craig Fisher.

The embroidered "shits" formed part of a site-specific installation, where they were placed to appear randomly splattered on an arrangement of fuchsia and grey planks of wood, concrete manholes, and hazard tape, crafted in plush, padded textiles.[23] As illustrated in Figure 13.2, the floor-based artwork occupied approximately 2 x 3 square meters of space, inviting the viewer to enter a scene of seductive detritus, where undesirable objects are playfully executed and adorned using the latest technology, presenting an ironic pairing of "hazardous materials" and craft.[24]

Fisher's paradoxical approach to textile embellishment was reinforced by Kane's review of the exhibition:

> Fisher's work underpinned the theme of ornamentation running through the show, but explicitly addressed the subversive potential of the decorative in relation to notions of masculinity … touching upon ideas of mechanization and industry … From an aesthetic perspective, Fisher's digitized piece was ambitious in its approach to surface … and perhaps glamorous.[25]

Danica Maier: "Harlequin Slit"

For Maier, "the act of drawing repetitive lines one after another, camouflaging letters and words within pretty patterns is in itself like the act of embroidery" and it is this repeated act of stitching, making, and drawing that she enjoys doing.[26] The works themselves have multiple levels of reading and understanding. First, the decorative image is seen, then the different stitching techniques or "marks"; finally—and only to those willing to look—does the text reveal itself and unravel the original understanding of the work.

For *Closely Held Secrets,* Maier used a combination of smooth, padded, and overstitching techniques to create a series of wall-mounted, parallelogram-shaped panels (Figure 13.3), featuring silver grey thread on dark grey (Figure 13.4: right) and scarlet silk. Maier enjoyed the physicality and practice of generating the digital element and worked very closely with Acti, learning how to program using the Wilcom software.

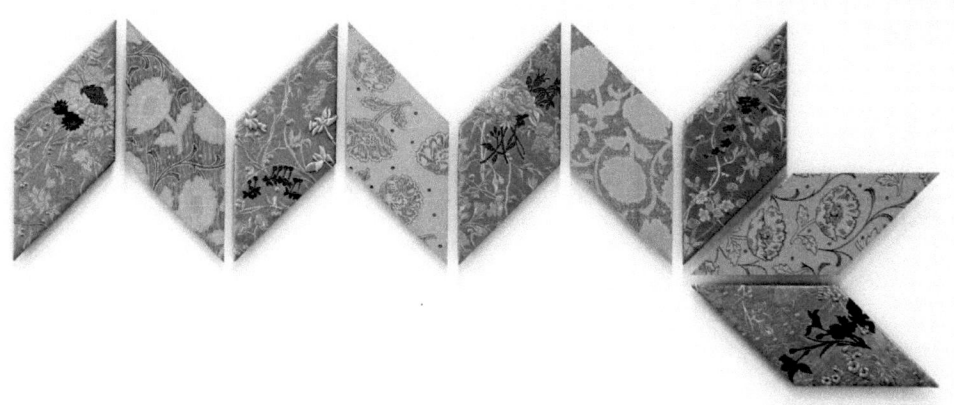

Figure 13.3 "Harlequin Slit," Danica Maier, 2010. Photograph: Danica Maier.

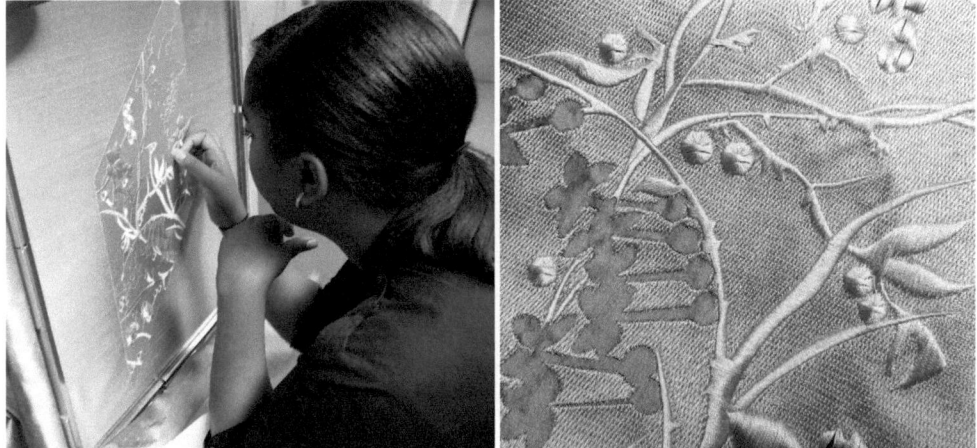

Figure 13.4 Left: Tessa Acti working on Danica Maier's "Harlequin Slit." Photograph: Debbie Whitmore. © Bonington Gallery. Right: Detail from one of Maier's panels, illustrating how the artist accentuated the negative space of the background silk by applying smooth and raised stitch effects. Photograph: Debbie Whitmore. © Danica Maier.

The repeated action of using a digital line to create the instructions for the machine to work from seemed to mimic the repeated action of drawing. While the repeated act of the embroidery machine hiding the lovely silk underneath seemed to inverse the expectation that in drawing the line is used to reveal. Stitched line, drawn line—both the same—a line used to direct the attention of the eye.[27]

Maier was shown how to digitize and asked for advice regarding technical (how to) detail alongside aesthetics. Her hand embroidery background helped her to visualize the pieces created with more ease than some of the other artists who had no embroidery knowledge. Acti reflected:

The people who worked more closely with me felt as though they had more control, investment and connection with the process and created a truer reflection of what they wanted to convey through the pieces. Also, Maier, Litherland, Townsend, and to some degree Fisher, had more appreciation of the time, limitations, and challenges which comes from the real-time engagement with the machine, i.e. being present during the stitching out process.[28]

Digital embroidery as an exploratory process

This section discusses Derek Sprawson's, Stella Whalley's, and Geoff Diego Litherland's artworks that were digitized by Taylor and stitched out by Acti, and Katherine Townsend's work, whose ideas were translated in collaboration with Acti. The members of this group had fewer preconceptions about the qualities and overall appearance of the final artworks, allowing the process to influence the outcome.

Derek Sprawson: "Evidence of 20,000 Saints"

For some time Sprawson had imagined how the imagery he painted would translate into embroidery. Finding himself undergoing a shake-up of his "comfortable mode of making," he was excited by the opportunity to collaborate with Taylor to produce something he hoped would satisfy his curiosity. Sprawson's starting point was globules of oil paint mixed with a solution of beeswax spattered onto stained canvas by pressing sheets of acetate onto the surface. The organic forms of the waxy, oily smears enthralled him. Having digitally scanned these shapes, he presented Taylor with a USB and asked him to explore how these scans might emerge as embroidered images. Following a week of artistic interpretation by Taylor, Sprawson's digitized artwork was uploaded to the multi-head machine by Acti and stitched out (Figure 13.5: right):

> Watching the thread, the needles dance over the surface of the cloth choreographed by the drawings Tony had extracted from my smears was probably the highlight of this whole experience for me. The precision and dexterity with which the form emerged was riveting. I could see the form of the smeared shape I had given to Tony but the colours of the thread, the scale of the shape and the tactility of the surface now read as something completely different.[29]

The translation of the smears presented Taylor with a particular challenge. Due to their amorphous nature, he processed the original scans by repeatedly rendering them in Paint Shop Pro, "enhancing the sharpness, and contrast, until they began to take the form of natural topographical features complete with contours as on an ordnance survey map, just as Derek hoped they might."[30] Sprawson and Taylor's conceptual collaboration raises parallels with the notion explored by Sol LeWitt that "an idea embodies its own logic of production and that its *narrative* potential could automatically unfold to achieve its full or total expression."[31]

Stella Whalley: "They Are Taking It to the People"

Stella Whalley's stylized graphics, based on a research visit to Tokyo,[32] provided Taylor with a completely different set of artistic parameters to work within. Whalley felt that Taylor had the skill to translate her different drawing styles into embroideries. Discussing her contrasting mark making approaches with him suggested the tone and textures of the threads and stitch techniques. For example, she wanted a stitch to reflect the scratchy pen drawing of the "Wolf" piece, with lots of long stitches and rough loose threads. She gave Taylor a challenge by using graduated tonal color, as on the "play girl's" body and "girl with fish" (Figure 13.5: left) where he applied a stitch that changed direction to effectively pick up various tones. Whalley was impressed by the amount of stitches Taylor had to plot to animate the qualities and characters in the drawings, using running stitches as outlines and infilling with satin stitch to create rich embossed 3D surfaces that caught the light. Like Sprawson, she was also mesmerized by the automated stitching process:

> I love watching the multi-head machine in its process, its robotic jabbing movement over the fabric; machines now can automatically snip threads, thread needles, and change colors, but there is still the hands-on skill of its operator in programming and setting up, making sure the fabric and needle work together without tearing the surface. I like the multiplicity of this process, as in print these stages can be separated.[33]

Whalley's account references what Harris (2012) refers to as "digital practice in material hands"[34]—how it is still dependent on the dexterity of nimble finger work and timely intervention to progress the technology strategically or prevent machine error. She was seduced by the relationship between man and machine, the programming and reprogramming activities of a "human computer."[35] Her enthusiasm for the medium followed initial reservations about its limitations, how it could enhance her work, and whether her ideas were practically possible to realize. However, it was clear to Taylor that the physicality of embroidery would be a perfect foil for her artwork and that the print and embroidery would "jump off" the surface in turns. The translation process necessitated "a leap into the unknown" since the scale of the pieces required multiple (and manual)

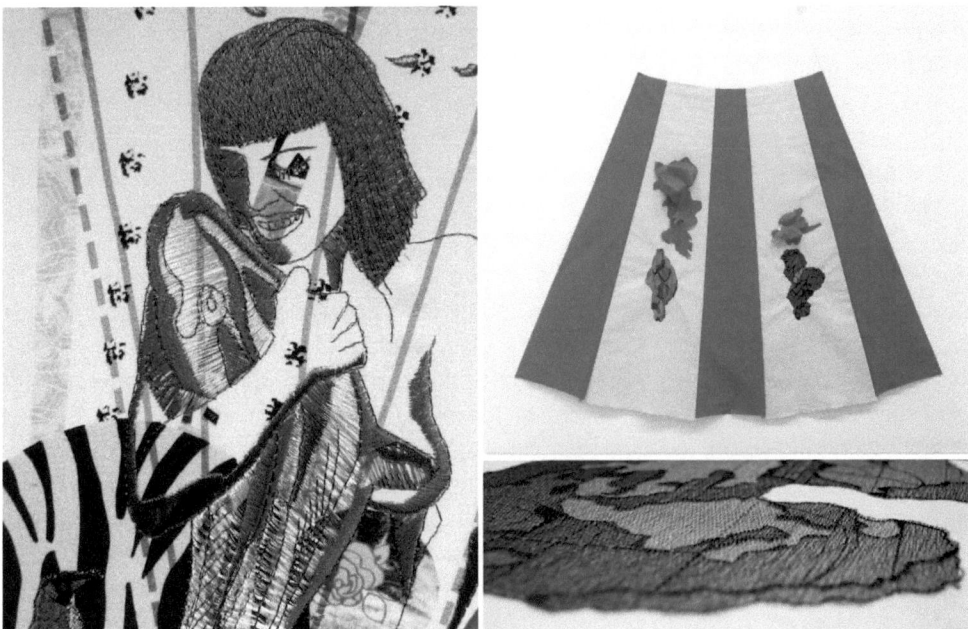

Figure 13.5 Left: "girl with fish" from "They Are Taking It to the People," showing satin-style stitches superimposed over digitally printed imagery, Stella Whalley, 2010. Photograph: Simon Beck Mather. © Stella Whalley. Right: "Part of Evidence of 20,000 Saints" and detail of motif based on oil smear, Derek Sprawson, 2010. Photograph: Debbie Whitmore. © Derek Sprawson.

manipulation of the fabric within the stitching frame for the embroidery to be accurately registered upon the printed substrate.[36]

While Taylor completed the digitizing aspect, the level of manual intervention required to superimpose stitches accurately over digital prints could not be outsourced.[37] Like most of the pieces, it was stitched out by Acti, who acknowledged that this was "the most difficult piece to navigate, as the fabric was larger than the surface area of the multi-head frame."[38] Despite Acti's rigorous approach, the disparity between the scale of printed and digitized visual elements resulted in some accidental, surreal effects, which contributed to the expressive style of the final textiles.

Geoff Diego Litherland: "All the Stars" and "Invaders"

Litherland experimented with integrating the digital embroidery into his painting practice. Like his paintings, which strongly reflect the actions and materiality of their making, it was important to him that the final outcomes for *Closely Held Secrets* were influenced by the various processes involved—from the initial conversations to the design of the motif and the embroidery itself. From the start he aimed to subvert the idea of the embroidered motif, "the default use of the technology and imagined what would happen if a malignant consciousness entered the machinery and took control of the production."[39]

> For "All the Stars" (Plate 22), I wanted to set up parameters that enabled an approach not dissimilar to the way that some minimalist composers create music, one layer at a time. And like Terry Riley's *In C* piece, I wanted to allow the performer—in this case Acti was controlling the multi-head machine—a space to be intuitive and improvise. The stars were digitized by Tony and I picked 24 colours and roughly laid out 5 layers of 10 stars each, but Acti picked the final colour combinations and layouts. I wanted the previous layer and background painting to direct but not dictate the overall composition.[40]

The initial imagery for "Invaders" was inspired by the 1980s arcade game Space Invaders; with its block-style pixels it had an obvious connection with digitization (Plate 23). Litherland was interested in exploring the sci-fi connotations "ghost in the machine." The first layer was based on a formal composition worked out in Photoshop. However, when stitched out, subsequent layers of the same composition were started from a different point and so on, resulting in a thick layer of stitching which mimicked the artist's impasto painting style and challenged the machine's technical capability. Litherland and Acti decided from the outset that there would be no specific aesthetic conclusion to the process but they would stop when there was a risk of breaking the embroidery equipment.[41] In order to promote this element of chaos, Litherland gave Acti some rules and parameters as to how to produce the pieces, with the aim of creating a generative image that was constructed not only by the limits of the technology, but also by intuition, communication or miscommunication, and error.[42]

Katherine Townsend: "Lace Flow 1–3"

The three textile lengths developed by Townsend for *Closely Held Secrets* were inspired by the patterning synergies between water and lace: the juxtaposition of an elemental fast-flowing rhythm with static, organically inspired fabrications.[43] The pieces explored the potential for combining multi-head embroidery with inkjet printing: how both processes can be used to photographically replicate visual and textural detail, but, more significantly, how these technologies can be applied non-prescriptively to abstract and innovate rather than duplicate.[44]

The Baradun multi-head machine used in this project has fifteen needles on each head and a working surface of 45 x 52 cm. Townsend became fixated on what would happen if she stripped the machine back to a single thread in a single color and how she could utilize the working canvas to stitch images that permeated lengths, rather than create small detailed samplers. The use of one needle and thread referenced traditional hand embroidery, which early machines had been devised to replicate.

In practice, this presented problems: the machine did not respond well to this limitation, and stopped regularly, due to the uneven tension created on the cloth's surface by the needle's piercing/threading action. This required Townsend or Acti to regularly

Figure 13.6 Left: "Lace Flow 1–3" by Katherine Townsend in *Closely Held Secrets* exhibition, Bonington Gallery. Top right: horseshoe collar motif on digitally printed silk surface. Bottom right: detail of a lace-inspired motif showing the use of short and elongated stitches within the same design. Photographs: Debbie Whitmore. © Katherine Townsend.

have to restart and rethread the machine needle, generating a complementary set of manual movements and a disjointed woman/machine rhythm. Other hands-on interventions included moving the digitally printed silk base to assimilate stitch and image sympathetically, or to create large-scale elements by joining mirrored motifs (such as the "horseshoe collar" and large "pylon") stitched in two halves to create embroidered motifs, some measuring 80 x 100 cm (Figure 13.6: top right).

The resulting lengths constituted three experimental textile "sketches". On "Lace Flow 1 and 2" the greyscale silk (digitally printed with abstract patterns of fast-flowing rivers) was embroidered with interpretations of lace collar and handkerchief designs from the Nottingham Trent Lace Archive. The motifs were stretched and distorted to replicate the idea of lace fragments being dropped into a fast-flowing current, translated through a combination of satin, short stabbed and long draped stitches in white matt cotton threads to create a contrast with the sheen of the base cloth (Figure 13.6: bottom right). On "Lace Flow 3", red, black and white, running, tacking-style, and floating stitches overlaid the print, leaving the viewer to decide which surface to look at first. This reflected the aim: to integrate the stitches so the threads followed and responded to the visual clues of the surface, adding a variable patina as opposed to a layer of embellishment.[45]

Conclusion

Closely Held Secrets challenged the process and perceptions of digital embroidery as a creative medium by highlighting its potential application within a visual arts context. The embroidered artworks formed a diverse collection of images, canvases, fabric lengths, and soft sculptures; they were in a sense all "super-objects"[46] in their own right—the process of collaborative exchange being as significant as the final crafted outcome.

The collaborations between Tony Taylor, Tessa Acti, and the artists provided valuable insights into the aesthetic responsibility of the technician during the digitization and stitching out stages of digital embroidery production. Decisions were made and applied by them in varying degrees, according to the tacit knowledge and aspirations of the practitioners they were working with. As mentioned earlier, the artists with the least hands-on experience of working with textiles seemed to be particularly open to the cross-disciplinary process, such as Beck Mather, Sprawson, and Litherland, who generally work with fine art materials such as wood, canvas, and paint. For Hodes and Whalley, Taylor's and Acti's input was necessarily more intensive; their sophisticated, illustrative artworks required skilled interpretation through multiple stitch techniques.

While each of the creative partnerships worked differently, everyone involved had to accept artistic and technical compromises in order to complete the artworks for the exhibition deadline—in a similar way to how textile designers work in the commercial industry. The cooperative process of artistic translation not only extended the artists' skill base, particularly in the case of Maier, Townsend, and Fisher, who were most familiar with working with stitch and textiles, but revealed and elevated the role of the technician *and* the technology beyond that of "faithful copier."[47] For long-standing collaborators Perry and Taylor, the way that they created the work for the exhibition was distinct from the other partnerships. They have evolved a tried and tested process over time, building on their embodied knowledge of working together with digital embroidery, which ensures that Perry's artistic intentions are realized through engagement with Taylor's aesthetic and technical expertise.

Significantly, the cross-disciplinary research making process demonstrated the flexibility of using both hand and computerized digitizing methods to translate contrasting visual constructs: from the intricate patterns of handmade lace, to untamed stitch structures that float across the surface. The artists using digital embroidery to "replicate" and envision carefully conceived compositions created artworks that were sophisticated, decorative, and in some cases quite traditional in terms of the application of the technology. However, all were challenging in their use of subject matter and/or their determination to interpret narratives inspired by elaborate hand-stitched effects, using craft as an aesthetic and political position.[48]

Conversely, some of the more experimental approaches adopted by the "exploratory" group were more focused on the unknown, serendipitous potential of the multi-head machine: how it could be played with or subverted to create unexpected material effects. Most artworks encompassed both replication and exploration of the medium simultaneously, with each artifact the result of a unique research journey. Whether traditional or experimental in terms of stitch application, of greatest significance was how the "research through making" journey acknowledged the reciprocal relationship between the artist and the technician. The project also highlighted the importance of supporting opportunities for non-specialists to access and "play" with digital textile technologies as alternative media to extend creative practice.

Closely Held Secrets celebrated the historical and conceptual significance of craft textiles. The project proved timely in a number of ways, preceding *The Power of Making* (2011) exhibition,[49] which celebrated the skill of the craftsperson, and *The Art of Not Making* (2012) publication,[50] which documented the emergence of a new kind of relationship between the artist and the artisan. Ultimately, the strength of the outcomes was not about the physical artifacts themselves, but how making artworks by "other means," even the flexible medium of digital textiles, requires a sophisticated level of communication and reliance on the embodied knowledge and skills of all parties.

Notes

1   Tony Taylor, quoted in Grayson Perry, artist's statement in *Closely Held Secrets* [exhibition catalog] (Nottingham: Nottingham Trent University Bonington Gallery, 2010), 3.
2   Jean Baudrillard, *The Vital Illusion* (New York: Colombia University Press, 2000), 177.
3   Jane Harris, "Digital Practice in Material Hands: How Craft and Computing Practices are Advancing Digital Aesthetic and Conceptual Methods," *Craft Research* 3 (1) (2012): 91.
4   Andrew Ure, *A Dictionary of Arts, Manufacture and Mines* (London: Longman, Orme, Brown, Green and Longmans, 1839), 429.
5   Tony Taylor, private interview with Katherine Townsend, Nottingham Trent University, July 20, 2011.

6 David Thomas, "Programming and Reprogramming Artworks: A Case of Painting and Practicing Conceptual and Media Art by Other Means," *Intermédialités Journal* 13 (Spring 2009): 89–113. http://id.erudit.org/iderudit/044042ar [accessed December 19, 2014].

7 Coleman Schneider, *Schiffli and Multi Head* (New Jersey: Coleman Schneider, 1978), 1.

8 Christopher Frayling, "Research in Art and Design," *Royal College of Art Research Papers* 1 (1) (1993): 5.

9 Ibid.

10 Jean McNiff, *Action Research, Principles and Practice* (London: Routledge, 1999).

11 Donald Schön, *Educating the Reflective Practitioner: Towards a New Design for Teaching and Learning in the Professions* (San Francisco: Jossey-Bass, 1987).

12 Julian Malins and Carole Gray, "Appropriate Research Methodologies for Artists, Designers & Crafts Persons: Research as a Learning Process," in *Proceedings of Making It, UK Crafts Council Conference* (Wakefield: Woolley Hall, 1995), 3. http://carolegray.net/Papers%20PDFs/cc.pdf [accessed January 7, 2014].

13 Taylor, private interview, 2011.

14 Taylor refers to Perry's "subversion" as being related to his "imprecise" use of controversial subject matter. This is a very different, but no less powerful, connotation to the feminist context addressed by Rozsika Parker in *The Subversive Stitch* (London: I.B.Tauris, 2010; originally printed in 1984 by The Women's Press).

15 Grayson Perry in Jacky Klein, *Grayson Perry* (London: Thames and Hudson, 2009), 113.

16 Taylor, private interview, 2011.

17 Ibid.

18 Charlotte Hodes, artist's statement in *Closely Held Secrets*, 7.

19 Taylor, private interview, 2011.

20 Craig Fisher, artist's statement in *Closely Held Secrets*, 6.

21 Ibid.

22 Tessa Acti, private interview with Katherine Townsend, Nottingham Trent University, March 21, 2011.

23 Neoprene, styrofoam, felt, cotton, Dupont silk, and car upholstery were used to create soft sculptures of industrial salvage for the "embroidered shits" to be placed on, as if left in the corner of a builder's yard.

24 Craig Fisher, *Hazardous Materials* [exhibition catalog] (Plymouth: Plymouth College of Art, 2008).

25 Faith Kane, "Digital Embroidery and Expression: A Review of *Closely Held Secrets*," *Craft Research* 1 (2) (2011): 161–8.

26 Danica Maier, private email correspondence with Katherine Townsend, September 11, 2011.

27 Ibid.

28 Acti, private interview, 2011.

29 Derek Sprawson, private email correspondence with Katherine Townsend, October 17, 2011.

30 Taylor, private interview, 2011.

31 Sol LeWitt, quoted in Thomas, *Programming and Reprogramming Artworks*, 32.

32 Stella Whalley, *Tokyo Tales* (England: Design United Worldwide, 2007).

33 Stella Whalley, private email correspondence with Katherine Townsend, September 14, 2011.

34 Harris, "Digital Practice in Material Hands."

35 Thomas, "Programming and Reprogramming Artworks," 24.
36 Taylor, private interview, 2011.
37 Taylor worked with Lace Market Embroidery, Nottingham, but their commercial production precludes the time or flexibility for them to be able to reposition the fabric around to assimilate the stitch with the digitally printed images on the fabric.
38 Acti, private interview, 2011.
39 Geoff Diego Litherland, private interview with Katherine Townsend, Nottingham Trent University, March, 21 2011.
40 Ibid.
41 The over-stitching process stresses the machine, as it is designed to operate on a smooth, taut surface, but as the design demonstrated, a multilayered effect can be achieved if this is not adhered to strictly.
42 Litherland, private interview, 2011.
43 See also Katherine Townsend and Joy Buttress, "High Falls: Water, Lace and the Body," *DUCK Textile Journal* 1 (2010).
44 Katherine Townsend, artist's statement in *Closely Held Secrets*, 12
45 Marguerite Dessanay, "Following the Thread: Art & Craft; An Embroidered Web," *Elephant: The Arts & Visual Culture Magazine* 9 (Winter 2011): 74–95.
46 Louise Manzanti, "Super-Objects: Craft as an Aesthetic Position," in Maria Elena Buzek (ed.), *Extra/Ordinary: Craft and Contemporary Art* (Durham, NC: Duke University Press, 2011), 60–81.
47 Tony Taylor, artist's statement in *Closely Held Secrets*, 3.
48 Louise Mazanti, "Super-Objects: Craft as an Aesthetic Position."
49 See Daniel Charny, *The Power of Making: The Importance of Being Skilled* (London: V&A and the Crafts Council, 2011).
50 The relationship between the artist and technical expert is also discussed in Michael Petry, *The Art of Not Making: The New Artist/Artisan Relationship* (London: Thames and Hudson, 2012).

Bibliography

Baudrillard, Jean, *The Vital Illusion* (New York: Colombia University Press, 2000).
Charny, Daniel, *The Power of Making: The Importance of Being Skilled* (London: V&A and the Crafts Council, 2011).
Dessanay, Marguerite, "Following the Thread: Art & Craft, An Embroidered Web," *Elephant: The Arts & Visual Culture Magazine* 9 (2011): 74–95.
Fisher, Craig, *Hazardous Materials* [exhibition catalog] (Plymouth: Plymouth College of Art, 2008).
Frayling, Christopher, *Research in Art and Design: Royal College of Art Research Paper* 1 (1) (1993).
Harris, Jane, "Digital Practice in Material Hands: How Craft and Computing Practices are Advancing Digital Aesthetic and Conceptual Methods," *Craft Research* 3 (1) (2012): 91–112.
Kane, Faith, "Digital Embroidery and Expression: A Review of Closely Held Secrets," *Craft Research* 1 (2) (2011): 161–8.
Klein, Jacky, *Grayson Perry* (London: Thames and Hudson, 2010).
Litherland, Geoff Diego, Tony Taylor, Katherine Townsend, Tessa Acti, and Helen Garrigan, *Closely*

Held Secrets [catalog of an exhibition held at Bonington Gallery, October 29–November 24, 2010] (Nottingham: Nottingham Trent University, 2010).

Malins, Julian, and Carole Gray, "Appropriate Research Methodologies for Artists, Designers & Crafts Persons: Research as a Learning Proces," in *Proceedings of "Making It". UK Crafts Council Conference* (Wakefield: Woolley Hall, 1995). http://carolegray.net/Papers%20PDFs/cc.pdf [accessed January 7, 2014].

Mazanti, Louise, "Super-Objects: Craft as an Aesthetic Position," in *Extra/Ordinary Craft: Craft and Contemporary Art*, ed. Maria Elena Buzek (Durham, NC: Duke University Press, 2011), 59–83.

McNiff, Jean, *Action Research, Principles and Practice* (London: Routledge, 1999).

Parker, Rozsika, *The Subversive Stitch* (London: I.B.Tauris, 2010; originally printed in 1984 by The Women's Press).

Petry, Michael, *The Art of Not Making: The New Artist/Artisan Relationship* (London: Thames and Hudson, 2012).

Schneider, Coleman, *Schiffli and Multi Head* (New Jersey, USA: Coleman Schneider, 1978).

Schön, Donald, *Educating the Reflective Practitioner: Towards a New Design for Teaching and Learning in the Professions* (San Francisco: Jossey-Bass, 1987).

Thomas, David, "Programming and Reprogramming Artworks: A Case of Painting and Practicing Conceptual and Media Art by Other Means," *Intermédialités Journal* 13 (Spring 2009): 89–113. http://id.erudit.org/iderudit/044042ar [accessed December 19, 2014].

Townsend, Katherine, and Joy Buttress, "High Falls: Water, Lace and the Body," *DUCK Textile Journal* (2010). http://www.lboro.ac.uk/microsites/sota/duck/volume1.htm [accessed December 19, 2014].

Ure, Andrew, *A Dictionary of Arts, Manufacture and Mines* (London: Longman, Orme, Brown, Green and Longmans, 1839).

Whalley, Stella, *Tokyo Tales* (England: Design United Worldwide, 2007).

INDEX

In this index, the principal subject matter of textiles, craft, and digital tools is categorized primarily by other headings and subheadings. Terms are generally indexed in abbreviated form. Project titles are in italics; the letters f., n., and t. indicate figures, notes, and a table.

active materials 28, 29f., 91–2, 98, 111–12
   active wear 104, 109, 110
   crafted control 95, 98, 99
   emotional factors 28
   environmental factors 105
   knowledge 40–1
   light 96
   risk 93
   scope 6, 95, 96, 97, 98, 99, 100
   3D 40–1, 41f.
   uniqueness and 105
   well-being 40
Adamson, Glenn xix, 1, 78
Adobe Flash 54
alginate process 125f., 126f.
   cooling properties 121, 127f., 127–8, 131–2
   scope 125–7
"All the Stars" (Litherland) 200
animation
   light 52, 53, 54f., 55, 56f.
   patterns 54–5, 55f., 57
   scope 4–5
A-POC (A Piece of Cloth) collection 147
Apple IIe computer 22f., 22–3
architecture 67
archives 97, 98
Arts and Crafts movement 159
automated production processes
   crafted control 93–4, 94f.
   distance and proximity 93–4, 94f.
   lasers 95, 96–7, 98, 100
   materials 6, 98
   scope 96, 99

Banishing Boundaries 48

Baradun machine 201–2
Barthes, Roland 173, 185
Basso and Brooke 21
Beck Mather, Simon 192, 193–4, 194f.
beeswax 198, 199f.
Bell, John Edgar 172, 177, 182, 184
black box knowledge 130–1
blindness 65
block patterns 54–5, 55f., 56f., 57, 58
block printing 19f., 20, 122–3
body 165
   absorption 159
   human and machine 154
   knowledge 160
   patterns 50–1
   paying attention 156–7, 158f., 159
   pleasure 159
   self-centered perception 164–5
   time factors 165
Bolton, Andrew 105
Boontje, Tord 81
Braddock, Sarah 7, 103
Brodsky, Joseph 155–6
Brooke, Christopher 21

CAD/CAM (computer-aided design/manufacture) 70–1
   authenticity and 68
   challenges 20
   history 20–1
   scope 67
   time factors 20, 62
   see also digital tools
"Cape Cornwall" (Treadaway) 25f.
capsule wardrobe 107, 108f., 109 *see also* iconic garments

Chalayan, Hussein 5, 21
chiffon 85f., 127
Closely Held Secrets 38f.
    challenges 43
    fragility of machine 43
    originator and agent 43, 189, 191–2 *see also* embroidery: originator and agent
    repetition 43
    scope 189, 190, 191, 192, 193, 202
codes 7, 26–8, 27f., 146 *see also* semiotics
collage 182f.
    color 182
    domesticity 184
    narratives 173, 177–9, 178f., 182–3, 184
    semiotics 177, 179–80, 181f., 182, 183–4, 185–6
Collins, Liz 144, 149 n.13
color 18, 53–4, 54f., 112–13, 115f., 198–9
    challenges 23–4
    lines 51
    metallic 22–3, 23f.
    optical blending 51, 58
    scope 20, 21, 51, 56f., 80, 114–16
    semiotics 182
    serendipity 114–15
"Coming Out Dress" (Perry) 193
commutation tests 175
Considerate Design 147
cooling properties 121, 127f., 130f.
    patent 121, 128
    scope 128, 131–2
    serendipity 127–8
    time factors 127
Corkhill, Betsan 70
cotton 105
Couwenberg, Henricus Wilhelmus 63f.
craft
    aesthetics 131
    authenticity 129
    communication and xix–xx
    cultural factors 18, 153
    definition xix, 177
    distance and proximity 93
    emotional factors 164
    history 99–100
    human and machine 99–100
    knowledge 9, 10, 99, 132
    learning 69
    limitations 9
    mass production and 93
    materials xix, 91–2, 93, 129
    old and new 103–4

    scope 1, 2, 99, 100–1, 131, 147, 166 n.4
    time factors 131
    viewer perception 171, 177
crafted control 92, 93–4, 94f., 95, 96, 99
    risk and 98, 101f.
craftsperson, designer, and technician *see* originator–agent relationships
Crawford, Matthew 154
crochet 144
crushed fabrics 83
Csikszentmihalyi, Mihaly 159
cultural heritage 10
customers and markets 86–7 *see also* fashion

damask 57
Delamore, Philip 22, 28
democratization of design 35, 45 n.1
de Saussure, Ferdinand 173
designing through making 2, 5, 79
Diderot, Denis 65
digital tools 11
    challenges 122
    change and xx, xxii
    communication and 10–11
    constraint 2
    control xxi
    flaws and xxi
    human and machine 121–2
    knowledge 10
    limitations xx
    loss and error xxi
    principles xx–xxii
    scope xix, 17
    studios 6
    time factors xxii, 66
    uniqueness and xx
Dissanayake, Ellen 156
domesticity 143, 143f., 171–2, 184
Dormer, Peter 50, 93, 160, 176–7
drawing 65–6, 67
dresses 28, 29f., 38f., 85f.
Driessen, Hil 21

Edelkoort, Lidewij 9–10
EEG (Electroencephalography) 69, 69f.
Eley Kishimoto 21–2
Emboscan 95
embroidery 38f.
    challenges 39–40, 42, 43, 44
    constraint 36
    democratization of design 35, 45 n.1

INDEX

fragility of machine 43
free machine 39
history 42
human and machine 37, 44, 45
human and materials 37
knowledge 4, 37, 40, 44–5
lasers 95
lines 42
materials 40–1, 41f., 42–3
materials and machine 37
originator and agent 8–9, 42–3, 45–6 n.9, 190, 192, 193–7, 194f., 195f., 196f., 197f., 198–203, 199f., 201f.
randomness 39f., 40
repetition 43
resists 83, 87–8
scope 35–7, 189, 190, 191, 192, 193, 202
spontaneity and 4
time factors 44, 191
see also hand stitching
emotional factors 26, 28, 155–6, 162f., 162–3, 164
love and hate 163, 164f.
Emotional Wardrobe 147
engraved roller printing 19f.
environmental factors 105, 106, 131
"Evidence of 20,000 Saints" (Sprawson) 198, 199f.
"Evolving Lace" (Kenning) 27f.
Exploration of Digital Technology, An 80–1
designing through making 79
error and 79
originator and agent 77, 78, 81, 83
resists 79, 80, 81, 82f., 83, 84f., 85f., 86–8
scope 77–8
"Extreme Scale Stitches" (Acti) 38f.

family 172
narratives 173, 177–9, 178f., 182, 184
semiotics 174f.
fashion 21–2
aesthetics 154
high end and high street 86
materials 104
multidisciplinary approaches 104–5
scope 147
urban factors 105
see also *individual names*; active materials; iconic garments
FDM (Fused Deposition Modeling) printers 25–6

feminism and gender 143, 143f., 145, 171–2, 184
figurative weaving 51, 57–8
Fisher, Craig 189, 195f., 195–6
Fiske, John 173
Flash player 54
fleece
materials 109, 114–15, 115f., 116–17
patterns 109, 114–15, 116–17
scope 109–10
flow 20, 159
Flusser, Vilém 122
fMRI (functional Magnetic Resonance Imaging) scanning 69
Foucault, Michel 145
Freedom of Creation 147
free machine embroidery 39
Frølund, Lise 51, 57–8

Garment ID 7, 106, 108f., 119 n.14
knowledge 107, 118
patterns and materials 106–7, 109, 110, 111t., 111–18, 113f., 115f., 116f., 117f.
scope 107, 109, 111, 111t., 118
gender issues 143, 143f., 145, 171–2, 184
Giard, Jacques 171
Gil, Luisa 40–1, 41f., 44–5
"girl with fish" (Whalley) 199f.
graffiti 144–5
grounded theory 124
Gschwandtner, Sabrina 140, 148 n.1
guerrilla knitters 144–5

habotai 82f., 84f., 85f.
"Hamefarers' Kist" (White) 141, 142f.
hand knitting 69f., 139
accessibility 148
codes 7, 146
constraint 140
gender issues 143, 143f.
history 140, 141
knowledge 7–8, 139, 140–1, 145, 148
lines 8
living craft 140–3, 142f.
make-do-and-mend 140
making and product 143–4
materials 109, 110, 112–14, 113f., 116f., 116–18, 117f.
memories 141, 142f.
narratives 144
online communities 145–6, 149 n.12

patterns 109, 112–14, 116f., 116–18, 117f., 141
political activism 144–5
scope 8, 109, 139, 143, 144, 147–8, 149 n.13
serendipity 69
trade links and 141
well-being 70
hands/hand skills 61f., 63f., 68, 121
absorption 159
aesthetics 154
challenges 122, 145
coming-up-against 155
constraint 2
crafted control 93–4, 94f.
distance and proximity 93–4, 94f.
drawing 65–6
emotional factors 155–6
flaws and 154
hidden knowledge 156
knowledge 18, 155
lasers 95, 96–7, 98
limitations xxi–xxii
making special 156
materials 96
pleasure 156, 159
printing and 24–6, 30 see also printing
scope 5, 17, 18, 62, 64, 68, 96, 154, 155
sensibility to change 64
sensory factors 64, 155
touch 64–5, 155
workmanship theory 78
hand stitching 154, 156, 161, 191
aesthetic perception 160f., 161
blending in 162f.
challenges 163
cultural factors 153
emotional factors 162f., 162–3, 164f.
knowledge 161–2
paying attention 156–7, 157f., 158f., 159, 163
pleasure 160
scope 8, 70, 153, 166 n.4
self-centered perception 165–6
sensory factors 161
time factors 153–4, 165
hand weaving 62
cultural heritage 10
materials 67f., 67–8, 71f.
scope 5, 71–2
sensibility to change 64
system and order 50

3D 62, 67f., 67–8, 71f.
time factors 66
uniqueness 68
see also jacquard weaving
handwriting 18, 39, 39f., 40, 43
Hansmeyer, Michael 67
"Harlequin Slit" (Maier) 196f., 196–7, 197f.
hate and love 163, 164f.
Hodes, Charlotte 194f., 194–5
"Hold Your Beliefs Lightly" (Perry) 189, 193
Holyoke, Julie 48
hyperbolic crochet 144

iconic garments 7, 106, 108f.
knowledge 118
patterns and materials 106, 109, 110, 111t., 111–18, 113f., 115f., 116f., 117f.
scope 107, 109, 111, 111t., 118
"Incompleta" (Auch) 67f.
Ingold, Tim 71–2, 155
inkjet printing 19f., 77–8, 80–1, 122
black box knowledge 130–1
chain of events 130
challenges 122
coating 126f., 127
color 18, 21
control 123
environmental factors 106
error and 123, 124
history 21
human and machine 123
knowledge 122
originator and agent 78, 81, 83, 201
resists 79, 80, 81, 82f., 83, 84, 84f., 85f., 86–8
scope 21–2, 24, 30, 80, 84, 132
subjectivity 123–4
Innovative Synthesis 121, 125f.
coating 126f., 127, 130f.
cooling properties 121, 127f., 127–8, 130f., 131–2
error and 124
knowledge 7, 124
scope 123, 124, 132
subjectivity 123–4
intelligent materials see active materials
interdisciplinary work see multidisciplinary approaches
"Invaders" (Litherland) 200

jacquard tapestry 48
jacquard weaving 47, 48, 50

history 48
    TC-1 looms 1–2, 48, 49f., 50–1, 53, 54, 57–9
    TC-2 looms 1–2
Jakob Schlaepfer see Schlaepfer
Jefferies, Janis 172, 189
jewelry 64, 65–6
John-Steiner, Vera 176
jumpers 109, 110, 113

Kalay, Yehuda E. xx
Kenning, Gail 27f.
Kishimoto, Wakako 21–2
Knitta 144–5
"Knitted Homes of Crime" (Robins) 143, 143f.
knitting 5, 104, 146–7 see also hand knitting
Knitting and Stitching Show, The 166 n.4
Knitting Nation 144, 149 n.13
Knit to Fit 147
Kuhn, Annette 179

lace 81, 82f., 83, 202
"Lace Flow 1–3" (Townsend) 201f., 201–2
lasers 94, 98
    materials 92, 95, 98, 100, 116–18, 117f.
    multidisciplinary approaches 96
    patterns 95, 116–18, 117f.
    scope 95, 96–7, 98
Latour, Bruno 130–1
Lenzing Group 105, 119 n.9
libraries 86
light
    crafted control 96
    patterns 52, 53, 54f., 55, 56f.
Litherland, Geoff Diego 43, 44–5, 192, 200
looms 47, 48, 50
    history 48
    system and order 50
    TC-1 1–2, 48, 49f., 50–1, 53, 54, 57–9
    TC-2 1–2
love and hate 163, 164f.
"Ludens" (Auch) 67f.

McCullough, Malcolm 5–6, 92, 145
    designing through making 79
    workmanship theory 91–2
McLean, George 64
Maeda, Kuniko 66
Maier, Danica 43, 44–5, 196f., 196–7, 197f.
make-do-and-mend 140
"Manual Work" (Nissen) 50–1
Margetts, Martina 155

mathematics xxi, 5, 62, 144, 146
Matthews, Rachael 144
medical science 61f.
    drawing 66
    knitting 69f.
    scope 61
    sensibility to change 64
    serendipity 69
    weaving 5, 62
memories 65, 141, 142f., 173, 179
metallic color 22–3, 23f.
metallic foil 25f.
Metcalf, Bruce 164
microscope 66
Minale and Maeda 66
Miyake, Issey 147
MMC (man-made cellulosic) fabrics 105
Morris, William 159
MRI (Magnetic Resonance Imaging) scanning 61f., 69
multidisciplinary approaches xx, 6–7, 30, 95–6, 100, 104–5
    challenges 10
    crafted control 96
    knowledge 42, 132
multi-head embroidery see embroidery

Nakamatsu, Yuri 42, 44–5
narratives and narratology 172
    gender issues 184
    memories 173, 179
    scope 175
    semiotics 173, 176, 177–9, 178f., 182–3, 184, 186 n.5
    unfinished pieces 144
    viewer perception 171
neoprene 112
    patterns 112–13, 115–16, 116f., 117f.
    scope 110
"Neurotubes" (Auch) 71f.
New Craft practice 146
Nissen, Kirsten 50–1, 57
Noten, Ted 65–6

oil paint 198, 199f.
online communities 145–6, 149 n.12, 150 n.29
originator–agent relationships 45–6 n.9, 81, 122–3, 190, 194f., 195f., 196f., 197f.
    challenges 194–5, 198, 199–200, 201–2
    color 198–9
    control 200
    cultural factors 193

fragility of machine 200
hidden knowledge 194
human and machine 43, 199
knowledge 78, 189, 191–2, 197, 202–3
materials 193, 198, 199f., 201f., 202
patterns 201
repetition 197
resists 81, 83
scope 8–9, 42–3, 77, 193–4, 195–6, 197, 198, 203
serendipity 203
surfaces 202

Paint Shop Pro 198
Pajaczkowska, Claire 159
Pallasmaa, Juhani 161
panels 182f.
    color 182
    domesticity 184
    narratives 172, 173, 176, 177–9, 178f., 182–3, 184
    originator and agent 196f., 196–7, 197f.
    scope 175
    semiotics 172, 176–7, 179–80, 181f., 182, 183–4, 185–6
    viewer perception 177
Parker, Rozsika 171–2
Parsons, Jean 21
passive materials 91, 92, 96, 97
patents 121, 128, 129
pattern cutting 42
patterns 52, 81, 82f., 95, 111t., 111–12, 201
    aesthetics 115–16
    block 54–5, 55f., 56f., 57, 58
    color 53, 54f., 56f., 112–13, 114–16, 115f.
    flow and harmony 20
    glossiness 53, 55
    history 81
    living craft 141
    lost and recreated 145–6
    repetition 20, 24f., 116–17
    scope 50–1, 52, 53, 54, 80, 81, 109, 118
    sharpness and 113, 115–16, 116f.
    surfaces 106–7, 110, 112, 114, 117f., 117–18
    3D 113f., 113–14, 116–17
    uniqueness and 81, 83, 84f.
pen plotter 22–3
Perry, Grayson 189, 190, 193
    cultural factors 193
    knowledge 192, 202–3
    materials 193

pleating 83, 84f.
Pluto Designer system 23, 24f.
Polanyi, Michael 128–9
Polartec 114–15, 115f., 116–17
political activism 144–5
Pollock, Griselda 171–2
porcelain 66
printing 19–20, 36
    block 19f., 20, 122–3
    code 26, 28
    color 22–4, 23f.
    designing through making 5
    4D 30
    history 18, 22f., 22–4, 23f., 24f.
    knowledge 7
    materials 4, 28, 29f.
    multidisciplinary approaches 30
    narratives 175
    patterns 20, 24f.
    risk 26
    roller 19f.
    scope 3–4, 6, 18–19, 30, 118
    semiotics 176, 182–3
    silkscreen 19f., 20, 112–14, 113f.
    sublimation 114–16, 115f., 116f.
    3D 22, 25f., 25–6, 27f., 28, 30, 65–6
    time factors 66
    see also inkjet printing; lasers
problem solving 175–7
Processing language 26
puff binder 113f., 113–14
Pye, David xix, 78, 91–2, 121, 128, 159

Queen Susan Shawl, The 145–6
quilting 166 n.4, 190
Quinn, Bradley 105

Rainbow Winters 28, 29f.
Ravelry 145–6, 150 n.29
Reas, Casey 26
reflection-in-action 107, 124, 175–7
resists 79, 80
    challenges 84
    color 80
    control 83
    knowledge 87, 88
    libraries and 86
    mass production and 86–7
    patterns 80, 81, 82f., 83, 84f.
    scope 79, 83, 87–8
    surfaces 80
    uniqueness and 85f., 86

INDEX

Riisberg, Vibeke 21
risk xix, 101f., 132
   emotional factors 26
   scope 78, 91–3, 98
Robins, Freddie 143f., 143–4
Rolf, Margot 64
roller printing 19f.
Rosenberg, Rikke 52

San Martin, Macarena 104
satin 127, 193, 199f.
Saunders, Jonathan 21–2
Schlaepfer 97f.
   archives 97, 98
   lasers 94, 95, 96, 98
   multidisciplinary approaches 6–7, 95–6
   scope 94, 97–8
   uniqueness 94
Schlein, Alice 48
Schlömer, Rudiger 146
Schön, Donald 107, 124, 176
Scott, Clive 173
screen printing 19f., 20, 112–14, 113f.
Scrivener, Stephen 124
semiotics 8, 172, 174f., 186 n.5
   challenges 176–7
   commutation tests 175
   history 173, 179–80, 182–3, 184–5
   intertextuality 179
   intratextuality 179
   paradigm 173, 175, 176, 180, 182, 185
   scope 172, 177, 180, 181f., 182–3, 185, 186
   sensory factors 183, 184
   surfaces 176, 183
   syntagm 173, 175, 176, 177–9, 178f., 185–6
   time factors 176
   viewer perception 179–80, 182, 183–6
serendipity and chance 2, 67, 69, 114–15, 127, 203
   control and 127–8
   error and 128
   invention and 128–9
Serres, Michel 155, 165
Seymour, Sabine 104
shibori 79
Shillito, Ann Marie 28, 68
"Signatures Exchanged for Passwords" (Rumble-Smith) 39f., 39–40
silk 125f.
   coating 126f., 127, 130f.
   cooling properties 127f., 127–8, 130, 130f.
   habotai 82f., 84f., 85f.
silkscreen printing 19f., 20, 112–14, 113f.
sketchbooks 129, 130f., 174f.
skin 155
smart materials *see* active materials
Sørensen, Grethe 51, 58
"Spina Aperta" (Auch) 67f.
"Spina Occlusive" (Auch) 67f.
sportswear 104, 110
Sprawson, Derek 192, 198, 199f.
starch 25f.
Starszakowna, Norma 21
Stitch_My_Brain 68, 69, 69f.
Stitch 'n' Bitch 149 n.12
Stitch_Your_Brain (SYB) 68, 70–1
sublimation printing 114–16, 115f., 116f.
Swammerdam, Jan 66
SYB (*Stitch_Your_Brain*) 68, 70–1

Taimina, Daina 144
tapestry 48
Taylor, Tony 190, 191, 193–5, 198
   color 198–9
   hidden knowledge 194
   knowledge 192, 202–3
   materials 193, 198
TC-1 (thread controller) looms 48, 49f., 50
   accessibility 48
   color 51, 58
   knowledge 57–8
   patterns 50–1, 54
   scope 1–2, 51, 53, 57, 58–9
TC-2 (thread controller) looms 1–2
Templeton, Rebecca 87–8
TENCEL 105
Textile Illusions group 47, 52 *see also* TWEEN
textiles
   aesthetics 105–6
   challenges 9–10
   change and 9
   error and 79
   knowledge 36, 78–9
   learning 2, 36
   materials 4
   old and new 103–4
   scope 1, 2, 9, 79, 106, 191
   uniqueness and 2
"They Are Taking It to the People" (Whalley) 189, 198–200, 199f.
"Thunderstorm" (Winters) 28, 29f.

tie-dyeing 79
timber 91, 92
touch 64–5, 155
"Tree of Death" (Perry) 190
tubular fabrics 147
TWEEN 47
   color 53–4
   jacquard weaving 53, 54
   light 53, 54f., 55, 56f.
   patterns 52, 54–5, 55f., 57, 58
   scope 4, 53
Twigger Holroyd, Amy 141

Udale, Jenny 105–6
uFOs (un-Finished Objects) 144
Ujiie, Hitoshi 21
Upper Street Events 166 n.4
urban factors 105

van Herpen, Iris 28, 30
Vestby, Vibeke 48
video 23
von Busch, Otto 141, 149 n.10

watercolor 22–3, 23f.
"Wave" (Hodes) 194f., 194–5
wearability 104, 105
weaving
   animation 4–5, 52, 53, 54f., 54–5, 55f., 56f., 57

color 53–4
figurative 51, 57–8
jacquard 48
multilayered 51, 58
patterns 52, 58
scope 50, 52, 53
tapestry 48
viewer perception 52
see also hand weaving
well-being and health 40, 70
Whalley, Stella 189, 198–200, 199f.
"What a Load of Shit" (Fisher) 189, 195f., 195–6
White, Hazel 141, 142f.
Williamson, Andrea 141
Wilson, Frank 62, 64
Winters, Amy 28, 29f.
"Women's Millennium" (Frølund) 51
woodblock printing 122–3
wool 109–10, 113, 116
workmanship
   of certainty 78, 91, 98, 101f., 121
   of risk xix, 26, 78, 91–3, 98, 101f., 132

"Yew Tree Avenue" (Beck Mather) 193–4, 194f.

Z Corp printers 25–6, 27f.
Zen of knitting 141
Ziek, Bhakti 48